D1557544

The Britannica Guide to
Analysis and Calculus

MATH EXPLAINED

The Britannica Guide to
Analysis and
Calculus

EDITED BY ERIK GREGERSEN,
ASSOCIATE EDITOR, ASTRONOMY AND SPACE EXPLORATION

Educational Publishing

IN ASSOCIATION WITH

EDUCATIONAL SERVICES

Published in 2011 by Britannica Educational Publishing
(a trademark of Encyclopædia Britannica, Inc.)
in association with Rosen Educational Services, LLC
29 East 21st Street, New York, NY 10010.

First Edition

Britannica Educational Publishing
Michael I. Levy: Executive Editor
J.E. Luebering: Senior Manager
Marilyn L. Barton: Senior Coordinator, Production Control
Steven Bosco: Director, Editorial Technologies
Lisa S. Braucher: Senior Producer and Data Editor
Yvette Charboneau: Senior Copy Editor
Kathy Nakamura: Manager, Media Acquisition
Erik Gregersen: Associate Editor, Astronomy and Space Exploration

Rosen Educational Services
Hope Lourie Killcoyne: Senior Editor and Project Manager
Joanne Randolph: Editor
Nelson Sá: Art Director
Cindy Reiman: Photography Manager
Nicole Russo: Design
Matthew Cauli: Cover Design
Introduction by John Strazzabosco

Library of Congress Cataloging-in-Publication Data

The Britannica guide to analysis and calculus / edited by Erik Gregersen.
    p. cm. — (Math explained)
"In association with Britannica Educational Publishing, Rosen Educational Services."
Includes bibliographical references and index.
ISBN 978-1-61530-123-2 (lib. bdg.)
1. Mathematical analysis. 2. Calculus. I. Gregersen, Erik.
QA300.B6955 2011
515 — dc22

                                                            2010001618

Manufactured in the United States of America

Cover Image Source/Getty Images

On page 12: In this engraving from Isaac Newton's 18th-century manuscript *De methodis serierum et fluxionum*, a hunter adjusts his aim as a group of ancient Greek mathematicians explain his movements with algebraic formulas. *SSPL via Getty Images*

On page 20: High school calculus teacher Tom Moriarty writes a problem during a multivariable "post-AP" calculus class. *Washington Post/Getty Images*

On pages 21, 35, 48, 64, 81, 106, 207, 282, 285, 289: Solution of the problem of the brachistochrone, or curve of quickest descent. The problem was first posed by Galileo, re-posed by Swiss mathematician Jakob Bernoulli, and solved here by English mathematician and physicist Isaac Newton. *Hulton Archive/Getty Images*

CONTENTS

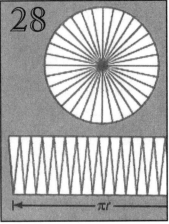

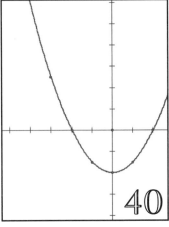

160

183

215

228

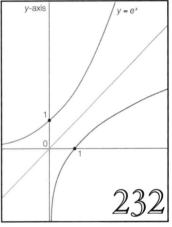

232

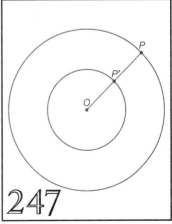

247

Τὰ κοινὰ καινῶς, τὰ καινὰ κοινῶς.

I n this volume, insight into the discoverers, their innovations, and how their achievements resulted in changing our world today is presented. The reader is invited to delve deeply into the mathematical workings or pursue these topics in a more general manner. A calculus student could do worse than to have readily available the history and development of calculus, its applications and examples, plus the major players of the math all gathered under one editorial roof.

Some old themes of human achievement and progress appear within these pages, such as the classic brilliant mathematical mind recognizing past accomplishment and subsequently forming that past brilliancy into yet another. Call this theme "cooperation." But it isn't always human nature to cooperate. Rather, sometimes competition rules the day, wherein brilliant minds who cannot accept the achievements of others are stirred to prove them wrong, but in so doing, also make great discoveries. And indeed, it turns out that not all of analysis and calculus discoveries have consisted of pleasant relationships—battles have even broken out within the same family.

One might suspect that, since the world awaited the discovery of calculus, we would have witnessed fireworks between the two men who suddenly—simultaneously and independently—discovered it. We might even suspect foul play, or at least remark to ourselves, "Come on, two guys discover calculus at the same time? What are the odds of that?"

But simultaneously discover calculus they did. And the times have proven convincingly that the approach of Sir Isaac Newton (circa 1680, England) differed from that of the other discoverer, Gottfried Wilhelm Leibniz (1684, Germany). Both discoveries are recognized today as legitimate.

That two people find an innovation that reshapes the world at any time, let alone the same time, is not so remote from believability when considering what was swirling around these men in the worldwide mathematics community. The 60-year span of 1610–1670 that immediately preceded calculus was filled with novel approaches both competitive and cooperative. Progress was sought on a broad scale. Newton and Leibniz were inspired by this activity.

Newton relied upon, among others, the works of Dutch mathematician Frans van Schooten and English mathematician John Wallis. Leibniz's influences included a 1672 visit from Dutch scientist Christiaan Huygens. Both Newton and Leibniz were influenced greatly by the work of Newton's teacher, Isaac Barrow (1670). But Barrow's geometrical lectures proceeded geometrically, thus limiting him from reaching the final plateau of the true calculus that was about to be found.

Newton was extremely committed to rigour with his mathematics. A man not given to making noise, he was slow to publish. Perhaps his calculus was discovered en route to pursuits of science. His treatise on fluxions, necessary for his calculus, was developed in 1671 but was not published until sixty-five years later, in 1736, long after the birth of his calculus.

Leibniz, on the contrary, favoured a vigorous approach and had a talent for attracting supporters. As it happened, the dispute between followers of Leibniz and Newton grew bitter, favouring Leibniz's ability to further his own works. Newton was less well known at the time. And not only did Leibniz's discovery catch hold because his followers helped push it—the locus of mathematics had now shifted from England to the Continent. Historian Michael Mahoney writes of a certain tragedy concerning Newton's mathematical isolation: "Whatever the revolutionary influence of [Newton's] *Principia*, math would have looked much the same if Newton had never existed.

In that endeavour he belonged to a community, and he was far from indispensable to it." While Mahoney refers here solely to Newton's mathematics notoriety, Newton's enormous science contributions remain another matter.

Calculus soon established the deep connection between geometry and physics, in the process transforming physics and giving new impetus to the study of geometry. Calculus became a prerequisite for the study of physics, chemistry, biology, economics, finance, actuarial sciences, engineering, and many other fields. Calculus was exploding into weighty fragments, each of which became an important subject of its own and taking on its own identity: ordinary calculus, partial differentiation, differential equations, calculus of variations, infinite series, and differential geometry. Applications to the sciences were discovered.

Both preceding and following the discovery of calculus, the Swiss Bernoulli family provided a compelling study of the strange ways in which brilliance is revealed. The Bernoulli brothers, Jakob (1655–1705) and Johann (1667–1748), were instructed by their father, a pharmacist, to take up vocations in theology and medicine, respectively. The kids didn't listen to Dad. They liked math better.

Brother Jakob went on to coin the term "integral" in this new field of calculus. Jakob also applied calculus to bridge building. His catenary studies of a chain suspended from two poles was an idea that found a home in the building of suspension bridges. Jakob's probability theory led to a formula still used in most high school intermediate algebra classes to determine the probability that, say, a baseball team will win three games out of four against another team if their past records are known.

Jakob's brother Johann made significant contributions to math applied to the building of clocks, ship sails, and optics. He also discovered what is now known as L'Hôpital's rule. (Oddly, Guillaume-François-Antoine de L'Hôpital took calculus lessons from Johann. Yet in L'Hôpital's widely accepted textbook (1696), *Analysis of the Infinitely Small*, the aforementioned innovation of Johann Bernoulli appeared as L'Hôpital's rule and notably was not called Bernoulli's rule.) Undaunted, Johann began serious study of other pursuits with his brother.

That endeavour proved to be a short-lived attempt at cooperation.

The two fell into a disagreement over the equation of the path of a particle if acted upon by gravity alone (a problem first tackled by Galileo, who had been dropping stones and other objects from the Leaning Tower of Pisa in the early 1600s). The path of the Bernoulli brothers' argument led to a protracted and bitter dispute between them. Jakob went so far as to offer a reward for the solution. Johann, seeing that move as a slap in the face, took up the challenge and solved it. Jakob, however, rejected Johann's solution. Ironically, the brothers were possibly the only two people in the world capable of understanding the concept. But whether they were engaged in cooperation, competition, or a combination of both, what emerged was yet another Bernoulli brilliancy, the calculus of variations. The mathematical world was grateful.

Jakob died a few years later. Johann went on to more fame. But with his battling brother gone, his new rival may very well have become his own son, Daniel.

Daniel Bernoulli was to become the most prolific and distinguished of the Bernoulli family. Oddly enough, this development does not appear to have sat well with his father, Johann. Usually a parent brags about his child, but not this time. The acorn may not have fallen far enough from the tree for Johann's liking, as his son's towering intellect cast his own accomplishments in shadow—or so the father seemed to think.

It wasn't long before Daniel was making great inroads into differential equations and probability theory, winning prizes for his work on astronomy, gravitation, tides, magnetism, ocean currents, and the behaviour of ships at sea. His aura grew with further achievements in medicine, mechanics, and physics. By 1738 father Johann had had enough. He is said to have published *Hydraulica* with as much intent to antagonize his son as to upstage him.

Daniel, perhaps as a peace offering, shared with his father a prize he, Daniel, won for the study of planetary orbits. But his father was vindictive. Johann Bernoulli threw Daniel out of the house and said the prize should have been his, Johann's, alone.

Despite the grand achievements and discoveries of Newton, Leibniz, the battling Bernoullis, and many others, the output of Leonhard Euler (1707–1783) is said to have dwarfed them all. Euler leaves hints of having been the cooperative type, taking advantage of what he saw as functional, rather than fretting over who was getting credit.

To understand Euler's contributions we should first remind ourselves of the branch of mathematics in which he worked. Analysis is defined as the branch of mathematics dealing with continuous change and certain emergent processes: limits, differentiation, integration, and more. Analysis had the attention of the mathematics world. Euler took advantage and apparently not in a selfish manner.

By way of example, 19-year-old Joseph-Louis Lagrange, who was to follow Euler as a leader of European mathematics, wrote to Euler in 1755 to announce a new symbol for calculus — it had no reference to geometric configuration, which was quite distinct from Euler's mathematics. Euler might have said, "Who is this upstart? At 19, what could he possibly know?" Euler used geometry. Lagrange didn't. Euler immediately adopted Lagrange's ideas, and the two revised the subject creating new techniques. Euler demonstrated the traits of a person with an open mind. That mind would make computer software applications possible for 21st century commercial transactions.

Euler's *Introduction to the Analysis of the Infinite* (1748) led to the zeta function, which strengthened proof that the set of prime numbers was an infinite set. A prime number has only two factors, 1 and itself. In other words, only two numbers multiply out to a prime number. Examples of the primes are 2, 3, 5, 7, 11, 13, and 17. The question was whether the set of primes was infinite. The answer from the man on the street might be, "Does it matter?"

The answer to that question is a word that boggles the mind of all new math students—and many mature ones. It's the word "rigour," associated with the term "hard work." Rigour means real proof and strictness of judgment—demonstrating something mathematically until we know that it is mathematically true.

That's what Euler's zeta function did for prime numbers—proved that the set was infinite. Today, prime numbers are the key to the security of most electronic transactions. Sensitive information such as our bank balances, account numbers, and Social Security numbers are "hidden" in the infinite number of primes. Had we not been assured that the set of primes was infinite through Euler's rigour, we could not have used primes for keeping our computer credit card transactions secure.

But just when it seems that rigour is crucial, it occasionally proves to be acceptable if delivered later. That story begins with the Pythagoras cult investigating music, which led to applications in understanding heat, sound, light, fluid dynamics, elasticity, and magnetism. First the music, then the rigour. The Pythagoreans discovered that ratios of 2:1 or 3:2 for violin string lengths yielded the most pleasing sounds. Some 2,000 years later, Brook Taylor (1714) elevated that theory and calculated the frequency today known as pitch. Jean Le Rond d'Alembert (1746) showed the intricacies by applying partial derivatives. Euler responded to that, and his response was held suspect by Daniel Bernoulli, who smelled an error with Euler's work but couldn't find it. The problem? Lack of rigour. In fact Euler *had* made a mistake. It would take another century to figure out this error of Euler's suspected by Bernoulli. But the lack of rigour did not get in the way. Discoveries were happening so fast both around this theory and caused by it, that math did not and could not wait for the rigour, which in this case was a good thing. French mathematician Pierre-Simon de Laplace (1770s) and Scottish physicist James Clerk Maxwell (1800s) extended and refined the theory that would later link Pythagorean harmony, the work of Taylor, d'Alembert, Laplace, Maxwell, and finally Euler's amended work, and others, with mathematical knowledge of waves that gave us radio, television, and radar. All because of music and generations of mathematicians' curiosity and desire to see knowledge stretched to the next destination.

One extra note on rigour and its relationship to analysis. Augustin-Louis Cauchy (1789–1857) proposed basing calculus on a sophisticated and difficult interpretation of two points arbitrarily close together. His students hated it. It was too hard. Cauchy was ordered to teach it anyway so students could learn and use it. His methods gradually became established and refined to form the core of modern rigorous calculus, the subject now called mathematical analysis. With rigour Cauchy proved that integration and differentiation are mutually inverse, giving for the first time the rigorous foundation to all elementary calculus of his day.

Rigour, vigour, cooperation, and competition: products of the mind, heart, soul, and psyche await readers in *The Britannica Guide to Analysis and Calculus*.

$$f(x,y) = x^4 + y^4 - 4$$

$$L_1: \quad y=0 \quad 0 \leq x \leq 2$$

$$f(x$$

CHAPTER I
MEASURING
CONTINUOUS CHANGE

Analysis is the branch of mathematics that deals with continuous change and with certain general types of processes that have emerged from the study of continuous change, such as limits, differentiation, and integration. Since the discovery of the differential and integral calculus by Isaac Newton and Gottfried Wilhelm Leibniz at the end of the 17th century, analysis has grown into an enormous and central field of mathematical research, with applications throughout the sciences and in areas such as finance, economics, and sociology.

The historical origins of analysis can be found in attempts to calculate spatial quantities such as the length of a curved line or the area enclosed by a curve. These problems can be stated purely as questions of mathematical technique, but they have a far wider importance because they possess a broad variety of interpretations in the physical world. The area inside a curve, for instance, is of direct interest in land measurement: how many acres does an irregularly shaped plot of land contain? But the same technique also determines the mass of a uniform sheet of material bounded by some chosen curve or the quantity of paint needed to cover an irregularly shaped surface. Less obviously, these techniques can be used to find the total distance traveled by a vehicle moving at varying speeds, the depth at which a ship will float when placed in the sea, or the total fuel consumption of a rocket.

Similarly, the mathematical technique for finding a tangent line to a curve at a given point can also be used to calculate the steepness of a curved hill or the angle through which a moving boat must turn to avoid a collision. Less directly, it is related to the extremely important question of the calculation of instantaneous velocity or other instantaneous rates of change, such as the cooling of a warm object in a cold room or the propagation of a disease organism through a human population.

BRIDGING THE GAP BETWEEN ARITHMETIC AND GEOMETRY

Mathematics divides phenomena into two broad classes, discrete and continuous, historically corresponding to the division between arithmetic and geometry. Discrete systems can be subdivided only so far, and they can be described in terms of whole numbers 0, 1, 2, 3, ... Continuous systems can be subdivided indefinitely, and their description requires the real numbers, numbers represented by decimal expansions such as 3.14159..., possibly going on forever. Understanding the true nature of such infinite decimals lies at the heart of analysis.

The distinction between discrete mathematics and continuous mathematics is a central issue for mathematical modeling, the art of representing features of the natural world in mathematical form. The universe does not contain or consist of actual mathematical objects, but many aspects of the universe closely resemble mathematical concepts. For example, the number 2 does not exist as a physical object, but it does describe an important feature of such things as human twins and binary stars. In a similar manner, the real numbers provide satisfactory models for a variety of phenomena, even though no physical quantity can be measured accurately to more than a dozen or so decimal places. It is not the values of infinitely many decimal places that apply to the real world but the deductive structures that they embody and enable.

Analysis came into being because many aspects of the natural world can profitably be considered as being continuous—at least, to an excellent degree of approximation. Again, this is a question of modeling, not of reality. Matter is not truly continuous. If matter is subdivided into sufficiently small pieces, then indivisible components, or atoms, will appear. But atoms are extremely small, and, for most applications, treating matter as though it were a continuum introduces negligible error while greatly simplifying the computations. For example, continuum modeling is standard engineering practice when studying the flow of fluids such as air or water, the bending of

The atom is one of the smallest pieces of matter. It is made up of three smaller pieces—the neutron, the proton, and the electron. There are branches of science that study matter on this tiny scale, but calculus takes a larger, more continuous view. Photodisc/Getty Images

elastic materials, the distribution or flow of electric current, and the flow of heat.

DISCOVERY OF THE CALCULUS AND THE SEARCH FOR FOUNDATIONS

Two major steps led to the creation of analysis. The first was the discovery of the surprising relationship, known as the fundamental theorem of calculus, between spatial problems involving the calculation of some total size or value, such as length, area, or volume (integration), and problems involving rates of change, such as slopes of tangents and velocities (differentiation). Credit for the independent discovery, about 1670, of the fundamental theorem of calculus together with the invention of techniques to apply this theorem goes jointly to Gottfried Wilhelm Leibniz and Isaac Newton.

While the utility of calculus in explaining physical phenomena was immediately apparent, its use of infinity in calculations (through the decomposition of curves, geometric bodies, and physical motions into infinitely many small parts) generated widespread unease. In particular, the Anglican bishop George Berkeley published a famous pamphlet, *The Analyst; or, A Discourse Addressed to an Infidel Mathematician* (1734), pointing out that calculus—at least, as presented by Newton and Leibniz—possessed serious logical flaws. Analysis grew out of the resulting painstakingly close examination of previously loosely defined concepts such as function and limit.

Newton's and Leibniz's approach to calculus had been primarily geometric, involving ratios with "almost zero" divisors—Newton's "fluxions" and Leibniz's "infinitesimals." During the 18th century calculus became increasingly algebraic, as mathematicians—most notably the Swiss

Leonhard Euler and the Italian French Joseph-Louis Lagrange—began to generalize the concepts of continuity and limits from geometric curves and bodies to more abstract algebraic functions and began to extend these ideas to complex numbers. Although these developments were not entirely satisfactory from a foundational standpoint, they were fundamental to the eventual refinement of a rigorous basis for calculus by the Frenchman Augustin-Louis Cauchy, the Bohemian Bernhard Bolzano, and above all the German Karl Weierstrass in the 19th century.

NUMBERS AND FUNCTIONS

NUMBER SYSTEMS

There are a variety of number systems — that is, collections of mathematical objects (numbers) that can be operated on by some or all of the standard operations of arithmetic: addition, multiplication, subtraction, and division. These main number systems are:

- The natural numbers **N**. These numbers are the positive (and zero) whole numbers 0, 1, 2, 3, 4, 5, ... If two such numbers are added or multiplied, the result is again a natural number.
- The integers **Z**. These numbers are the positive and negative whole numbers ... , -5, -4, -3, -2, -1, 0, 1, 2, 3, 4, 5, ... If two such numbers are added, subtracted, or multiplied, the result is again an integer.
- The rational numbers **Q**. These numbers are the positive and negative fractions p/q where p and q are integers and $q \neq 0$. If two such numbers are added, subtracted, multiplied, or

divided (except by 0), the result is again a rational number.

- The real numbers **R**. These numbers are the positive and negative infinite decimals (including terminating decimals that can be considered as having an infinite sequence of zeros on the end). If two such numbers are added, subtracted, multiplied, or divided (except by 0), the result is again a real number.
- The complex numbers **C**. These numbers are of the form $x + iy$ where x and y are real numbers and $i = \sqrt{-1}$. If two such numbers are added, subtracted, multiplied, or divided (except by 0), the result is again a complex number.

FUNCTIONS

In simple terms, a function f is a mathematical rule that assigns to a number x (in some number system and possibly with certain limitations on its value) another number $f(x)$. For example, the function "square" assigns to each number x its square x^2. Note that it is the general rule, not specific values, that constitutes the function.

The common functions that arise in analysis are usually definable by formulas, such as $f(x) = x^2$. They include the trigonometric functions sin (x), cos (x), tan (x), and so on; the logarithmic function log (x); the exponential function exp (x) or e^x (where $e = 2.71828...$ is a special constant called the base of natural logarithms); and the square root function $\sqrt{x}$. However, functions need not be defined by single formulas (indeed by any formulas). For example, the absolute value function $|x|$ is defined to be x when $x \geq 0$ but $-x$ when $x < 0$ (where $\geq$ indicates greater than or equal to and $<$ indicates less than).

THE PROBLEM OF CONTINUITY

The logical difficulties involved in setting up calculus on a sound basis are all related to one central problem, the notion of continuity. This in turn leads to questions about the meaning of quantities that become infinitely large or infinitely small—concepts riddled with logical pitfalls. For example, a circle of radius r has circumference $2\pi r$ and area πr^2, where π is the famous constant 3.14159.... Establishing these two properties is not entirely straightforward, although an adequate approach was developed by the geometers of ancient Greece, especially Eudoxus and Archimedes. It is harder than one might expect to show that the circumference of a circle is proportional to its radius and that its area is proportional to the square of its radius. The really difficult problem, though, is to show that the constant of proportionality for the circumference is precisely twice the constant of proportionality for the area—that is, to show that the constant now called π really is the same in both formulas. This boils down to proving a theorem (first proved by Archimedes) that does not mention π explicitly at all: the area of a circle is the same as that of a rectangle, one of whose sides is equal to the circle's radius and the other to half the circle's circumference.

APPROXIMATIONS IN GEOMETRY

A simple geometric argument shows that such an equality must hold to a high degree of approximation. The idea is to slice the circle like a pie, into a large number of equal pieces, and to reassemble the pieces to form an approximate rectangle. Then the area of the "rectangle" is closely approximated by its height, which equals the circle's radius, multiplied by the length of one set of curved sides—which together form one-half of the circle's circumference. Unfortunately, because of the approximations involved, this argument does not prove the theorem about the area of a circle. Further thought suggests that as the slices get very thin, the error in the approximation becomes very small. But that still does not prove the theorem, for an error, however tiny, remains an error. If it made sense to talk of the slices being infinitesimally thin, however, then the error would disappear altogether, or at least it would become infinitesimal.

Actually, there exist subtle problems with such a construction. It might justifiably be argued that if the slices are infinitesimally thin, then each has zero area; hence, joining them together produces a rectangle with

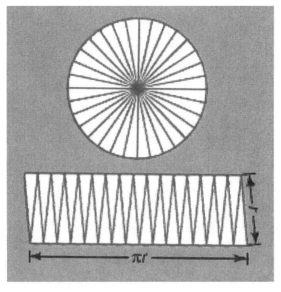

Geometry is a study in approximations in many ways. Mathematicians discovered the area of a circle by breaking it into ever-smaller triangles and then fitting those triangles into a rectangle, a shape for which they knew how to measure the area. Copyright Encyclopædia Britannica; rendering for this edition by Rosen Educational Services

zero total area since 0 + 0 + 0 +··· = 0. Indeed, the very idea of an infinitesimal quantity is paradoxical because the only number that is smaller than every positive number is 0 itself.

The same problem shows up in many different guises. When calculating the length of the circumference of a circle, it is attractive to think of the circle as a regular polygon with infinitely many straight sides, each infinitesimally long. (Indeed, a circle is the limiting case for a regular polygon as the number of its sides increases.) But while this picture makes sense for some purposes—illustrating that the circumference is proportional to the radius—for others it makes no sense at all. For example, the "sides" of the infinitely many-sided polygon must have length 0, which implies that the circumference is 0 + 0 + 0 + ··· = 0, clearly nonsense.

Infinite Series

Similar paradoxes occur in the manipulation of infinite series, such as

$$\tfrac{1}{2} + \tfrac{1}{4} + \tfrac{1}{8} + \cdots \tag{1}$$

continuing forever. This particular series is relatively harmless, and its value is precisely 1. To see why this should be so, consider the partial sums formed by stopping after a finite number of terms. The more terms, the closer the partial sum is to 1. It can be made as close to 1 as desired by including enough terms. Moreover, 1 is the only number for which the above statements are true. It therefore makes sense to define the infinite sum to be exactly 1. (Series whose successive terms differ by a common ratio, in this example by $\tfrac{1}{2}$, are known as geometric series.)

Other infinite series are less well-behaved—for example, the series

$$1 - 1 + 1 - 1 + 1 - 1 + \cdots . \qquad (2)$$

If the terms are grouped one way, $(1 - 1) + (1 - 1) + (1 - 1) + \cdots$, then the sum appears to be $0 + 0 + 0 + \cdots = 0$. But if the terms are grouped differently, $1 + (-1 + 1) + (-1 + 1) + (-1 + 1) + \cdots$, then the sum appears to be $1 + 0 + 0 + 0 + \cdots = 1$. It would be foolish to conclude that $0 = 1$. Instead, the conclusion is that infinite series do not always obey the traditional rules of algebra, such as those that permit the arbitrary regrouping of terms.

The difference between series (1) and (2) is clear from their partial sums. The partial sums of (1) get closer and closer to a single fixed value—namely, 1. The partial sums of (2) alternate between 0 and 1, so that the series never settles down. A series that does settle down to some definite value, as more and more terms are added, is said to converge, and the value to which it converges is known as the limit of the partial sums. All other series are said to diverge.

THE LIMIT OF A SEQUENCE

All the great mathematicians who contributed to the development of calculus had an intuitive concept of limits, but it was only with the work of the German mathematician Karl Weierstrass that a completely satisfactory formal definition of the limit of a sequence was obtained.

Consider a sequence (a_n) of real numbers, by which is meant an infinite list $a_0, a_1, a_2, \ldots$. It is said that a_n converges to (or approaches) the limit a as n tends to infinity, if the following mathematical statement holds true: For every $\varepsilon > 0$, there exists a whole number N such that $|a_n - a| < \varepsilon$

for all $n > N$. Intuitively, this statement says that, for any chosen degree of approximation (ε), there is some point in the sequence (N) such that, from that point onward ($n > N$), every number in the sequence (a_n) approximates a within an error less than the chosen amount ($|a_n - a| < \varepsilon$). Stated less formally, when n becomes large enough, a_n can be made as close to a as desired.

For example, consider the sequence in which $a_n = 1/(n + 1)$, that is, the sequence $1, \frac{1}{2}, \frac{1}{3}, \frac{1}{4}, \frac{1}{5}, \ldots$, going on forever. Every number in the sequence is greater than zero, but, the farther along the sequence goes, the closer the numbers get to zero. For example, all terms from the 10th onward are less than or equal to 0.1, all terms from the 100th onward are less than or equal to 0.01, and so on. Terms smaller than 0.000000001, for instance, are found from the 1,000,000,000th term onward. In Weierstrass's terminology, this sequence converges to its limit 0 as n tends to infinity. The difference $|a_n - 0|$ can be made smaller than any ε by choosing n sufficiently large. In fact, $n > \frac{1}{\varepsilon}$ suffices. So, in Weierstrass's formal definition, N is taken to be the smallest integer $> \frac{1}{\varepsilon}$.

This example brings out several key features of Weierstrass's idea. First, it does not involve any mystical notion of infinitesimals. All quantities involved are ordinary real numbers. Second, it is precise. If a sequence possesses a limit, then there is exactly one real number that satisfies the Weierstrass definition. Finally, although the numbers in the sequence tend to the limit 0, they need not actually reach that value.

CONTINUITY OF FUNCTIONS

The same basic approach makes it possible to formalize the notion of continuity of a function. Intuitively, a function $f(t)$ approaches a limit L as t approaches a value p if, whatever size error can be tolerated, $f(t)$ differs from L by less than the tolerable error for all t sufficiently close to p. But what exactly is meant by phrases such as "error," "prepared to tolerate," and "sufficiently close"?

Just as for limits of sequences, the formalization of these ideas is achieved by assigning symbols to "tolerable error" (ε) and to "sufficiently close" (δ). Then the definition becomes: A function $f(t)$ approaches a limit L as t approaches a value p if for all $\varepsilon > 0$ there exists $\delta > 0$ such that $|f(t) - L| < \varepsilon$ whenever $|t - p| < \delta$. (Note carefully that first the size of the tolerable error must be decided upon. Only then can it be determined what it means to be "sufficiently close.")

Having defined the notion of limit in this context, it is straightforward to define continuity of a function. Continuous functions preserve limits. This means that a function f is continuous at a point p if the limit of $f(t)$ as t approaches p is equal to $f(p)$. And f is continuous if it is continuous at every p for which $f(p)$ is defined. Intuitively, continuity means that small changes in t produce small changes in $f(t)$—there are no sudden jumps.

PROPERTIES OF THE REAL NUMBERS

Earlier, the real numbers were described as infinite decimals, although such a description makes no logical sense without the formal concept of a limit. This is because an infinite decimal expansion such as 3.14159... (the value of the constant π) actually corresponds to the sum of an infinite series $3 + \frac{1}{10} + \frac{4}{100} + \frac{1}{1,000} + \frac{5}{10,000} + \frac{9}{100,000} + \cdots$, and the concept of limit is required to give such a sum meaning.

It turns out that the real numbers (unlike, say, the rational numbers) have important properties that correspond to intuitive notions of continuity. For example, consider the function $x^2 - 2$. This function takes the value -1 when $x = 1$ and the value +2 when $x = 2$. Moreover, it varies continuously with x. It seems intuitively plausible that, if a continuous function is negative at one value of x (here at $x = 1$) and positive at another value of x (here at $x = 2$), then it must equal zero for some value of x that lies between these values (here for some value between 1 and 2). This expectation is correct if x is a real number: the expression is zero when $x = \sqrt{2} = 1.41421....$ However, it is false if x is restricted to rational values because there is no rational number x for which $x^2 = \sqrt{2}$. (The fact that 2 is irrational has been known since the time of the ancient Greeks.)

In effect, there are gaps in the system of rational numbers. By exploiting those gaps, continuously varying quantities can change sign without passing through zero. The real numbers fill in the gaps by providing additional numbers that are the limits of sequences of approximating rational numbers. Formally, this feature of the real numbers is captured by the concept of completeness.

One awkward aspect of the concept of the limit of a sequence (a_n) is that it can sometimes be problematic to find what the limit a actually is. However, there is a closely related concept, attributable to the French mathematician Augustin-Louis Cauchy, in which the limit need not be specified. The intuitive idea is simple. Suppose that a sequence (a_n) converges to some unknown limit a. Given two sufficiently large values of n, say r and s, then both a_r and a_s are very close to a, which in particular means that they are very close to each other. The sequence (a_n) is said to be a Cauchy sequence if it behaves in this manner. Specifically, (a_n) is Cauchy if, for every $\varepsilon > 0$, there exists some N such that, whenever $r, s > N, |a_r - a_s| < \varepsilon$. Convergent sequences are always Cauchy, but is every Cauchy sequence convergent? The answer is yes for sequences of real numbers but no for sequences of rational numbers (in the sense that they may not have a rational limit).

A number system is said to be complete if every Cauchy sequence converges. The real numbers are complete, while the rational numbers are not. Completeness is one of the key features of the real number system, and it is a major reason why analysis is often carried out within that system.

The real numbers have several other features that are important for analysis. They satisfy various ordering properties associated with the relation less than ($<$). The simplest of these properties for real numbers x, y, and z are:

- Trichotomy law. One and only one of the statements $x < y$, $x = y$, and $x > y$ is true.
- Transitive law. If $x < y$ and $y < z$, then $x < z$.
- If $x < y$, then $x + z < y + z$ for all z.
- If $x < y$ and $z > 0$, then $xz < yz$.

More subtly, the real number system is Archimedean. This means that, if x and y are real numbers and both $x, y > 0$, then $x + x + \cdots + x > y$ for some finite sum of x's. The Archimedean property indicates that the real numbers contain no infinitesimals. Arithmetic, completeness, ordering, and the Archimedean property completely characterize the real number system.

CHAPTER 2
CALCULUS

With the technical preliminaries out of the way, the two fundamental aspects of calculus may be examined:

- Finding the instantaneous rate of change of a variable quantity.
- Calculating areas, volumes, and related "totals" by adding together many small parts.

Although it is not immediately obvious, each process is the inverse of the other, and this is why the two are brought together under the same overall heading. The first process is called differentiation, the second integration.

DIFFERENTIATION

Differentiation is about rates of change. For geometric curves and figures, this means determining the slope, or tangent, along a given direction. Being able to calculate rates of change also allows one to determine where maximum and minimum values occur—the title of Leibniz's first calculus publication was "*Nova Methodus pro Maximis et Minimis, Itemque Tangentibus, qua nec Fractas nec Irrationales Quantitates Moratur, et Singulare pro illi Calculi Genus*" (1684; "A New Method for Maxima and Minima, as Well as Tangents, Which Is Impeded Neither by Fractional nor by Irrational Quantities, and a Remarkable Type of Calculus for This"). Early applications for calculus included the study of gravity and planetary motion, fluid flow and ship design, and geometric curves and bridge engineering.

Average Rates of Change

A simple illustrative example of rates of change is the speed of a moving object. An object moving at a constant speed travels a distance that is proportional to the time. For example, a car moving at 50 kilometres per hour (km/hr) travels 50 km (31 miles) in 1 hr, 100 km (62 miles) in 2 hr, 150 km (93 miles) in 3 hr, and so on. A graph of the distance traveled against the time elapsed looks like a straight line whose slope, or gradient, yields the speed.

Constant speeds pose no particular problems—in the example above, any time interval yields the same speed—but variable speeds are less straightforward. Nevertheless, a similar approach can be used to calculate the average speed of an object traveling at varying speeds: simply divide the total distance traveled by the time taken to traverse it. Thus, a car that takes 2 hr to travel 100 km moves with an average speed of 50 km/hr. However, it may not travel at the same speed for the entire period. It may slow down, stop, or even go backward for parts of the time, provided that during other parts it speeds up enough to cover the total distance of 100 km. Thus, average speeds—certainly if the average is taken over long intervals of time—do not tell us the actual speed at any given moment.

Instantaneous Rates of Change

In fact, it is not so easy to make sense of the concept of "speed at a given moment." How long is a moment? Zeno of Elea, a Greek philosopher who flourished about 450 BCE, pointed out in one of his celebrated paradoxes that a moving arrow, at any instant of time, is fixed. During zero time it must travel zero distance. Another way to say this is that the instantaneous speed of a moving object cannot be calculated by dividing the distance that it travels in zero time by the time that it takes to travel that distance. This calculation leads to a fraction, $\frac{0}{0}$, that does not possess any well-defined meaning. Normally, a fraction indicates a specific quotient. For example, $\frac{6}{3}$ means 2, the number that, when multiplied by 3, yields 6. Similarly, $\frac{0}{0}$ should mean the number that, when multiplied by 0, yields 0. But any number multiplied by 0 yields 0. In principle, then, $\frac{0}{0}$ can take any value whatsoever, and in practice it is best considered meaningless.

Despite these arguments, there is a strong feeling that a moving object does move at a well-defined speed at each instant. Passengers know when a car is traveling faster or slower. So the meaninglessness of $\frac{0}{0}$ is by no means the end of the story. Various mathematicians—both before and after Newton and Leibniz—argued that good approximations to the instantaneous speed can be obtained by finding the average speed over short intervals of time. If a car travels 5 metres (16.4 feet) in one second, then its average speed is 18 km/hr (11 mph), and, unless the speed is varying wildly, its instantaneous speed must be close to 18 km/hr. A shorter time period can be used to refine the estimate further.

If a mathematical formula is available for the total distance traveled in a given time, then this idea can be turned into a formal calculation. For example, suppose that after time t seconds an object travels a distance t^2 metres. (Similar formulas occur for bodies falling freely under gravity, so this is a reasonable choice.) To determine the object's instantaneous speed after precisely one second, its average speed over successively shorter time intervals will be calculated.

To start the calculation, observe that between time $t = 1$ and $t = 1.1$ the distance traveled is $1.1^2 - 1 = 0.21$. The average speed over that interval is therefore $0.21/0.1 = 2.1$

metres (6.9 feet) per second. For a finer approximation, the distance traveled between times $t = 1$ and $t = 1.01$ is $1.01^2 - 1 = 0.0201$, and the average speed is $0.0201/0.01 = 2.01$ metres per second. Table 1 displays successively finer approximations to the average speed after one second. It is clear that the smaller the interval of time, the closer the average speed is to 2 metres (6.6 feet) per second.

Table 1: Approximations to a rate of change				
start time	end time	distance traveled	elapsed time	average speed
1	1.1	0.21	0.1	2.1
1	1.01	0.0201	0.01	2.01
1	1.001	0.002001	0.001	2.001
1	1.0001	0.00020001	0.0001	2.0001
1	1.00001	0.0000200001	0.00001	2.00001

The structure of the entire table points very compellingly to an exact value for the instantaneous speed—namely, 2 metres per second. Unfortunately, 2 cannot be found anywhere in the table. However far it is extended, every entry in the table looks like 2.000...0001, with perhaps a huge number of zeros, but always with a 1 on the end. Neither is there the option of choosing a time interval of 0, because then the distance traveled is also 0, which leads back to the meaningless fraction $\frac{0}{0}$.

FORMAL DEFINITION OF THE DERIVATIVE

More generally, suppose an arbitrary time interval h starts from the time $t = 1$. Then the distance traveled is $(1 + h)^2 - 1^2$, which simplifies to give $2h + h^2$. The time taken is h. Therefore, the average speed over that time interval is $(2h + h^2)/h$, which equals $2 + h$, provided $h \neq 0$. Obviously, as h approaches zero, this average speed approaches 2. Therefore, the definition of instantaneous speed is satisfied by the value 2 and only that value. What has not been done here—indeed, what the whole procedure deliberately avoids—is to set h equal to 0. As Bishop George Berkeley pointed out in the 18th century, to replace $(2h + h^2)/h$ by $2 + h$, one must assume h is not zero, and that is what the rigorous definition of a limit achieves.

Even more generally, suppose the calculation starts from an arbitrary time t instead of a fixed $t = 1$. Then the distance traveled is $(t + h)^2 - t^2$, which simplifies to $2th + h^2$. The time taken is again h. Therefore, the average speed over that time interval is $(2th + h^2)/h$, or $2t + h$. Obviously, as h approaches zero, this average speed approaches the limit $2t$.

This procedure is so important that it is given a special name: the derivative of t^2 is $2t$, and this result is obtained by differentiating t^2 with respect to t.

One can now go even further and replace t^2 by any other function f of time. The distance traveled between times t and $t + h$ is $f(t + h) - f(t)$. The time taken is h. So the average speed is

$$(f(t + h) - f(t))/h. \qquad (3)$$

If (3) tends to a limit as h tends to zero, then that limit is defined as the derivative of $f(t)$, written $f'(t)$. Another common notation for the derivative is df/dt, symbolizing a small change in f divided by a small change in t. A function is differentiable at t if its derivative exists for that specific value of t. It is differentiable if the derivative exists for all t for which $f(t)$ is defined. A differentiable function must be continuous, but the converse is false. (Indeed, in 1872 Weierstrass produced the first example of a continuous function that cannot be differentiated at any point—a function now known as a nowhere differentiable function.)

GRAPHICAL INTERPRETATION

The above ideas have a graphical interpretation. Associated with any function $f(t)$ is a graph in which the horizontal axis represents the variable t and the vertical axis represents the value of the function. Choose a value for t, calculate $f(t)$, and draw the corresponding point. Now repeat for all appropriate t. The result is a curve, the graph of f. For example, if $f(t) = t^2$, then $f(t) = 0$ when $t = 0$, $f(t) = 1$ when $t = 1$, $f(t) = 4$ when $t = 2$, $f(t) = 9$ when $t = 3$, and so on, leading to the curve known as a parabola.

Expression (3), the numerical calculation of the average speed traveled between times t and $t + h$, also can be represented graphically. The two times can be plotted as two points on the curve, and a line can be drawn joining the two points. This line is called a secant, or chord, of the curve, and its slope corresponds to the change in distance with respect to time—that is, the average speed traveled

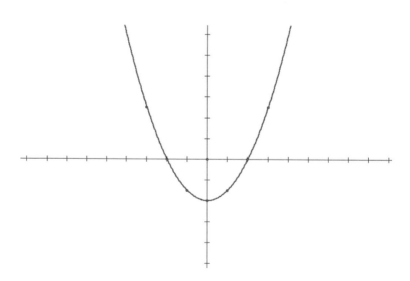

A graph showing a classic parabola. Rosen Educational Services

between t and $t + h$. If, as h becomes smaller and smaller, this slope tends to a limiting value, then the direction of the chord stabilizes and the chord approximates more and more closely the tangent to the graph at t. Thus, the numerical notion of instantaneous rate of change of $f(t)$ with respect to t corresponds to the geometric notion of the slope of the tangent to the graph.

The graphical interpretation suggests a number of useful problem-solving techniques. An example is finding the maximum value of a continuously differentiable function $f(x)$ defined in some interval $a \leq x \leq b$. Either f attains its maximum at an endpoint, $x = a$ or $x = b$, or it attains a maximum for some x inside this interval. In the latter case, as x approaches the maximum value, the curve defined by f rises more and more slowly, levels out, and then starts to fall. In other words, as x increases from a to b, the derivative $f'(x)$ is positive while the function $f(x)$ rises to its maximum value, $f'(x)$ is 0 at the value of x for which $f(x)$ has a maximum value, and $f'(x)$ is negative while $f(x)$ declines from its maximum value. Simply stated, maximum values can be located by solving the equation $f'(x) = 0$.

It is necessary to check whether the resulting value genuinely is a maximum, however. First, all of the above reasoning applies at any local maximum—a place where $f(x)$ is larger than all values of $f(x)$ for nearby values of x. A function can have several local maxima, not all of which are overall ("global") maxima. Moreover, the derivative $f'(x)$ vanishes at any (local) minimum value inside the interval. Indeed, it can sometimes vanish at places where the value is neither a maximum nor a minimum. An example is $f(x) = x^3$ for $-1 \leq x \leq 1$. Here $f'(x) = 3x^2$ so $f'(0) = 0$, but 0 is neither a maximum nor a minimum. For $x < 0$ the value of $f(x)$ gets smaller than the value $f(0) = 0$, but for $x > 0$ it gets larger. Such a point is called a point of inflection. In general, solutions of $f'(x) = 0$ are called critical points of f.

Local maxima, local minima, and points of inflection are useful features of a function f that can aid in sketching its graph. Solving the equation $f'(x) = 0$ provides a list of critical values of x near which the shape of the curve is determined—concave up near a local minimum, concave down near a local maximum, and changing concavity at an inflection point. Moreover, between any two adjacent critical points of f, the values of f either increase steadily or decrease steadily—that is, the direction of the slope cannot change. By combining such information, the general qualitative shape of the graph of f can often be determined.

For example, suppose that $f(x) = x^3 - 3x + 2$ is defined for $-3 \leq x \leq 3$. The critical points are solutions x of $0 = f'(x) = 3x^2 - 3$. That is, $x = -1$ and $x = 1$. When $x < -1$ the slope is positive; for $-1 < x < 1$ the slope is negative; for $x > 1$ the slope is positive again. Thus, $x = -1$ is a local maximum, and $x = 1$ is a local minimum. Therefore, the graph of f slopes upward from left to right as x runs from -3 to -1, then slopes downward as x runs from -1 to 1, and finally slopes upward again as x runs from 1 to 3.

HIGHER-ORDER DERIVATIVES

The process of differentiation can be applied several times in succession, leading in particular to the second derivative f'' of the function f, which is just the derivative of the derivative f'. The second derivative often has a useful physical interpretation. For example, if $f(t)$ is the position of an object at time t, then $f'(t)$ is its speed at time t and $f''(t)$ is its acceleration at time t. Newton's laws of motion state that the acceleration of an object is proportional to the total force acting on it. This means that second derivatives are of central importance in dynamics. The second derivative is also useful for graphing functions, because it can quickly determine whether each critical point, c, corresponds to a local maximum ($f''(c) < 0$), a local minimum ($f''(c) > 0$), or a change in concavity ($f''(c) = 0$). Third derivatives occur in such concepts as curvature. Even fourth derivatives have their uses, notably in elasticity. The nth derivative of $f(x)$ is denoted by $f^{(n)}(x)$ or $d^n f/dx^n$ and has important applications in power series.

An infinite series of the form $a_0 + a_1 x + a_2 x^2 + \cdots$, where x and the a_j are real numbers, is called a power series. The a_j are the coefficients. The series has a legitimate meaning, provided the series converges. In general, there exists a real number R such that the series converges when $-R < x < R$ but diverges if $x < -R$ or $x > R$. The range of values $-R < x < R$ is called the interval of convergence. The behaviour of the series at $x = R$ or $x = -R$ is more delicate and depends on the coefficients. If $R = 0$ the series has little utility, but when $R > 0$ the sum of the infinite series defines a function $f(x)$. Any function f that can be defined by a convergent power series is said to be real-analytic.

The coefficients of the power series of a real-analytic function can be expressed in terms of derivatives of that function. For values of x inside the interval of convergence, the series can be differentiated term by term. That is, $f'(x) = a_1 + 2a_2 x + 3a_3 x^2 + \cdots$, and this series also converges. Repeating this procedure and then setting $x = 0$ in the resulting expressions shows that $a_0 = f(0)$, $a_1 = f'(0)$, $a_2 = f''(0)/2$, $a_3 = f'''(0)/6$, and, in general, $a_j = f^{(j)}(0)/j!$. That is, within the interval of convergence of f,

$$f(x) = f(0) + f'(0)x + \frac{f''(0)x^2}{2!} + \frac{f'''(0)x^3}{3!} + \cdots.$$

This expression is the Maclaurin series of f, otherwise known as the Taylor series of f about o. A slight generalization leads to the Taylor series of f about a general value x:

$$f(x+h) = f(x) + f'(x)h + \frac{f''(x)h^2}{2!} + \frac{f'''(x)h^3}{3!} + \cdots.$$

All these series are meaningful only if they converge.

For example, it can be shown that $e^x = 1 + x + \frac{x^2}{2!} + \frac{x^3}{3!} + \cdots$, $\sin(x) = x - \frac{x^3}{3!} + \frac{x^5}{5!} - \cdots$, $\cos(x) = 1 - \frac{x^2}{2!} + \frac{x^4}{4!} - \cdots$, and these series converge for all x.

INTEGRATION

Like differentiation, integration has its roots in ancient problems—particularly, finding the area or volume of irregular objects and finding their centre of mass. Essentially, integration generalizes the process of summing up many small factors to determine some whole.

Also like differentiation, integration has a geometric interpretation. The (definite) integral of the function f, between initial and final values $t = a$ and $t = b$, is the area of the region enclosed by the graph of f, the horizontal axis, and the vertical lines $t = a$ and $t = b$. It is denoted by the symbol $\int_a^b f(t)dt$. Here the symbol $\int$ is an elongated s, for sum, because the integral is the limit of a particular kind of sum. The values a and b are often, confusingly, called the limits of the integral; this terminology is unrelated to the limit concept introduced above.

THE FUNDAMENTAL THEOREM OF CALCULUS

The process of calculating integrals is called integration. Integration is related to differentiation by the fundamental theorem of calculus, which states that (subject to the mild technical condition that the function be continuous) the derivative of the integral is the original function. In symbols, the fundamental theorem is stated as $\frac{d}{dt}(\int_a^t f(u)\,du) = f(t)$.

The reasoning behind this theorem can be demonstrated in a logical progression, as follows: Let $A(t)$ be the integral of f from a to t. Then the derivative of $A(t)$ is very closely approximated by the quotient $(A(t + h) - A(t))/h$. This is $\frac{1}{h}$ times the area under the graph of f between t and $t + h$. For continuous functions f the value of $f(t)$, for t in the interval, changes only slightly, so it must be very close to $f(t)$. The area is therefore close to $h\,f(t)$, so the quotient is close to $h\,f(t)/h = f(t)$. Taking the limit as h tends to zero, the result follows.

ANTIDIFFERENTIATION

Strict mathematical logic aside, the importance of the fundamental theorem of calculus is that it allows one to find areas by antidifferentiation—the reverse process to differentiation. To integrate a given function f, just find a function F whose derivative F' is equal to f. Then the value of the integral is the difference $F(b) - F(a)$ between the value of F at the two limits. For example, since the derivative of t^3 is $3t^2$, take the antiderivative of $3t^2$ to be t^3. The area of the region enclosed by the graph of the function $y = 3t^2$, the horizontal axis, and the vertical lines $t = 1$ and $t = 2$, for example, is given by the integral $\int_1^2 3t^2\,dt$. By the fundamental theorem of calculus, this is the difference between the values of t^3 when $t = 2$ and $t = 1$. That is, $2^3 - 1^3 = 7$.

All the basic techniques of calculus for finding integrals work in this manner. They provide a repertoire of tricks for finding a function whose derivative is a given function. Most of what is taught in schools and colleges

THE BRITANNICA GUIDE TO ANALYSIS AND CALCULUS

under the name *calculus* consists of rules for calculating the derivatives and integrals of functions of various forms and of particular applications of those techniques, such as finding the length of a curve or the surface area of a solid of revolution.

Table 2: Derivatives and integrals of some elementary functions		
function $f(x)$	derivative $f'(x)$	integral $\int f(x)dx$
1	0	$x + c$
x	1	$\frac{x^2}{2} + c$
x^2	$2x$	$\frac{x^3}{3} + c$
x^a	ax^{a-1}	$\frac{x^{a+1}}{a+1} + c$ (when $a \neq -1$)
e^x	e^x	$e^x + c$
$\log x$	$\frac{1}{x}$	$x \log x - x + c$
$\sin x$	$\cos x$	$-\cos x + c$
$\cos x$	$-\sin x$	$\sin x + c$

The symbol c is an arbitrary constant.

Table 2 lists the derivatives and integrals of a small number of elementary functions. In the table, the symbol c denotes an arbitrary constant. (Because the derivative of a constant is zero, the antiderivative of a function is not unique: adding a constant makes no difference. When an integral is evaluated between two specific limits, this constant is subtracted from itself and thus cancels out. In the indefinite integral, another name for the antiderivative, the constant must be included.)

THE RIEMANN INTEGRAL

The task of analysis is to provide not a computational method but a sound logical foundation for limiting processes. Oddly enough, when it comes to formalizing the integral, the most difficult part is to define the term *area*.

It is easy to define the area of a shape whose edges are straight. For example, the area of a rectangle is just the product of the lengths of two adjoining sides. But the area of a shape with curved edges can be more elusive. The answer, again, is to set up a suitable limiting process that approximates the desired area with simpler regions whose areas can be calculated.

The first successful general method for accomplishing this is usually credited to the German mathematician Bernhard Riemann in 1853, although it has many precursors (both in ancient Greece and in China). Given some function $f(t)$, consider the area of the region enclosed by the graph of f, the horizontal axis, and the vertical lines $t = a$ and $t = b$. Riemann's approach is to slice this region into thin vertical strips and to approximate its area by sums of areas of rectangles, both from the inside and from the outside. If both of these sums converge to the same limiting value as the thickness of the slices tends to zero, then their common value is defined to be the Riemann integral of f between the limits a and b. If this limit exists for all a, b, then f is said to be (Riemann) integrable. Every continuous function is integrable.

CHAPTER 3
DIFFERENTIAL EQUATIONS

How far does an object fall in a certain time? How fast does radioactive material decay? How does a capacitor discharge? The answers to all these questions can be found using differential equations.

ORDINARY DIFFERENTIAL EQUATIONS

NEWTON AND DIFFERENTIAL EQUATIONS

Analysis is one of the cornerstones of mathematics. It is important not only within mathematics itself but also because of its extensive applications to the sciences. The main vehicles for the application of analysis are differential equations, which relate the rates of change of various quantities to their current values, making it possible—in principle and often in practice—to predict future behaviour. Differential equations arose from the work of Isaac Newton on dynamics in the 17th century.

NEWTON'S LAWS OF MOTION

Imagine a body moving along a line, whose distance from some chosen point is given by the function $x(t)$ at time t. (The symbol x is traditional here rather than the symbol f for a general function, but this is purely a notational convention.) The instantaneous velocity of the moving body is the rate of change of distance—that is, the derivative $x'(t)$. Its instantaneous acceleration is the rate of change of velocity—that is, the second derivative $x''(t)$. According to the most important of Newton's laws of motion, the acceleration experienced by a body of mass m is proportional to the force F applied, a principle that can be expressed by the equation

$$F = mx''. \tag{4}$$

Suppose that m and F (which may vary with time) are specified, and one wishes to calculate the motion of the body. Knowing its acceleration alone is not satisfactory; one wishes to know its position x at an arbitrary time t. In order to apply equation (4), one must solve for x, not for its second derivative x''. Thus, one must solve an equation for the quantity x when that equation involves derivatives of x. Such equations are called differential equations, and their solution requires techniques that go well beyond the usual methods for solving algebraic equations.

For example, consider the simplest case, in which the mass m and force F are constant, as is the case for a body falling under terrestrial gravity. Then equation (4) can be written as

$$x''(t) = {}^{F}\!/_{m}. \tag{5}$$

Integrating (5) once with respect to time gives

$$x'(t) = {}^{Ft}\!/_{m} + b \tag{6}$$

where b is an arbitrary constant. Integrating (6) with respect to time yields $x(t) = {}^{Ft^2}\!/_{2m} + bt + c$ with a second constant c. The values of the constants b and c depend upon initial conditions. Indeed, c is the initial position, and b is the initial velocity.

A crash test is a prime illustration of Newton's first law of motion, which has to do with inertia. An object in motion will remain in motion until a force acts upon it. If a car hits a wall, the passenger keeps moving until a seat belt stops him or he comes into contact with another object that applies a force. TRL Ltd. Photo Researchers, Inc

EXPONENTIAL GROWTH AND DECAY

Newton's equation for the laws of motion could be solved as above, by integrating twice with respect to time, because time is the only variable term within the function x''. Not all differential equations can be solved in such a simple manner. For example, the radioactive decay of a substance is governed by the differential equation

$$x'(t) = -kx(t) \qquad (7)$$

where k is a positive constant and $x(t)$ is the amount of substance that remains radioactive at time t. The equation can be solved by rewriting it as

$$\frac{x'(t)}{x(t)} = -k. \qquad (8)$$

The left-hand side of (8) can be shown to be the derivative of $\ln x(t)$, so the equation can be integrated to yield $\ln x(t) + c = -k\,t$ for a constant c that is determined by initial conditions. Equivalently, $x(t) = e^{-(kt + c)}$. This solution represents exponential decay: in any fixed period of time, the same proportion of the substance decays. This property of radioactivity is reflected in the concept of the half-life of a given radioactive substance—that is, the time taken for half the material to decay.

A surprisingly large number of natural processes display exponential decay or growth. [Change the sign from negative to positive on the right-hand side of (7) to obtain the differential equation for exponential growth.] However, this is not quite so surprising if consideration is given to the fact that the only functions whose derivatives are proportional to themselves are exponential functions. In other words, the rate of change of exponential functions directly depends upon their current value. This accounts for their ubiquity in mathematical models. For instance, the more radioactive material present, the more radiation is produced. Similarly, the greater the temperature difference between a "hot body" in a "cold room," the faster the heat loss (known as Newton's law of cooling and an essential tool in the coroner's arsenal). The larger the savings, the greater the compounded interest. And the larger the population (in an unrestricted environment), the greater the population explosion.

DYNAMICAL SYSTEMS THEORY AND CHAOS

The classical methods of analysis have their limitations. For example, differential equations describing the motion of the solar system do not admit solutions by power series (i.e., infinite sums of multiples of powers). Ultimately, this is because the dynamics of the solar system is too complicated to be captured by such simple, well-behaved objects as power series. One of the most important modern theoretical developments has been the qualitative theory of differential equations, otherwise known as dynamical systems theory, which seeks to establish general properties of solutions from general principles without writing down any explicit solutions at all. Dynamical systems theory combines local analytic information, collected in small "neighbourhoods" around points of special interest, with global geometric and topological properties of the shape and structure of the manifold in which all the possible solutions, or paths, reside—the qualitative aspect of the theory. (A manifold, also known as the state space or phase space, is the multidimensional analog of a curved surface.) This approach is especially powerful when employed in conjunction with numerical methods, which use computers to approximate the solution.

The qualitative theory of differential equations was the brainchild of the French mathematician Henri Poincaré at the end of the 19th century. A major stimulus to the development of dynamical systems theory was a prize offered in 1885 by King Oscar II of Sweden and Norway for a solution to the problem of determining the stability of the solar system. The problem was stated essentially as follows: Will the planets of the solar system continue forever in much the same arrangement as they do at present? Or could something dramatic happen, such as a planet being flung out of the solar system entirely or colliding with the Sun? Mathematicians already knew that considerable difficulties arise in answering any such questions as soon as the number of bodies involved exceeds two. For two bodies moving under Newtonian gravitation, it is possible to solve the differential equation and deduce an exact formula for their motion. That is, they move in ellipses about their mutual centre of gravity. Newton carried out this calculation when he showed that the inverse square law of gravitation explains Johannes Kepler's discovery that planetary orbits are elliptical. The motion of three bodies proved less tractable—indeed, nobody could solve the "three-body problem"—and the solar system is a ten-body problem (or something like a thirty-body problem if one includes the satellites of the planets and a many-thousand-body problem if one includes asteroids).

Undaunted, Poincaré set up a general framework for the problem, but, in order to make serious progress, he was forced to specialize to three bodies and to assume that one of them has negligible mass in comparison with the other two. This approach is known as the "restricted" three-body problem, and his work on it won Poincaré the prize.

Ironically, the prizewinning memoir contained a serious mistake, and Poincaré's biggest discovery in the area came when he hastened to put the error right (costing him more in printing expenses than the value of the prize). It turned out that even the restricted three-body problem was still too difficult to be solved. What Poincaré did manage to understand, though, was why it is so hard to solve. By ingenious geometric arguments, he showed that planetary orbits in the restricted three-body problem are too complicated to be describable by any explicit formula. He did so by introducing a novel idea, now called a Poincaré section. Suppose one knows some solution path and wants to find out how nearby solution paths behave. Imagine a surface that slices through the known path. Nearby paths will also cross this surface and may eventually return to it. By studying how this "point of first return" behaves, information is gained about these nearby solution paths.

Today the term *chaos* is used to refer to Poincaré's discovery. Sporadically during the 1930s and '40s and with increasing frequency in the 1960s, mathematicians and scientists began to notice that simple differential equations can sometimes possess extremely complex solutions. The American mathematician Stephen Smale, continuing to develop Poincaré's insights on qualitative properties of differential equations, proved that in some cases the behaviour of the solutions is effectively random. Even when there is no hint of randomness in the equations, there can be genuine elements of randomness in the solutions. The Russian school of dynamicists under Andrey Kolmogorov and Vladimir Arnold developed similar ideas at much the same time.

These discoveries challenged the classical view of determinism, the idea of a "clockwork universe" that merely works out the consequences of fixed laws of nature, starting from given initial conditions. By the end of the 20th century, Poincaré's discovery of chaos had grown into a major discipline within mathematics, connecting with many areas of applied science. Chaos was found not just in the motion of the planets but in weather, disease epidemics, ecology, fluid flow, electrochemistry, acoustics, even quantum mechanics. The most important feature of the new viewpoint on dynamics—popularly known as chaos theory but really just a subdiscipline of dynamical systems theory—is not the realization that many processes are unpredictable. Rather, it is the development of a whole series of novel techniques for extracting useful information from apparently random behaviour. Chaos theory has led to the discovery of new and more efficient ways to send space probes to the Moon or to distant comets, new kinds of solid-state lasers, new ways to forecast weather and estimate the accuracy of such forecasts, and new designs for heart pacemakers. It has even been turned into a quality-control technique for the wire- and spring-making industries.

PARTIAL DIFFERENTIAL EQUATIONS

From the 18th century onward, huge strides were made in the application of mathematical ideas to problems arising in the physical sciences: heat, sound, light, fluid dynamics, elasticity, electricity, and magnetism. The complicated interplay between the mathematics and its applications led to many new discoveries in both. The main unifying theme in much of this work is the notion of a partial differential equation.

MUSICAL ORIGINS

The problem that sparked the entire development was deceptively simple, and it was surprisingly far removed from any serious practical application, coming not so much from the physical sciences but from music: What is the appropriate mathematical description of the motion of a violin string?

HARMONY

The students of Pythagoras in ancient Greece also found inspiration in music, especially musical harmony. They experimented with the notes sounded by strings of various lengths, and one of their great discoveries was that two notes sound pleasing together, or harmonious, if the lengths of the corresponding strings are in simple numerical ratios such as 2:1 or 3:2. It took more than two millennia before mathematics could explain why these ratios arise naturally from the motion of elastic strings.

NORMAL MODES

Probably the earliest major result was obtained in 1714 by the English mathematician Brook Taylor, who calculated the fundamental vibrational frequency of a violin string in terms of its length, tension, and density. The ancient Greeks knew that a vibrating string can produce many different musical notes, depending on the position of the nodes, or rest-points. Today it is known that musical pitch is governed by the frequency of the vibration—the number of complete cycles of vibrations every second. The faster the string moves, the higher the frequency and the higher the note that it produces. For the fundamental frequency, only the end points are at rest. If the string has a node at its centre, then it produces a note at exactly double the frequency (heard by the human ear as one octave higher).

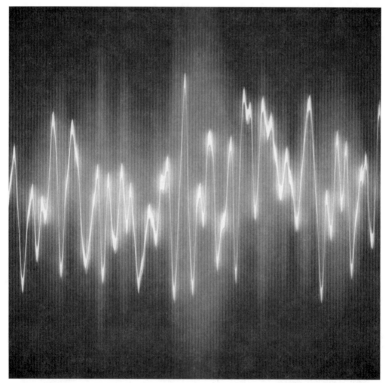

This is a sound wave. There are peaks and troughs, or highs and lows. These highs and lows define the amplitude of a sound wave. © www.istockphoto. com/Phil Morley

The more nodes there are, the higher the frequency of the note. These higher vibrations are called overtones.

The vibrations produced are standing waves. That is, the shape of the string at any instant is the same, except that it is stretched or compressed in a direction at right angles to its length. The maximum amount of stretching is the amplitude of the wave, which physically determines how loud the note sounds. The waveforms shown are sinusoidal in shape—given by the sine function from trigonometry—and their amplitudes vary sinusoidally with time. Standing waves of this simple kind are called normal modes. Their frequencies are integer multiples of a single fundamental frequency—the mathematical source of the Pythagoreans' simple numerical ratios.

PARTIAL DERIVATIVES

In 1746 the French mathematician Jean Le Rond d'Alembert showed that the full story is not quite that simple. There are many vibrations of a violin string that are not normal modes. In fact, d'Alembert proved that the shape of the wave at time $t = 0$ can be arbitrary.

Imagine a string of length l, stretched along the x-axis from $(0, 0)$ to $(l, 0)$, and suppose that at time t the point $(x, 0)$ is displaced by an amount $y(x, t)$ in the y-direction. The function $y(x, t)$—or, more briefly, just y—is a function of two variables. That is, it depends not on a single variable t but upon x as well. If some value for x is selected and kept fixed, it is still possible for t to vary. Therefore a function $f(t)$ can be defined by $f(t) = y(x, t)$ for this fixed x. The derivative $f'(t)$ of this function is called the partial derivative of y with respect to t, and the procedure that produces it is called partial differentiation with respect to t. The partial derivative of f with respect to t is written $\partial y/\partial t$, where the symbol ∂ is a special form of the letter d reserved for this particular operation. An alternative, simpler notation is y_t. Analogously, fixing t instead of x gives the partial derivative of y with respect to x, written $\partial y/\partial x$ or y_x. In both cases, the way to calculate a partial derivative is to treat all other variables as constants and then find the usual derivative of the resulting function with respect to the chosen variable. For example, if $y(x, t) = x^2 + t^3$, then $y_t = 3t^2$ and $y_x = 2x$.

Both y_x and y_t are again functions of the two variables x and t, so they in turn can be partially differentiated with respect to either x or t. The partial derivative of y_t with respect to t is written y_{tt} or $\partial^2 y/\partial t^2$; the partial derivative of y_t with respect to x is written y_{tx} or $\partial^2 y/\partial t \partial x$; and so on. Henceforth the simpler subscript notation will be used.

D'ALEMBERT'S WAVE EQUATION

D'Alembert's wave equation takes the form

$$y_{tt} = c^2 y_{xx}. \tag{9}$$

Here c is a constant related to the stiffness of the string. The physical interpretation of (9) is that the acceleration (y_{tt}) of a small piece of the string is proportional to the tension (y_{xx}) within it. Because the equation involves partial derivatives, it is known as a partial differential equation—in contrast to the previously described differential equations, which, involving derivatives with respect to only one variable, are called ordinary differential equations. Since partial differentiation is applied twice (for instance, to get y_{tt} from y), the equation is said to be of second order.

In order to specify physically realistic solutions, d'Alembert's wave equation must be supplemented by boundary conditions, which express the fact that the ends of a violin string are fixed. Here the boundary conditions take the form

$$y(0, t) = 0 \text{ and } y(l, t) = 0 \text{ for all } t. \qquad (10)$$

D'Alembert showed that the general solution to (10) is

$$y(x, t) = f(x + c\,t) + g(x - ct) \qquad (11)$$

where f and g are arbitrary functions (of one variable). The physical interpretation of this solution is that f represents the shape of a wave that travels with speed c along the x-axis in the negative direction, while g represents the shape of a wave that travels along the x-axis in the positive direction. The general solution is a superposition of two traveling waves.

In order to satisfy the boundary conditions given in (10), the functions f and g must be related by the equations $f(-ct) + g(ct) = 0$ and $f(l - ct) + g(l + ct) = 0$ for all t. These equations imply that $g = -f$, that f is an odd function—one satisfying $f(-u) = -f(u)$—and that f is periodic with period $2l$, meaning that $f(u + 2l) = f(u)$ for all u. Notice that the part of f lying between $x = 0$ and $x = l$ is arbitrary, which corresponds to the physical fact that a violin string can be started vibrating from any shape whatsoever (subject to its ends being fixed). In particular, its shape need not be sinusoidal, proving that solutions other than normal modes can occur.

TRIGONOMETRIC SERIES SOLUTIONS

In 1748, in response to d'Alembert's work, the Swiss mathematician Leonhard Euler wrote a paper, *Sur la vibration des cordes* ("On the Vibrations of Strings"). In it he repeated d'Alembert's derivation of the wave equation for a string, but he obtained a new solution. Euler's innovation was to permit f and g to be what he called discontinuous curves (though in modern terminology it is their derivatives that are discontinuous, not the functions themselves). To Euler, who thought in terms of formulas, this meant that the shapes of the curves were defined by different formulas in different intervals. In 1749 he went on to explain that if several normal mode solutions of the wave equation are superposed, the result is a solution of the form

$$y(x,t) = a_1 \sin\frac{x}{l}\cos\frac{ct}{l} + a_2 \sin\frac{2x}{l}\cos\frac{2ct}{l} + a_3 \sin\frac{3x}{l}\cos\frac{3ct}{l} + \cdots \quad (12)$$

where the coefficients a_1, a_2, a_3, ... are arbitrary constants. Euler did not state whether the series should be finite or infinite. Nonetheless it eventually turned out that infinite series held the key to a central mystery, the relation between d'Alembert's arbitrary function solutions (11) and Euler's trigonometric series solutions (12). Every solution of Euler's type can also be written in the form of d'Alembert's solution, but is the converse true? This question was the subject of a lengthy controversy, whose final conclusion was that all possible vibrations of the string can be obtained by superposing infinitely many normal modes in suitable proportions. The normal modes are the basic components. The vibrations that can occur are all possible sums of constant multiples of finitely or infinitely many normal modes. As the Swiss mathematician Daniel Bernoulli expressed it in 1753: "All new curves given by d'Alembert and Euler are only combinations of the Taylor vibrations."

The controversy was not really about the wave equation. It was about the meaning of the word *function*. Euler wanted it to include his discontinuous functions, but he thought—wrongly as it turned out—that a trigonometric series cannot represent a discontinuous function, because it provides a single formula valid throughout the entire interval $0 \leq x \leq l$. Bernoulli, mostly on physical grounds, was happy with the discontinuous functions, but he thought—correctly but without much justification—that Euler was wrong about their not being representable by trigonometric series. It took roughly a century to sort out the answers—and, along the way, mathematicians were forced to take what might seem to be logical hairsplitting very seriously indeed, because it was only by being very careful about logical rigour that the problem could be resolved in a satisfactory and reliable manner.

Mathematics did not wait for this resolution, though. It plowed ahead into the disputed territory, and every new discovery made the eventual resolution that much more important. The first development was to extend the wave equation to other kinds of vibrations—for example, the vibrations of drums. The first work here was also Euler's, in 1759. Again he derived a wave equation, describing how the displacement of the drum skin in the vertical direction varies over time. Drums differ from violin strings not only in their dimensionality—a drum is a flat two-dimensional membrane—but in having a much more interesting boundary. If $z(x, y, t)$ denotes the displacement at time t in the z-direction of the portion of drum skin that lies at the point (x, y) in the plane, then Euler's wave equation takes the form

$$z_{tt} = c^2(z_{xx} + z_{yy}) \tag{13}$$

with boundary conditions

$$z(x, y, t) = 0 \tag{14}$$

whenever (x, y) lies on the boundary of the drum. Equation (13) is strikingly similar to the wave equation for a violin string. Its physical interpretation is that the acceleration of a small piece of the drum skin is proportional to the average tension exerted on it by all nearby parts of the drum skin. Equation (14) states that the rim of the drum skin remains fixed. In this whole subject, boundaries are absolutely crucial.

The mathematicians of the 18th century were able to solve the equations for the motion of drums of various shapes. Again they found that all vibrations can be built up from simpler ones, the normal modes. The simplest case is the rectangular drum, whose normal modes are combinations of sinusoidal ripples in the two perpendicular directions.

FOURIER ANALYSIS

Nowadays, trigonometric series solutions (12) are called Fourier series, after Joseph Fourier, who in 1822 published one of the great mathematical classics, *The Analytical Theory of Heat*. Fourier began with a problem closely analogous to the vibrating violin string: the conduction of heat in a rigid rod of length l. If $T(x, t)$ denotes the temperature at position x and time t, then it satisfies a partial differential equation

$$T_t = a^2 T_{xx} \qquad (15)$$

that differs from the wave equation only in having the first time derivative T_t instead of the second, T_{tt}. This apparently minor change has huge consequences, both mathematical and physical. Again there are boundary conditions, expressing the fact that the temperatures at the ends of the rod are held fixed—for example,

$$T(0, t) = 0 \text{ and } T(l, t) = 0, \qquad (16)$$

if the ends are held at zero temperature. The physical effect of the first time derivative is profound: instead of getting persistent vibrational waves, the heat spreads out more and more smoothly—it diffuses.

Fourier showed that his heat equation can be solved using trigonometric series. He invented a method (now called Fourier analysis) of finding appropriate coefficients $a_1, a_2, a_3, \ldots$ in equation (12) for any given initial temperature distribution. He did not solve the problem of providing rigorous logical foundations for such series—indeed, along with most of his contemporaries, he failed to appreciate the need for such foundations—but he provided major motivation for those who eventually did establish foundations.

These developments were not just of theoretical interest. The wave equation, in particular, is exceedingly important. Waves arise not only in musical instruments but in all sources of sound and in light. Euler found a three-dimensional version of the wave equation, which he applied to sound waves. It takes the form

$$w_{tt} = c^2(w_{xx} + w_{yy} + w_{zz}) \qquad (17)$$

where now $w(x, y, z, t)$ is the pressure of the sound wave at point (x, y, z) at time t. The expression $w_{xx} + w_{yy} + w_{zz}$ is called the Laplacian, after the French mathematician Pierre-Simon de Laplace, and is central to classical mathematical physics. Roughly a century after Euler, the Scottish physicist James Clerk Maxwell extracted the three-dimensional wave equation from his equations for electromagnetism, and in consequence he was able to predict the existence of radio waves. It is probably fair to suggest that radio, television, and radar would not exist today without the early mathematicians' work on the analytic aspects of musical instruments.

Profl I

Investiganda est curva linea ADB ... Z C
qua grave a dato quovis puncto A ad
...

CHAPTER 4
OTHER AREAS
OF ANALYSIS

Modern analysis is far too broad to describe in detail. Instead, a small selection of other major areas is explored below to convey some flavour of the subject.

COMPLEX ANALYSIS

In the 18th century a far-reaching generalization of analysis was discovered, centred on the so-called imaginary number $i = \sqrt{-1}$. (In engineering this number is usually denoted by j.) The numbers commonly used in everyday life are known as real numbers, but in one sense this name is misleading. Numbers are abstract concepts, not objects in the physical universe. So mathematicians consider real numbers to be an abstraction on exactly the same logical level as imaginary numbers.

The name *imaginary* arises because squares of real numbers are always positive. In consequence, positive numbers have two distinct square roots—one positive, one negative. Zero has a single square root—namely, zero. And negative numbers have no "real" square roots at all. However, it has proved extremely fruitful and useful to enlarge the number concept to include square roots of negative numbers. The resulting objects are numbers in the sense that arithmetic and algebra can be extended to them in a simple and natural manner. They are imaginary in the sense that their relation to the physical world is less direct than that of the real numbers. Numbers formed by combining real and imaginary components, such as $2 + 3i$, are said to be complex (meaning they are composed of several parts rather than complicated).

The first indications that complex numbers might prove useful emerged in the 16th century from the solution of certain algebraic equations by the Italian mathematicians Girolamo Cardano and Raphael Bombelli. By the 18th century, after a lengthy and controversial history, they became fully established as sensible mathematical concepts. They remained on the mathematical fringes until it was discovered that analysis, too, can be extended to the complex domain. The result was such a powerful extension of the mathematical tool kit that philosophical questions about the meaning of complex numbers became submerged amid the rush to exploit them. Soon the mathematical community had become so used to complex numbers that it became hard to recall that there had been a philosophical problem at all.

FORMAL DEFINITION OF COMPLEX NUMBERS

The modern approach is to define a complex number $x + iy$ as a pair of real numbers (x, y) subject to certain algebraic operations. Thus one wishes to add or subtract, $(a, b) \pm (c, d)$, and to multiply, $(a, b) \times (c, d)$, or divide, $(a, b)/(c, d)$, these quantities. These are inspired by the wish to make $(x, 0)$ behave like the real number x and, crucially, to arrange that $(0, 1)^2 = (-1, 0)$—all the while preserving as many of the rules of algebra as possible. This is a formal way to set up a situation which, in effect, ensures that one may operate with expressions $x + iy$ using all the standard algebraic rules but recalling when necessary that i^2 may be replaced by -1. For example, $(1 + 3i)^2 = 1^2 + 2 \cdot 3i + (3i)^2 = 1 + 6i + 9i^2 = 1 + 6i - 9 = -8 + 6i$.

A geometric interpretation of complex numbers is readily available, inasmuch as a pair (x, y) represents a point in a plane. Whereas real numbers can be described by a single number line, with negative numbers to the left and positive numbers to the right, the complex numbers require a number plane with two axes, real and imaginary.

EXTENSION OF ANALYTIC CONCEPTS TO COMPLEX NUMBERS

Analytic concepts such as limits, derivatives, integrals, and infinite series are based upon algebraic ideas, together with error estimates that define the limiting process: certain numbers must be arbitrarily well approximated by particular algebraic expressions. In order to represent the concept of an approximation, all that is needed is a well-defined way to measure how "small" a number is. For real numbers this is achieved by using the absolute value $|x|$. Geometrically, it is the distance along the real number line between x and the origin o. Distances also make sense in the complex plane, and they can be calculated, using Pythagoras's theorem from elementary geometry (the square of the hypotenuse of a right triangle is equal to the sum of the squares of its two sides), by constructing a right triangle such that its hypotenuse spans the distance between two points and its sides are drawn parallel to the coordinate axes. This line of thought leads to the idea that for complex numbers the quantity analogous to $|x|$ is

$$|x+iy| = \sqrt{x^2+y^2}.$$

Since all the rules of real algebra extend to complex numbers and the absolute value is defined by an algebraic formula, it follows that analysis also extends to the complex numbers. Formal definitions are taken from the real case, real numbers are replaced by complex numbers, and the real absolute value is replaced by the complex absolute value. Indeed, this is one of the advantages of analytic rigour: without this, it would be far less obvious how to extend such notions as tangent or limit from the real case to the complex.

In a similar vein, the Taylor series for the real exponential and trigonometric functions shows how to extend these definitions to include complex numbers—just use the same series but replace the real variable x by the complex variable z. This idea leads to complex-analytic functions as an extension of real-analytic ones.

Because complex numbers differ in certain ways from real numbers—their structure is simpler in some respects and richer in others—there are differences in detail between real and complex analysis. Complex integration, in particular, has features of complete novelty. A real function must be integrated between limits a and b, and the Riemann integral is defined in terms of a sum involving values spread along the interval from a to b. On the real number line, the only path between two points a and b is the interval whose ends they form. But in the complex plane there are many different paths between two given points. The integral of a function between two points is therefore not defined until a path between the endpoints is specified. This done, the definition of the Riemann integral can be extended to the complex case. However, the result may depend on the path that is chosen.

Surprisingly, this dependence is very weak. Indeed, sometimes there is no dependence at all. But when there is, the situation becomes extremely interesting. The value of the integral depends only on certain qualitative features of the path—in modern terms, on its topology. (Topology, often characterized as "rubber sheet geometry," studies those properties of a shape that are unchanged if it is continuously deformed by being bent, stretched, and twisted but not torn.) So complex analysis possesses a new ingredient, a kind of flexible geometry, that is totally lacking in real analysis. This gives it a very different flavour.

All this became clear in 1811 when, in a letter to the German astronomer Friedrich Bessel, the German mathematician Carl Friedrich Gauss stated the central theorem of complex analysis:

> *I affirm now that the integral...has only one value even if taken over different paths, provided [the function]... does not become infinite in the space enclosed by the two paths.*

A proof was published by Cauchy in 1825, and this result is now named Cauchy's theorem. Cauchy went on to develop a vast theory of complex analysis and its applications.

Part of the importance of complex analysis is that it is generally better-behaved than real analysis, the many-valued nature of integrals notwithstanding. Problems in the real domain can often be solved by extending them to the complex domain, applying the powerful techniques peculiar to that area, and then restricting the results back to the real domain again. From the mid-19th century onward, the progress of complex analysis was strong and steady. A system of numbers once rejected as impossible and nonsensical led to a powerful and aesthetically satisfying theory with practical applications to aerodynamics, fluid mechanics, electric power generation, and mathematical physics. No area of mathematics has remained untouched by this far-reaching enrichment of the number concept.

SOME KEY IDEAS OF COMPLEX ANALYSIS

A complex number is normally denoted by $z = x + iy$. A complex-valued function f assigns to each z in some region Ω of the complex plane a complex number $w = f(z)$. Usually it is assumed that the region Ω is connected (all in one piece) and open (each point of Ω can be surrounded by a small disk that lies entirely within Ω). Such a function f is differentiable at a point z_0 in Ω if the limit exists as z approaches z_0 of the expression

$$\frac{f(z) - f(z_0)}{z - z_0} .$$

This limit is the derivative $f'(z)$. Unlike real analysis, if a complex function is differentiable in some region, then its derivative is always differentiable in that region, so $f''(z)$ exists. Indeed, derivatives $f^{(n)}(z)$ of all orders $n = 1, 2, 3, \ldots$ exist. Even more strongly, $f(z)$ has a power series expansion $f(z) = c_0 + c_1(z - z_0) + c_2(z - z_0)^2 + \cdots$ with complex coefficients c_j. This series converges for all z lying in some disk with centre z_0. The radius of the largest such disk is called the radius of convergence of the series. Because of this power series representation, a differentiable complex function is said to be analytic.

The elementary functions of real analysis, such as polynomials, trigonometric functions, and exponential functions, can be extended to complex numbers. For example, the exponential of a complex number is defined by $e^z = 1 + z + \frac{z^2}{2!} + \frac{z^3}{3!} + \cdots$ where $n! = n(n - 1)\cdots 3 \cdot 2 \cdot 1$. It turns out that the trigonometric functions are related to the exponential by way of Euler's famous formula $e^{i\theta} = \cos(\theta) + i\sin(\theta)$, which leads to the expressions $\cos(z) = \frac{(e^{iz} + e^{-iz})}{2}$, $\sin(z) = \frac{(e^{iz} - e^{-iz})}{2i}$. Every complex number can be written in the form $z = re^{i\theta}$ for real $r \geq 0$ and real θ. Here r is the absolute value (or modulus) of z, and θ is known as its argument. The value of θ is not unique, but the possible values differ only by integer multiples of 2π. In consequence, the complex logarithm is many-valued: $\log(z) = \log(re^{i\theta}) = \log|r| + i(\theta + 2n\pi)$ for any integer n.

The integral $\int_C f(z)dz$ of an analytic function f along a curve (or contour) C in the complex plane is defined in a similar manner to the real Riemann integral. Cauchy's theorem, mentioned above, states that the value of such an integral is the same for two contours C_1 and C_2, provided both curves lie inside a simply connected region Ω—a region with no "holes." When Ω has holes, the value of the integral depends on the topology of the curve C but not its precise form. The essential feature is how many times C winds around a given hole—a number that is related to the many-valued nature of the complex logarithm.

MEASURE THEORY

A rigorous basis for the new discipline of analysis was achieved in the 19th century, in particular by the German mathematician Karl Weierstrass. Modern analysis, however, differs from that of Weierstrass's time in many ways, and the most obvious is the level of abstraction. Today's analysis is set in a variety of general contexts, of which the real line and the complex plane are merely two rather simple examples. One of the most important spurs to these developments was the invention of a new—and improved—definition of the integral by the French mathematician Henri-Léon Lebesgue about 1900. Lebesgue's contribution made possible the subbranch of analysis known as measure theory.

In Lebesgue's day, mathematicians had noticed a number of deficiencies in Riemann's way of defining the integral. Many functions with reasonable properties turned out not to possess integrals in Riemann's sense. Moreover, certain limiting procedures, when applied to sequences not of numbers but of functions, behaved in very strange ways as far as integration was concerned. Several mathematicians tried to develop better ways to define the integral, and the best of all was Lebesgue's.

Consider, for example, the function f defined by $f(x) = 0$ whenever x is a rational number but $f(x) = 1$ whenever x is irrational. What is a sensible value for $\int_0^1 f(x)dx$? Using Riemann's definition, this function does not possess a well-defined integral. The reason is that within any interval it takes values both 0 and 1, so that it hops wildly up and down between those two values. Unfortunately for this example, Riemann's integral is based on the assumption that over sufficiently small intervals the value of the function changes by only a very small amount.

However, there is a sense in which the rational numbers form a very tiny proportion of the real numbers. In fact, "almost all" real numbers are irrational. Specifically, the set of all rational numbers can be surrounded by a collection of intervals whose total length is as small as is wanted. In a well-defined sense, then, the "length" of the set of rational numbers is zero. There are good reasons why values on a set of zero length ought not to affect the integral of a function—the "rectangle" based on that set ought to have zero area in any sensible interpretation of such a statement. Granted this, if the definition of the function f is changed so that it takes value 1 on the rational numbers instead of 0, its integral should not be altered. However, the resulting function g now takes the form $g(x) = 1$ for all x, and this function does possess a Riemann integral. In fact, $\int_a^b g(x)dx = b - a$. Lebesgue reasoned that the same result ought to hold for f—but he knew that it would not if the integral were defined in Riemann's manner.

The reason why Riemann's method failed to work for f is that the values of f oscillate wildly over arbitrarily small intervals. Riemann's approach relied upon approximating the area under a graph by slicing it, in the vertical direction, into very thin slices. The problem with his method was that vertical direction: vertical slices permit wild variation in the value of the function within a slice. So

Lebesgue sliced the graph horizontally instead. The variation within such a slice is no more than the thickness of the slice, and this can be made very small. The price to be paid for keeping the variation small, though, is that the set of x for which $f(x)$ lies in a given horizontal slice can be very complicated. For example, for the function f defined earlier, $f(x)$ lies in a thin slice around o whenever x is rational and in a thin slice around 1 whenever x is irrational.

However, it does not matter if such a set is complicated: it is sufficient that it should possess a well-defined generalization of length. Then that part of the graph of f corresponding to a given horizontal slice will have a well-defined approximate area, found by multiplying the value of the function that determines the slice by the "length" of the set of x whose functional values lie inside that slice. So the central problem faced by Lebesgue was not integration as such at all. It was to generalize the concept of length to sufficiently complicated sets. This Lebesgue managed to do. Basically, his method is to enclose the set in a collection of intervals. Since the generalized length of the set is surely smaller than the total length of the intervals, it only remains to choose the intervals that make the total length as small as possible.

This generalized concept of length is known as the Lebesgue measure. Once the measure is established, Lebesgue's generalization of the Riemann integral can be defined, and it turns out to be far superior to Riemann's integral. The concept of a measure can be extended considerably—for example, into higher dimensions, where it generalizes such notions as area and volume—leading to the subbranch known as measure theory. One fundamental application of measure theory is to probability and statistics, a development initiated by Russian mathematician Andrey Kolmogorov in the 1930s.

FUNCTIONAL ANALYSIS

In the 1920s and '30s a number of apparently different areas of analysis all came together in a single generalization—rather, two generalizations, one more general than the other. These were the notions of a Hilbert space and a Banach space, named after the German mathematician David Hilbert and the Polish mathematician Stefan Banach, respectively. Together they laid the foundations for what is now called functional analysis.

Functional analysis starts from the principle that, in order to define basic analytic notions such as limits or the derivative, it is sufficient to be able to carry out certain algebraic operations and to have a suitable notion of size. For real analysis, size is measured by the absolute value $|x|$; for complex analysis, it is measured by the absolute value $|x + i\,y|$. Analysis of functions of several variables—that is, the theory of partial derivatives—can also be brought under the same umbrella. In the real case, the set of real numbers is replaced by the vector space R^n of all n-tuples of real numbers $x = (x_1, ..., x_n)$ where each x_j is a real number. Used in place of the absolute value is the length of the vector x, which is defined to be

$$\|x\| = \sqrt{x_1^2 + \cdots + x_n^2}.$$

In fact there is a closely related notion, called an inner product, written $\langle x, y \rangle$, where x, y are vectors. It is equal to $x_1 y_1 + \cdots + x_n y_n$. The inner product relates not just to the sizes of x and y but to the angle between them. For example, $\langle x, y \rangle = 0$ if and only if x and y are orthogonal—at right angles to each other. Moreover, the inner product determines the length, because $\|x\| = \sqrt{\langle x, x \rangle}$. If $F(x) = (f_1(x), ..., f_k(x))$ is a vector-valued function of a vector $x = (x_1, ..., x_n)$, the derivative no longer has numerical values. Instead, it is a linear operator, a special kind of function.

Functions of several complex variables similarly reduce to a study of the space C^n of n-tuples of complex numbers $x + iy = (x_1 + iy_1, ..., x_n + iy_n)$. Used in place of the absolute value is

$$\|x\| = \sqrt{x_1^2 + y_1^2 + \cdots + x_n^2 + y_n^2}.$$

However, the correct concept of an analytic function of several complex variables is subtle and was developed only in the 20th century. Henceforth only the real case is considered here.

Hilbert realized that these ideas could be extended from vectors—which are finite sequences of real numbers—to infinite sequences of real numbers. Define (the simplest example of) Hilbert space to consist of all infinite sequences $x = (x_0, x_1, x_2, ...)$ of real numbers, subject to the condition that the sequence is square-summable, meaning that the infinite series $x_0^2 + x_1^2 + x_2^2 + \cdots$ converges to a finite value. Now define the inner product of two such sequences to be $\langle x, y \rangle = x_0 y_0 + x_1 y_1 + x_2 y_2 + \cdots$. It can be shown that this also takes a finite value. Hilbert discovered that it is possible to carry out the basic operations of analysis on Hilbert space. For example, it is possible to define convergence of a sequence $b_0, b_1, b_2, ...$ where the b_j are not numbers but elements of the Hilbert space—infinite sequences in their own right. Crucially, with this definition of convergence, Hilbert space is complete: every Cauchy sequence is convergent. Completeness is central to analysis for real-valued functions, and the same goes for functions on a Hilbert space.

More generally, a Hilbert space in the broad sense can be defined to be a (real or complex) vector space with an inner product that makes it complete, as well as determining a norm—a notion of length subject to certain constraints. There are numerous examples. Furthermore, this notion is very useful because it unifies large areas of classical analysis. It makes excellent sense of Fourier analysis, providing a satisfactory setting in which convergence questions are relatively unsubtle and straightforward. Instead of resolving various delicate classical issues, it bypasses them entirely. It organizes Lebesgue's theory of measures. The theory of integral equations—like differential equations but with integrals instead of derivatives—was very popular in Hilbert's day, and that, too, could be brought into the same framework. What Hilbert could not anticipate, since he died before the necessary physical theories were discovered, was that Hilbert space would also turn out to be ideal for quantum mechanics. In classical physics an observable value is just a number. Today a quantum mechanical observable value is defined as an operator on a Hilbert space.

Banach extended Hilbert's ideas considerably. A Banach space is a vector space with a norm, but not necessarily given by an inner product. Again the space must be complete. The theory of Banach spaces is extremely important as a framework for studying partial differential equations, which can be viewed as algebraic equations whose variables lie in a suitable Banach space. For instance, solving the wave equation for a violin string is equivalent to finding solutions of the equation $P(u) = 0$, where u is a member of the Banach space of functions $u(x)$ defined on the interval $0 \leq x \leq l$ and where P is the wave operator

$$P = \frac{\partial^2}{\partial t^2} - c^2 \frac{\partial^2}{\partial x^2} .$$

VARIATIONAL PRINCIPLES AND GLOBAL ANALYSIS

The great mathematicians of Classical times were very interested in variational problems. An example is the famous problem of the brachistochrone: find the shape of a curve with given start and end points along which a body will fall in the shortest possible time. The answer is (part of) an upside-down cycloid, where a cycloid is the path traced by a point on the rim of a rolling circle. More important for the purposes of this book is the nature of the problem: from among a class of curves, select the one that minimizes some quantity.

Variational problems can be put into Banach space language too. The space of curves is the Banach space, the quantity to be minimized is some functional (a function with functions, rather than simply numbers, as input) defined on the Banach space, and the methods of analysis can be used to determine the minimum. This approach can be generalized even further, leading to what is now called global analysis.

Pierre-Louis Moreau de Maupertuis. Royal Astronomical Society/Photo Researchers, Inc.

Global analysis has many applications to mathematical physics. Euler and the French mathematician Pierre-Louis Moreau de Maupertuis discovered that the whole of Newtonian mechanics can be restated in terms of a variational principle: mechanical systems move in a manner that minimizes (or, more technically, extremizes) a functional known as action. The French mathematician Pierre de Fermat stated a similar principle for optics, known as the principle of least time: light rays follow paths that minimize the total time of travel. Later the Irish mathematician William Rowan Hamilton found a unified theory that includes both optics and mechanics under the general notion of a Hamiltonian system—nowadays subsumed into a yet more general and abstract theory known as symplectic geometry.

An especially fascinating area of global analysis concerns the Plateau problem. The blind Belgian physicist Joseph Plateau (using an assistant as his eyes) spent many years observing the form of soap films and bubbles. He found that if a wire frame in the form of some curve is dipped in a soap solution, then the film forms beautiful curved surfaces. They are called minimal surfaces because they have minimal area subject to spanning the curve. (Their surface tension is proportional to their area, and their energy is proportional to surface tension, so they are actually energy-minimizing films.) For example, a soap bubble is spherical because a sphere has the smallest surface area, subject to enclosing a given volume of air.

The mathematics of minimal surfaces is an exciting area of current research with many attractive unsolved problems and conjectures. One of the major triumphs of global analysis occurred in 1976 when the American mathematicians Jean Taylor and Frederick Almgren obtained the mathematical derivation of the Plateau conjecture, which states that, when several soap films join together (for example, when several bubbles meet each other along common interfaces), the angles at which the films meet are either 120 degrees (for three films) or approximately 108

Joseph Plateau (1801–1883) became a professor of physics in Ghent in 1835. He was blinded by the Sun during his investigations into the Sun's effect on the human eye. He continued his work in physics, including his work on minimal surfaces, using the help of an assistant. SSPL via Getty Images

degrees (for four films). Plateau had conjectured this from his experiments.

CONSTRUCTIVE ANALYSIS

One philosophical feature of traditional analysis, which worries mathematicians whose outlook is especially concrete, is that many basic theorems assert the existence of various numbers or functions but do not specify what those numbers or functions are. For instance, the completeness property of the real numbers indicates that every Cauchy sequence converges but not what it converges to. A school of analysis initiated by the American mathematician Errett Bishop has developed a new framework for analysis in which no object can be deemed to exist unless a specific rule is given for constructing it. This school is known as constructive analysis, and its devotees have shown that it is just as rich in structure as traditional analysis and that most of the traditional theorems have analogs within the constructive framework. This philosophy has its origins in the earlier work of the Dutch mathematician-logician L.E.J. Brouwer, who criticized "mainstream" mathematical logicians for accepting proofs that mathematical objects exist without there being any specific construction of them (for example, a proof that some series converges without any specification of the limit which it converges to). Brouwer founded an entire school of mathematical logic, known as intuitionism, to advance his views.

However, constructive analysis remains on the fringes of the mathematical mainstream, probably because most mathematicians accept classical existence proofs and see no need for the additional mathematical baggage involved in carrying out analysis constructively. Nevertheless, constructive analysis is very much in the same algorithmic spirit as computer science, and in the future there may be some fruitful interaction with this area.

NONSTANDARD ANALYSIS

A very different philosophy—pretty much the exact opposite of constructive analysis—leads to nonstandard analysis, a slightly misleading name. Nonstandard analysis arose from the work of the German-born mathematician Abraham Robinson in mathematical logic, and it is best described as a variant of real analysis in which infinitesimals and infinities genuinely exist—without any paradoxes. In nonstandard analysis, for example, one can define the limit a of a sequence a_n to be the unique real number (if any) such that $|a_n - a|$ is infinitesimal for all infinite integers n.

Generations of students have spent years learning, painfully, not to think that way when studying analysis. Now it turns out that such thinking is entirely rigorous, provided that it is carried out in a rather subtle context. As well as the usual systems of real numbers $\mathbf{R}$ and natural numbers $\mathbf{N}$, nonstandard analysis introduces two more extensive systems of nonstandard real numbers $\mathbf{R}^*$ and nonstandard natural numbers $\mathbf{N}^*$. The system $\mathbf{R}^*$ includes numbers that are infinitesimal relative to ordinary real numbers **R**. That is, nonzero nonstandard real numbers exist that are smaller than any nonzero standard real number. (What cannot be done is to have nonzero nonstandard real numbers that are smaller than any nonzero nonstandard real number, which is impossible for the same reason that no infinitesimal real numbers exist.) In a similar way, **R*** also includes numbers that are infinite relative to ordinary real numbers.

In a very strong sense, it can be shown that nonstandard analysis accurately mimics the whole of traditional analysis. However, it brings dramatic new methods to bear, and it has turned out, for example, to offer an interesting new approach to stochastic differential equations—like standard differential equations but subject to random noise. As with constructive analysis, nonstandard analysis sits outside the mathematical mainstream, but its prospects of joining the mainstream seem excellent.

CHAPTER 5
HISTORY OF ANALYSIS

Analysis has its roots in the speculations of the ancient Greeks. They wondered about the nature of numbers, of motion, and the infinite. Over the past 2,500 years, mathematicians have built upon those earliest speculations to create the rich discipline of analysis.

THE GREEKS ENCOUNTER CONTINUOUS MAGNITUDES

Analysis consists of those parts of mathematics in which continuous change is important. These include the study of motion and the geometry of smooth curves and surfaces — in particular, the calculation of tangents, areas, and volumes. Ancient Greek mathematicians made great progress in both the theory and practice of analysis. Theory was forced upon them about 500 BCE by the Pythagorean discovery of irrational magnitudes and about 450 BCE by Zeno's paradoxes of motion.

THE PYTHAGOREANS AND IRRATIONAL NUMBERS

Initially, the Pythagoreans believed that all things could be measured by the discrete natural numbers (1, 2, 3, ...) and their ratios (ordinary fractions, or the rational numbers). This belief was shaken, however, by the discovery that the diagonal of a unit square (that is, a square whose sides have a length of 1) cannot be expressed as a rational number. This discovery was brought about by their own Pythagorean theorem, which established that the square on the hypotenuse of a right triangle is equal to the sum of

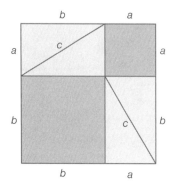 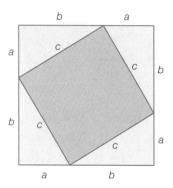

Visual demonstration of the Pythagorean theorem. This may be the original proof of the ancient theorem, which states that the sum of the squares on the sides of a right triangle equals the square on the hypotenuse ($a^2 + b^2 = c^2$). In the box on the left, the green-shaded a^2 and b^2 represent the squares on the sides of any one of the identical right triangles. On the right, the four triangles are rearranged, leaving c^2, the square on the hypotenuse, whose area by simple arithmetic equals the sum of a^2 and b^2. For the proof to work, one must only see that c^2 is indeed a square. This is done by demonstrating that each of its angles must be 90 degrees, since all the angles of a triangle must add up to 180 degrees. Encyclopædia Britannica, Inc.

the squares on the other two sides—in modern notation, $c^2 = a^2 + b^2$. In a unit square, the diagonal is the hypotenuse of a right triangle, with sides $a = b = 1$, hence its measure is $\sqrt{2}$—an irrational number. Against their own intentions, the Pythagoreans had thereby shown that rational numbers did not suffice for measuring even simple geometric objects. Their reaction was to create an arithmetic of line segments, as found in Book II of Euclid's *Elements* (*c.* 300 BCE), that included a geometric interpretation of rational numbers. For the Greeks, line segments were more general than numbers because they included continuous as well as discrete magnitudes.

Indeed, $\sqrt{2}$ can be related to the rational numbers only via an infinite process. This was realized by Euclid, who studied the arithmetic of both rational numbers and line segments. His famous Euclidean algorithm, when applied to a pair of natural numbers, leads in a finite number of steps to their greatest common divisor. However, when applied to a pair of line segments with an irrational ratio, such as √2 and 1, it fails to terminate. Euclid even used this nontermination property as a criterion for irrationality. Thus, irrationality challenged the Greek concept of number by forcing them to deal with infinite processes.

ZENO'S PARADOXES AND THE CONCEPT OF MOTION

Just as √2 was a challenge to the Greeks' concept of number, Zeno's paradoxes were a challenge to their concept of motion. In his *Physics* (c. 350 BCE), Aristotle quoted Zeno as saying:

> *There is no motion because that which is moved must arrive at the middle [of the course] before it arrives at the end.*

Zeno's arguments are known only through Aristotle, who quoted them mainly to refute them. Presumably, Zeno meant that, to get anywhere, one must first go half way and before that one-fourth of the way and before that one-eighth of the way and so on. Because this process of halving distances would go on into infinity (a concept that the Greeks would not accept as possible), Zeno claimed to "prove" that reality consists of changeless being. Still, despite their loathing of infinity, the Greeks found that the concept was indispensable in the mathematics of continuous magnitudes. So they reasoned about infinity as finitely as possible, in a logical framework called the theory of proportions and using the method of exhaustion.

The theory of proportions was created by Eudoxus about 350 BCE and preserved in Book V of Euclid's *Elements*. It established an exact relationship between rational magnitudes and arbitrary magnitudes by defining two magnitudes to be equal if the rational magnitudes less than them were the same. In other words, two magnitudes were different only if there was a rational magnitude strictly between them. This definition served mathematicians for two millennia and paved the way for the arithmetization of analysis in the 19th century, in which arbitrary numbers were rigorously defined in terms of the rational numbers. The theory of proportions was the first rigorous treatment of the concept of limits, an idea that is at the core of modern analysis. In modern terms, Eudoxus's theory defined arbitrary magnitudes as limits of rational magnitudes, and basic theorems about the sum, difference, and product of magnitudes were equivalent to theorems about the sum, difference, and product of limits.

THE METHOD OF EXHAUSTION

The method of exhaustion, also due to Eudoxus, was a generalization of the theory of proportions. Eudoxus's idea was to measure arbitrary objects by defining them as combinations of multiple polygons or polyhedra. In this way, he could compute volumes and areas of many objects with the help of a few shapes, such as triangles and triangular prisms, of known dimensions. For example, by using stacks of prisms, Eudoxus was able to prove that the volume of a pyramid is one-third of the area of its base B multiplied by its height h, or in modern notation $Bh/3$. Loosely speaking, the volume of the pyramid is "exhausted" by stacks of prisms as the thickness of the prisms becomes progressively smaller. More precisely, what Eudoxus proved is that any volume less than $Bh/3$ may be exceeded by a stack of prisms inside the pyramid, and any volume greater than $Bh/3$ may be undercut by a stack of prisms containing the pyramid. Hence, the volume of the pyramid itself can be only $Bh/3$—all other possibilities have been "exhausted." Similarly, Eudoxus proved that the area of a circular disk is proportional to the square of its radius and that the volume of a cone (obtained by exhausting it by pyramids) is also $Bh/3$, where B is again the area of the base and h is the height of the cone.

The greatest exponent of the method of exhaustion was Archimedes (c. 285–212/211 BCE). Among his discoveries using exhaustion were the area of a parabolic segment, the volume of a paraboloid, the tangent to a spiral, and a proof that the volume of a sphere is two-thirds the volume of the circumscribing cylinder. His calculation of the area of the parabolic segment involved the application of infinite series to geometry. In this case, the infinite geometric series $1 + \frac{1}{4} + \frac{1}{16} + \frac{1}{64} + \cdots = \frac{4}{3}$ is obtained by successively adding a triangle with unit area, then triangles that total $\frac{1}{4}$ unit area, then triangles of $\frac{1}{16}$, and so forth, until the area is exhausted. Archimedes avoided actual contact with infinity, however, by showing that the series obtained by stopping after a finite number of terms could be made to exceed any number less than $\frac{4}{3}$. In modern terms, $\frac{4}{3}$ is the limit of the partial sums.

MODELS OF MOTION IN MEDIEVAL EUROPE

The ancient Greeks applied analysis only to static problems—either to pure geometry or to forces in equilibrium. Problems involving motion were not well understood, perhaps because of the philosophical doubts exemplified by Zeno's paradoxes or because of Aristotle's erroneous theory that motion required the continuous application of force.

Analysis began its long and fruitful association with dynamics in the Middle Ages, when mathematicians in England and France studied motion under constant acceleration. They correctly concluded that, for a body under constant acceleration over a given time interval, total displacement = time × velocity at the middle instant.

This result was discovered by mathematicians at Merton College, Oxford, in the 1330s, and for that reason it is sometimes called the Merton acceleration theorem. A very simple graphical proof was given about 1361 by the French bishop and Aristotelian scholar Nicholas Oresme. He observed that the graph of velocity versus time is a straight line for constant acceleration and that the total displacement of an object is represented by the area under the line. This area equals the width (length of the time interval) times the height (velocity) at the middle of the interval.

In making this translation of dynamics into geometry, Oresme was probably the first to explicitly use coordinates outside of cartography. He also helped to demystify dynamics by showing that the geometric equivalent of motion could be quite familiar and tractable. For example, from the Merton acceleration theorem the distance traveled in time t by a body undergoing constant acceleration from rest is proportional to t^2. At the time, it was not known whether such motion occurs in nature, but in 1604 the Italian mathematician and physicist Galileo discovered that this model precisely fits free-falling bodies.

Galileo also overthrew the mistaken dogma of Aristotle that motion requires the continual application of force by asserting the principle of inertia: in the absence of external forces, a body has zero acceleration. That is, a motionless body remains at rest, and a moving body travels with constant velocity. From this he concluded that a projectile—which is subject to the vertical force of gravity but negligible horizontal forces—has constant horizontal velocity, with its horizontal displacement proportional to time t. Combining this with his knowledge that the vertical displacement of any projectile is proportional to t^2, Galileo discovered that a projectile's trajectory is a parabola.

The three conic sections (ellipse, parabola, and hyperbola) had been studied since antiquity, and Galileo's models of motion gave further proof that dynamics could be studied with the help of geometry. In 1609 the German astronomer Johannes Kepler took this idea to the cosmic level by showing that the planets orbit the Sun in ellipses. Eventually, Newton uncovered deeper reasons for the occurrence of conic sections with his theory of gravitation.

During the period from Oresme to Galileo, there were also some remarkable discoveries concerning infinite series. Oresme summed the series $\frac{1}{2} + \frac{2}{2^2} + \frac{3}{2^3} + \frac{4}{2^4} + \cdots = 2$, and he also showed that the harmonic series $1 + \frac{1}{2} + \frac{1}{3} + \frac{1}{4} + \cdots$ does not have a finite sum, because in the successive groups of

This image shows an alleged experiment performed by Galileo Galilei (1564–1642) around 1620 in which he dropped a wooden ball and a heavier cannonball from the Leaning Tower of Pisa. This experiment was designed to prove to the Aristotelian followers that all objects, regardless of weight, fall at the same speed. Hulton Archive/Getty Images

terms $\frac{1}{2}$, $\frac{1}{3} + \frac{1}{4}$, $\frac{1}{5} + \frac{1}{6} + \frac{1}{7} + \frac{1}{8}$, ... each group has a sum greater than $\frac{1}{2}$. With his use of infinite series, coordinates, and graphical interpretations of motion, Oresme was on the brink of a decisive advance beyond the discoveries of Archimedes. All that Oresme lacked was a symbolic language to unite his ideas and allow them to be manipulated mathematically. That symbolic language was to be found in the emerging mathematical discipline of algebra.

ANALYTIC GEOMETRY

About 1630 the French mathematicians Pierre de Fermat and René Descartes independently realized that algebra was a tool of wondrous power in geometry and invented what is now known as analytic geometry. If a curve in the plane can be expressed by an equation of the form $p(x, y) = 0$, where $p(x, y)$ is any polynomial in the two variables, then its basic properties can be found by algebra. (For example, the polynomial equation $x^2 + y^2 = 1$ describes a simple circle of radius 1 about the origin.) In particular, it is possible to find the tangent anywhere along the curve. Thus, what Archimedes could solve only with difficulty and for isolated cases, Fermat and Descartes solved in routine fashion and for a huge class of curves (now known as the algebraic curves).

It is easy to find the tangent by algebra, but it is somewhat harder to justify the steps involved. In general, the slope of any curve $y = f(x)$ at any value of x can be found by computing the slope of the chord

$$\frac{f(x+h) - f(x)}{h}$$

and taking its limit as h tends to zero. This limit, written as $f'(x)$, is called the derivative of the function f. Fermat's method showed that the derivative of x^2 is $2x$ and, by extension, that the derivative of x^k is kx^{k-1} for any natural number k.

THE FUNDAMENTAL THEOREM OF CALCULUS

DIFFERENTIALS AND INTEGRALS

The method of Fermat and Descartes is part of what is now known as differential calculus, and indeed it deserves the name *calculus*, being a systematic and general method for calculating tangents. At the same time, mathematicians were trying to calculate other properties of curved figures, such as their arc length, area, and volume. These calculations are part of what is now known as integral calculus. A general method for integral problems was not immediately apparent in the 17th century, although algebraic techniques worked well in certain cases, often in combination with geometric arguments. In particular, contemporaries of Fermat and Descartes struggled to understand the properties of the cycloid, a curve not studied by the ancients. The cycloid, as you may recall, is traced by a point on the circumference of a circle as it rolls along a straight line.

The cycloid was commended to the mathematicians of Europe by Marin Mersenne, a French priest who directed much of the scientific research in the first half of the 16th century by coordinating correspondence between scientists. About 1634 the French mathematician Gilles Personne de Roberval first took up the challenge, by proving a conjecture of Galileo that the area enclosed by one arch of the cycloid is three times the area of the generating circle.

Roberval also found the volume of the solid formed by rotating the cycloid about the straight line through its endpoints. Because his position at the Collège Royal had to be reclaimed every three years in a mathematical contest—in which the incumbent set the questions—he was secretive about his methods. It is now known that his calculations used indivisibles (loosely speaking, "nearly" dimensionless elements) and that he found the area beneath the sine curve, a result previously obtained by Kepler. In modern language, Kepler and Roberval knew how to integrate the sine function.

Results on the cycloid were discovered and rediscovered over the next two decades by Fermat, Descartes, and Blaise Pascal in France, Evangelista Torricelli in Italy, and John Wallis and Christopher Wren in England. In particular, Wren found that the length (as measured along the curve) of one arch of the cycloid is eight times the radius of the generating circle, demolishing a speculation of Descartes that the lengths of curves could never be known. Such was the acrimony and national rivalry stirred up by the cycloid that it became known as the Helen of geometers because of its beauty and ability to provoke discord. Its importance in the development of mathematics was somewhat like solving the cubic equation—a small technical achievement but a large encouragement to solve more difficult problems.

A more elementary, but fundamental, problem was to integrate x^k—that is, to find the area beneath the curves $y = x^k$ where $k = 1, 2, 3, \dots$. For $k = 2$ the curve is a parabola, and the area of this shape had been found in the 3rd century BCE by Archimedes. For an arbitrary number k, the area can be found if a formula for $1^k + 2^k + \dots + n^k$ is known. One of Archimedes' approaches to the area of the parabola was, in fact, to find this sum for $k = 2$. The sums for $k = 3$ and $k = 4$ had been found by the Arab mathematician Abū ʿAlī al-Ḥasan ibn al-Haytham (c. 965–1040) and for k

up to 13 by Johann Faulhaber in Germany in 1622. Finally, in the 1630s, the area under $y = x^k$ was found for all natural numbers k. It turned out that the area between 0 and x is simply $x^{k+1}/(k + 1)$, a solution independently discovered by Fermat, Roberval, and the Italian mathematician Bonaventura Cavalieri.

DISCOVERY OF THE THEOREM

This hard-won result became almost a triviality with the discovery of the fundamental theorem of calculus a few decades later. The fundamental theorem states that the area under the curve $y = f(x)$ is given by a function $F(x)$ whose derivative is $f(x)$, $F'(x) = f(x)$. The fundamental theorem reduced integration to the problem of finding a function with a given derivative; for example, $x^{k+1}/(k + 1)$ is an integral of x^k because its derivative equals x^k.

The fundamental theorem was first discovered by James Gregory in Scotland in 1668 and by Isaac Barrow (Newton's predecessor at the University of Cambridge) about 1670, but in a geometric form that concealed its computational advantages. Newton discovered the result for himself about the same time and immediately realized its power. In fact, from his viewpoint the fundamental theorem completely solved the problem of integration. However, he failed to publish his work, and in Germany Leibniz independently discovered the same theorem and published it in 1686. This led to a bitter dispute over priority and over the relative merits of Newtonian and Leibnizian methods. This dispute isolated and impoverished British mathematics until the 19th century.

For Newton, analysis meant finding power series for functions $f(x)$—i.e., infinite sums of multiples of powers of x. A few examples were known before his time—for example, the geometric series for $1/(1 - x)$, $\frac{1}{(1-x)} = 1 + x + x^2 + x^3 + x^4 + \cdots$, which is implicit in Greek mathematics, and series for sin (x), cos (x), and $\tan^{-1}(x)$, discovered about 1500 in India although not communicated to Europe. Newton created a calculus of power series by showing how to differentiate, integrate, and invert them. Thanks to the fundamental theorem, differentiation and integration were easy, as they were needed only for powers x^k. Newton's more difficult achievement was inversion: given $y = f(x)$ as a sum of powers of x, find x as a sum of powers of y. This allowed him, for example, to find the sine series from the inverse sine and the exponential series from the logarithm.

For Leibniz the meaning of calculus was somewhat different. He did not begin with a fixed idea about the form of functions, and so the operations he developed were quite general. In fact, modern derivative and integral symbols are derived from Leibniz's d for difference and $\int$ for sum. He applied these operations to variables and functions in a calculus of infinitesimals. When applied to a variable x, the difference operator d produces dx, an infinitesimal increase in x that is somehow as small as desired without ever quite being zero. Corresponding to this infinitesimal increase, a function $f(x)$ experiences an increase $df = f'dx$, which Leibniz regarded as the difference between values of the function f at two values of x a distance of dx apart. Thus the derivative $f' = df/dx$ was a quotient of infinitesimals. Similarly, Leibniz viewed the integral $\int f(x)dx$ of $f(x)$ as a sum of infinitesimals—infinitesimal strips of area under the curve $y = f(x)$—so that the fundamental theorem of calculus was for him the truism that the difference between successive sums is the last term in the sum: $d\int f(x)dx = f(x)dx$.

In effect, Leibniz reasoned with continuous quantities as if they were discrete. The idea was even more dubious

Gottfried Wilhelm Leibniz (1646–1716) reached the same conclusions as did Isaac Newton regarding integral and differential calculus. He published his work before Newton, however, in 1686. Archive Photos/Getty Images

than indivisibles, but, combined with a perfectly apt notation that facilitated calculations, mathematicians initially ignored any logical difficulties in their joy at being able to solve problems that until then were intractable. Both Leibniz and Newton (who also took advantage of mysterious nonzero quantities that vanished when convenient) knew the calculus was a method of unparalleled scope and power, and they both wanted the credit for inventing it. True, the underlying infinitesimals were ridiculous—as the Anglican bishop George Berkeley remarked in his *The Analyst; or, A Discourse Addressed to an Infidel Mathematician* (1734):

> *They are neither finite quantities...nor yet nothing. May we not call them ghosts of departed quantities?*

However, results found with their help could be confirmed (given sufficient, if not quite infinite, patience) by the method of exhaustion. So calculus forged ahead, and eventually the credit for it was distributed evenly, with Newton getting his share for originality and Leibniz his share for finding an appropriate symbolism.

CALCULUS FLOURISHES

Newton had become the world's leading scientist, thanks to the publication of his *Principia* (1687), which explained Kepler's laws and much more with his theory of gravitation. Assuming that the gravitational force between bodies is inversely proportional to the distance between them, he found that in a system of two bodies the orbit of one relative to the other must be an ellipse. Unfortunately, Newton's preference for classical geometric methods obscured the essential calculus. The result was that Newton had admirers but few followers in Britain, notable exceptions being

Brook Taylor and Colin Maclaurin. Instead, calculus flourished on the Continent, where the power of Leibniz's notation was not curbed by Newton's authority.

For the next few decades, calculus belonged to Leibniz and the Swiss brothers Jakob and Johann Bernoulli. Between them they developed most of the standard material found in calculus courses: the rules for differentiation, the integration of rational functions, the theory of elementary functions, applications to mechanics, and the geometry of curves. To Newton's chagrin, Johann even presented a Leibniz-style proof that the inverse square law of gravitation implies elliptical orbits. He claimed, with some justice, that Newton had not been clear on this point. The first calculus textbook was also due to Johann—his lecture notes *Analyse des infiniment petits* ("Infinitesimal Analysis") was published by the marquis de l'Hôpital in 1696—and calculus in the next century was dominated by his great Swiss student Leonhard Euler, who was invited to Russia by Catherine the Great and thus helped to spread the Leibniz doctrine to all corners of Europe.

Perhaps the only basic calculus result missed by the Leibniz school was one on Newton's specialty of power series, given by Taylor in 1715. The Taylor series neatly wraps up the power series for $1/(1 - x)$, sin (x), cos (x), tan^{-1} (x) and many other functions in a single formula:

$$f(x) = f(a) + \frac{x-a}{1!} f'(a) + \frac{(x-a)^2}{2!} f''(a) + \frac{(x-a)^3}{3!} f'''(a) + \cdots$$

Here $f'(a)$ is the derivative of f at $x = a$, $f''(a)$ is the derivative of the derivative (the "second derivative") at $x = a$, and so on (*see* Higher-Order Derivatives on page 42). Taylor's formula pointed toward Newton's original goal—the general study of functions by power series—but the actual meaning of this goal awaited clarification of the function concept.

ELABORATION AND GENERALIZATION

EULER AND INFINITE SERIES

The 17th-century techniques of differentiation, integration, and infinite processes were of enormous power and scope, and their use expanded in the next century. The output of Euler alone was enough to dwarf the combined discoveries of Newton, Leibniz, and the Bernoullis. Much of his work elaborated on theirs, developing the mechanics of heavenly bodies, fluids, and flexible and elastic media. For example, Euler studied the difficult problem of describing the motion of three masses under mutual gravitational attraction (now known as the three-body problem). Applied to the Sun-Moon-Earth system, Euler's work greatly increased the accuracy of the lunar tables used in navigation—for which the British Board of Longitude awarded him a monetary prize. He also applied analysis to the bending of a thin elastic beam and in the design of sails.

Euler also took analysis in new directions. In 1734 he solved a problem in infinite series that had defeated his predecessors: the summation of the series $\frac{1}{1^2} + \frac{1}{2^2} + \frac{1}{3^2} + \frac{1}{4^2} + \cdots$. Euler found the sum to be $\frac{\pi^2}{6}$ by the bold step of comparing the series with the sum of the roots of the following infinite polynomial equation (obtained from the power series for the sine function): $\frac{\sin(\sqrt{x})}{\sqrt{x}} = 1 - \frac{x}{3!} + \frac{x^2}{5!} - \frac{x^3}{7!} + \cdots = 0$. Euler was later able to generalize this result to find the values of the function

$$\zeta(s) = \frac{1}{1^s} + \frac{1}{2^s} + \frac{1}{3^s} + \frac{1}{4^s} + \cdots$$

for all even natural numbers s.

The function $\zeta(s)$, later known as the Riemann zeta function, is a concept that really belongs to the 19th century. Euler caught a glimpse of the future when he discovered the fundamental property of $\zeta(s)$ in his *Introduction to Analysis of the Infinite* (1748): the sum over the integers 1, 2, 3, 4, ... equals a product over the prime numbers 2, 3, 5, 7, 11, 13, 17, ..., namely

$$\zeta(s) = \frac{1}{1^s} + \frac{1}{2^s} + \frac{1}{3^s} + \cdots = \frac{1}{1-2^{-s}} \cdot \frac{1}{1-3^{-s}} \cdot \frac{1}{1-5^{-s}} \cdot \frac{1}{1-7^{-s}} \cdot \frac{1}{1-11^{-s}} \cdots$$

This startling formula was the first intimation that analysis—the theory of the continuous—could say something about the discrete and mysterious prime numbers. The zeta function unlocks many of the secrets of the primes—for example, that there are infinitely many of them. To see why, suppose there were only finitely many primes. Then the product for $\zeta(s)$ would have only finitely many terms and hence would have a finite value for $s = 1$. But for $s = 1$ the sum on the left would be the harmonic series, which Oresme showed to be infinite, thus producing a contradiction.

Of course it was already known that there were infinitely many primes—this is a famous theorem of Euclid—but Euler's proof gave deeper insight into the result. By the end of the 20th century, prime numbers had become the key to the security of most electronic transactions, with sensitive information being "hidden" in the process of multiplying large prime numbers. This demands an infinite supply of primes, to avoid repeating primes used in other transactions, so that the infinitude of primes has become one of the foundations of electronic commerce.

COMPLEX EXPONENTIALS

As a final example of Euler's work, consider his famous formula for complex exponentials $e^{i\theta} = \cos(\theta) + i\sin(\theta)$, where

$i = \sqrt{-1}$. Like his formula for $\zeta(2)$, which surprisingly relates π to the squares of the natural numbers, the formula for $e^{i\theta}$ relates all the most famous numbers—e, i, and π—in a miraculously simple way. Substituting π for θ in the formula gives $e^{i\pi} = -1$, which is surely the most remarkable formula in mathematics.

The formula for $e^{i\theta}$ appeared in Euler's *Introduction*, where he proved it by comparing the Taylor series for the two sides. The formula is really a reworking of other formulas due to Newton's contemporaries in England, Roger Cotes and Abraham de Moivre—and Euler may also have been influenced by discussions with his mentor Johann Bernoulli—but it definitively shows how the sine and cosine functions are just parts of the exponential function. This, too, was a glimpse of the future, where many a pair of real functions would be fused into a single "complex" function. Before explaining what this means, more needs to be said about the evolution of the function concept in the 18th century.

FUNCTIONS

Calculus introduced mathematicians to many new functions by providing new ways to define them, such as with infinite series and with integrals. More generally, functions arose as solutions of ordinary differential equations (involving a function of one variable and its derivatives) and partial differential equations (involving a function of several variables and derivatives with respect to these variables). Many physical quantities depend on more than one variable, so the equations of mathematical physics typically involve partial derivatives.

In the 18th century the most fertile equation of this kind was the vibrating string equation, discussed previously, that had been derived by the French mathematician Jean

Le Rond d'Alembert in 1747. As noted, this equation related to rates of change of quantities arising in the vibration of a taut violin string. This led to the amazing conclusion that an arbitrary continuous function $f(x)$ can be expressed, between 0 and 2π, as a sum of sine and cosine functions in a series (later called a Fourier series) of the form $y = f(x) = a_0/2 + (a_1 \cos(\pi x) + b_1 \sin(\pi x)) + (a_2 \cos(2\pi x) + b_2 \sin(2\pi x)) + \cdots$.

But what is an arbitrary continuous function, and is it always correctly expressed by such a series? Indeed, does such a series necessarily represent a continuous function at all? The French mathematician Joseph Fourier addressed these questions in his *The Analytical Theory of Heat* (1822). Subsequent investigations turned up many surprises, leading not only to a better understanding of continuous functions but also of discontinuous functions, which do indeed occur as Fourier series. This in turn led to important generalizations of the concept of integral designed to integrate highly discontinuous functions — the Riemann integral of 1854 and the Lebesgue integral of 1902.

Fluid Flow

Evolution in a different direction began when the French mathematicians Alexis Clairaut in 1740 and d'Alembert in 1752 discovered equations for fluid flow. Their equations govern the velocity components u and v at a point (x, y) in a steady two-dimensional flow. Like a vibrating string, the motion of a fluid is rather arbitrary, although not completely — d'Alembert was surprised to notice that a combination of the velocity components, $u + iv$, was a differentiable function of $x + iy$. Like Euler, he had discovered a function of a complex variable, with u and v its real and imaginary parts, respectively.

This property of $u + iv$ was rediscovered in France by Augustin-Louis Cauchy in 1827 and in Germany by

Bernhard Riemann in 1851. By this time complex numbers had become an accepted part of mathematics, obeying the same algebraic rules as real numbers and having a clear geometric interpretation as points in the plane. Any complex function $f(z)$ can be written in the form $f(z) = f(x + iy) = u(x, y) + iv(x, y)$, where u and v are real-valued functions of x and y. Complex differentiable functions are those for which the limit $f'(z)$ of $(f(z + h) - f(z))/h$ exists as h tends to zero. However, unlike real numbers, which can approach zero only along the real line, complex numbers reside in the plane, and an infinite number of paths lead to zero. It turned out that, in order to give the same limit $f'(z)$ as h tends to zero from any direction, u and v must satisfy the constraints imposed by the Clairaut and d'Alembert equations.

A way to visualize differentiability is to interpret the function f as a mapping from one plane to another. For $f'(z)$ to exist, the function f must be "similarity preserving in the small," or conformal, meaning that infinitesimal regions are faithfully mapped to regions of the same shape, though possibly rotated and magnified by some factor. This makes differentiable complex functions useful in actual mapping problems, and they were used for this purpose even before Cauchy and Riemann recognized their theoretical importance.

Differentiability is a much more significant property for complex functions than for real functions. Cauchy discovered that, if a function's first derivative exists, then all its derivatives exist, and therefore it can be represented by a power series in z—its Taylor series. Such a function is called analytic. In contrast to real differentiable functions, which are as "flexible" as string, complex differentiable functions are "rigid" in the sense that any region of the function determines the entire function. This is because the values of the function over any region, no matter how small, determine all its derivatives, and hence they determine its power series. Thus, it became feasible to study analytic functions via power series, a program attempted by the Italian French mathematician Joseph-Louis Lagrange for real functions in the 18th century but first carried out successfully by the German mathematician Karl Weierstrass in the 19th century, after the appropriate subject matter of complex analytic functions had been discovered.

REBUILDING THE FOUNDATIONS

ARITHMETIZATION OF ANALYSIS

Before the 19th century, analysis rested on makeshift foundations of arithmetic and geometry, supporting the discrete and continuous sides of the subject, respectively. Mathematicians since the time of Eudoxus had doubted that "all is number," and when in doubt they used geometry. This pragmatic compromise began to fall apart in 1799, when Gauss found himself obliged to use continuity in a result that seemed to be discrete—the fundamental theorem of algebra.

The theorem says that any polynomial equation has a solution in the complex numbers. Gauss's first proof fell short (although this was not immediately recognized) because it assumed as obvious a geometric result actually harder than the theorem itself. In 1816 Gauss attempted another proof, this time relying on a weaker assumption known as the intermediate value theorem: if $f(x)$ is a continuous function of a real variable x and if $f(a) < 0$ and $f(b) > 0$, then there is a c between a and b such that $f(c) = 0$.

The importance of proving the intermediate value theorem was recognized in 1817 by the Bohemian mathematician Bernhard Bolzano, who saw an opportunity to remove geometric assumptions from algebra. His attempted proof introduced essentially the modern condition for continuity of a function f at a point x: $f(x + h) - f(x)$ can be made smaller than any given quantity, provided h can be made arbitrarily close to zero. Bolzano also relied on an assumption—the existence of a greatest lower bound: if a certain property M holds only for values greater than some quantity l, then there is a greatest quantity u such that M holds only for values greater than or equal to u. Bolzano could go no further than this, because in his time the notion of quantity was still too vague. Was it a number? Was it a line segment? And in any case how does one decide whether points on a line have a greatest lower bound?

The same problem was encountered by the German mathematician Richard Dedekind when teaching calculus, and he later described his frustration with appeals to geometric intuition:

> For myself this feeling of dissatisfaction was so overpowering that I made a fixed resolve to keep meditating on the question till I should find a purely arithmetic and perfectly rigorous foundation for the principles of infinitesimal analysis....I succeeded on November 24, 1858.

Dedekind eliminated geometry by going back to an idea of Eudoxus but taking it a step further. Eudoxus said, in effect, that a point on the line is uniquely determined by its position among the rationals. That is, two points are equal if the rationals less than them (and the rationals greater than them) are the same. Thus, each point creates a unique "cut" (L, U) in the rationals, a partition of the set of rationals into sets L and U with each member of L less than every member of U.

Dedekind's small but crucial step was to dispense with the geometric points supposed to create the cuts.

He defined the real numbers to be the cuts (L, U) just described—that is, as partitions of the rationals with each member of L less than every member of U. Cuts included representatives of all rational and irrational quantities previously considered, but now the existence of greatest lower bounds became provable and hence also the intermediate value theorem and all its consequences. In fact, all the basic theorems about limits and continuous functions followed from Dedekind's definition—an outcome called the arithmetization of analysis.

The full program of arithmetization, based on a different but equivalent definition of real number, is mainly due to Weierstrass in the 1870s. He relied on rigorous definitions of real numbers and limits to justify the computations previously made with infinitesimals. Bolzano's 1817 definition of continuity of a function f at a point x, mentioned above, came close to saying what it meant for the limit of $f(x + h)$ to be $f(x)$. The final touch of precision was added with Cauchy's "epsilon-delta" definition of 1821: for each $\varepsilon > 0$ there is a $\delta > 0$ such that $|f(x + h) - f(x)| < \varepsilon$ for all $|h| < \delta$.

ANALYSIS IN HIGHER DIMENSIONS

While geometry was being purged from the foundations of analysis, its spirit was taking over the superstructure. The study of complex functions, or functions with two or more variables, became allied with the rich geometry of higher-dimensional spaces. Sometimes the geometry guided the development of concepts in analysis, and sometimes it was the reverse. A beautiful example of this interaction was the concept of a Riemann surface. The complex numbers can be viewed as a plane (as pointed out in the section on fluid flow), so a function of a complex variable can be viewed as a function on the plane. Riemann's insight was

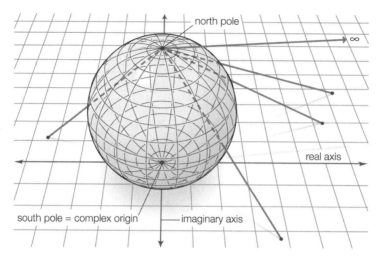

This model of the Riemann sphere has its south pole resting on the origin of the complex plane. Each point on the surface of the Riemann sphere corresponds to a unique point in the complex plane and vice versa. This is indicated by the rays extending from the sphere's north pole through some point on the sphere's surface and through some point in the plane. Because a ray that is tangent to the north pole does not intersect the complex plane, the north pole corresponds to infinity. Encyclopædia Britannica, Inc.

that other surfaces can also be provided with complex coordinates, and certain classes of functions belong to certain surfaces. For example, by mapping the plane stereographically onto the sphere, each point of the sphere except the north pole is given a complex coordinate, and it is natural to map the north pole to infinity, ∞. When this is done, all rational functions make sense on the sphere. For example, $\frac{1}{z}$ is defined for all points of the sphere by making the natural assumptions that $\frac{1}{0} = \infty$ and $\frac{1}{\infty} = 0$. This leads to a remarkable geometric characterization of the class of rational complex functions—they are the differentiable functions on the sphere. One similarly finds that the elliptic functions (complex functions that are periodic in two directions) are the differentiable functions on the torus.

Functions of three, four, … variables are naturally studied with reference to spaces of three, four, … dimensions, but these are not necessarily the ordinary Euclidean spaces. The idea of differentiable functions on the sphere or torus was generalized to differentiable functions on manifolds (topological spaces of arbitrary dimension). Riemann surfaces, for example, are two-dimensional manifolds.

Manifolds can be complicated, but it turned out that their geometry, and the nature of the functions on them, is largely controlled by their topology, the rather coarse properties invariant under one-to-one continuous mappings. In particular, Riemann observed that the topology of a Riemann surface is determined by its genus, the number of closed curves that can be drawn on the surface without splitting it into separate pieces. For example, the genus of a sphere is zero and the genus of a torus is one. Thus, a single integer controls whether the functions on the surface are rational, elliptic, or something else.

The topology of higher-dimensional manifolds is subtle, and it became a major field of 20th-century mathematics. The first inroads were made in 1895 by the French mathematician Henri Poincaré, who was drawn into topology from complex function theory and differential equations. The concepts of topology, by virtue of their coarse and qualitative nature, are capable of detecting order where the concepts of geometry and analysis can see only chaos. Poincaré found this to be the case in studying the three-body problem, and it continues with the intense study of chaotic dynamical systems.

The moral of these developments is perhaps the following: It may be possible and desirable to eliminate geometry from the foundations of analysis, but geometry still remains present as a higher-level concept. Continuity can be arithmetized, but the theory of continuity involves topology, which is part of geometry. Thus, the ancient complementarity between arithmetic and geometry remains the essence of analysis.

Probl. I

Investiganda est curva linea ADB in Z C P A
que grave a dato quovis puncto A ad ...
...
A dato ... parallel
...
ADC cujus basis et altitudo sit ad prioris basem et altitudinem re-
spective ut AQ ad AQ. Et Hac Cyclois novissima transibit per
... in qua grave a puncto A ...

CHAPTER 6

GREAT FIGURES IN THE HISTORY OF ANALYSIS

THE ANCIENT AND MEDIEVAL PERIOD

Although we know almost nothing about the lives of such great ancient mathematicians as Euclid and Pythagoras, the work that they did still stands among humanity's greatest intellectual achievements. Their work paved the way for those great figures of the Middle Ages, Nicholas Oresme and Ibn al-Haytham, who prepared the way for calculus.

ARCHIMEDES

(b. *c.* 290–280, Syracuse, Sicily [now in Italy]—d. 212/211 BCE, Syracuse)

Archimedes was the most famous mathematician and inventor of ancient Greece. He is especially important for his discovery of the relation between the surface and volume of a sphere and its circumscribing cylinder. He is known for his formulation of a hydrostatic principle (known as Archimedes' principle) and a device for raising water, still used in developing countries, known as the Archimedes screw.

Archimedes probably spent some time in Egypt early in his career, but he resided for most of his life in Syracuse, the principal Greek city-state in Sicily, where he was on intimate terms with its king, Hieron II. Archimedes published his works in the form of correspondence with the principal mathematicians of his time, including the Alexandrian scholars Conon of Samos and Eratosthenes of Cyrene. He played an important role in the defense of Syracuse against the siege laid by the Romans in 213 BCE by constructing war machines so effective that they long delayed the capture of the city. When Syracuse eventually fell to the Roman general Marcus Claudius Marcellus in the autumn of 212 or spring of 211 BCE, Archimedes was killed in the sack of the city.

Far more details survive about the life of Archimedes than about any other ancient scientist, but they are largely anecdotal, reflecting the impression that his mechanical genius made on the popular imagination. Thus, he is credited with inventing the Archimedes screw, and he is supposed to have made two "spheres" that Marcellus

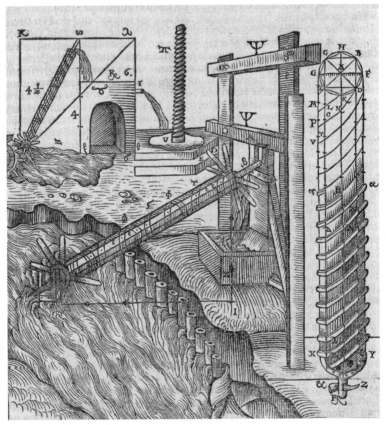

The Archimedes screw is shown in this 1548 woodcut from a text on architecture published in 1548. The Archimedes screw was devised by Archimedes in the 3rd century BCE and is still in use today. SSPL via Getty Images

took back to Rome—one a star globe and the other a device (the details of which are uncertain) for mechanically representing the motions of the Sun, the Moon, and the planets. The story that he determined the proportion of gold and silver in a wreath made for Hieron by weighing it in water is probably true, but the version that has him leaping from the bath in which he supposedly got the idea and running naked through the streets shouting "*Heurēka!*" ("I have found it!") is popular embellishment. Equally apocryphal are the stories that he used a huge array of mirrors to burn the Roman ships besieging Syracuse; that he said, "Give me a place to stand and I will move the Earth"; and that a Roman soldier killed him because he refused to leave his mathematical diagrams—although all are popular reflections of his real interest in catoptrics (the branch of optics dealing with the reflection of light from mirrors, plane or curved), mechanics, and pure mathematics.

According to Plutarch (*c.* 46–119 CE), Archimedes had so low an opinion of the kind of practical invention at which he excelled and to which he owed his contemporary fame that he left no written work on such subjects. While it is true that—apart from a dubious reference to a treatise, "On Sphere-Making"—all of his known works were of a theoretical character, his interest in mechanics nevertheless deeply influenced his mathematical thinking. Not only did he write works on theoretical mechanics and hydrostatics, but his treatise *Method Concerning Mechanical Theorems* shows that he used mechanical reasoning as a heuristic device for the discovery of new mathematical theorems.

There are nine extant treatises by Archimedes in Greek. The principal results in *On the Sphere and Cylinder* (in two books) are that the surface area of any sphere of radius r is four times that of its greatest circle (in modern notation, $S = 4\pi r^2$) and that the volume of a sphere is two-thirds that of the cylinder in which it is inscribed (leading immediately to the formula for the volume, $V = \frac{4}{3}\pi r^3$). Archimedes was proud enough of the latter discovery to leave instructions for his tomb to be marked with a sphere inscribed in a cylinder. Marcus Tullius Cicero (106–43 BCE) found the tomb, overgrown with vegetation, a century and a half after Archimedes' death.

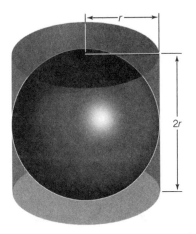

The surface area of a sphere is $4\pi r^2$ and the surface area of the circumscribing cylinder is $6\pi r^2$. Hence, any sphere has two-thirds the surface area of its circumscribing cylinder. Archimedes (d. 212/211 BCE) was so proud of his discovery of this relationship that he had the formula chiseled on his tomb. Encyclopædia Britannica, Inc.

Measurement of the Circle is a fragment of a longer work in which π (pi), the ratio of the circumference to the diameter of a circle, is shown to lie between the limits of $3\frac{10}{71}$ and $3\frac{1}{7}$. Archimedes' approach to determining π, which consists of inscribing and circumscribing regular polygons with a large number of sides, was followed by everyone until the development of infinite series expansions in India during the 15th century and in Europe during the 17th century. This work also contains accurate approximations (expressed as ratios of integers) to the square roots of 3 and several large numbers.

On Conoids and Spheroids deals with determining the volumes of the segments of solids formed by the revolution of a conic section (circle, ellipse, parabola, or hyperbola) about its axis. In modern terms, these are problems of integration. *On Spirals* develops many properties of tangents to, and areas associated with, the spiral of

Archimedes—i.e., the locus of a point moving with uniform speed along a straight line that itself is rotating with uniform speed about a fixed point. It was one of only a few curves beyond the straight line and the conic sections known in antiquity.

On the Equilibrium of Planes (or *Centres of Gravity of Planes*; in two books) is mainly concerned with establishing the centres of gravity of various rectilinear plane figures and segments of the parabola and the paraboloid. The first book purports to establish the "law of the lever" (magnitudes balance at distances from the fulcrum in inverse ratio to their weights), and it is mainly on the basis of this treatise that Archimedes has been called the founder of theoretical mechanics. Much of this book, however, is undoubtedly not authentic, consisting as it does of inept later additions or reworkings, and it seems likely that the basic principle of the law of the lever and—possibly—the concept of the centre of gravity were established on a mathematical basis by scholars earlier than Archimedes. His contribution was rather to extend these concepts to conic sections.

Quadrature of the Parabola demonstrates, first by "mechanical" means (as in *Method*, below) and then by conventional geometric methods, that the area of any segment of a parabola is $\frac{4}{3}$ of the area of the triangle having the same base and height as that segment. This is, again, a problem in integration.

Method Concerning Mechanical Theorems describes a process of discovery in mathematics. It is the sole surviving work from antiquity, and one of the few from any period, that deals with this topic. In it Archimedes recounts how he used a "mechanical" method to arrive at some of his key discoveries, including the area of a parabolic segment and the surface area and volume of a sphere. The technique consists of dividing each of two figures into an infinite but equal number of infinitesimally thin strips, then "weighing" each corresponding pair of these strips against each other on a notional balance to obtain the ratio of the two original figures. Archimedes emphasizes that, though useful as a heuristic method, this procedure does not constitute a rigorous proof.

On Floating Bodies (in two books) survives only partly in Greek, the rest in medieval Latin translation from the Greek. It is the first known work on hydrostatics, of which Archimedes is recognized as the founder. Its purpose is to determine the positions that various solids will assume when floating in a fluid, according to their form and the variation in their specific gravities. In the first book various general principles are established, notably what has come to be known as Archimedes' principle: a solid denser than a fluid will, when immersed in that fluid, be lighter by the weight of the fluid it displaces.

Archimedes' mathematical proofs and presentation exhibit great boldness and originality of thought on the one hand and extreme rigour on the other, meeting the highest standards of contemporary geometry. While the *Method* shows that he arrived at the formulas for the surface area and volume of a sphere by "mechanical" reasoning involving infinitesimals, in his actual proofs of the results in *Sphere and Cylinder* he uses only the rigorous methods of successive finite approximation that had been invented by Eudoxus of Cnidus in the 4th century BCE. These methods, of which Archimedes was a master, are the standard procedure in all his works on higher geometry that deal with proving results about areas and volumes. Their mathematical rigour stands in strong contrast to the "proofs" of the first practitioners of integral calculus in the 17th century, when infinitesimals were reintroduced into mathematics. Yet Archimedes' results are no less impressive than theirs.

The greatest impact of Archimedes' work on later mathematicians came in the 16th and 17th centuries with the printing of texts derived from the Greek, and eventually of the Greek text itself, the *Editio Princeps*, in Basel in 1544. The Latin translation of many of Archimedes' works by Federico Commandino in 1558 contributed greatly to the spread of knowledge of them, which was reflected in the work of the foremost mathematicians and physicists of the time, including Johannes Kepler and Galileo Galilei. David Rivault's edition and Latin translation (1615) of the complete works, including the ancient commentaries, was enormously influential in the work of some of the best mathematicians of the 17th century, notably René Descartes and Pierre de Fermat. Without the background of the rediscovered ancient mathematicians, among whom Archimedes was paramount, the development of mathematics in Europe in the century between 1550 and 1650 is inconceivable. It is unfortunate that *Method* remained unknown to both Arabic and Renaissance mathematicians (it was only rediscovered in the late 19th century), for they might have fulfilled Archimedes' hope that the work would prove useful in the discovery of theorems.

EUCLID

(b. *c.* 300 BCE, Alexandria, Egypt)

The most prominent mathematician of Greco-Roman antiquity was Euclid (Greek: Eukleides), who was best known for his treatise on geometry, the *Elements*.

Of Euclid's life nothing is known except what the Greek philosopher Proclus (*c.* 410–485 CE) reports in his "summary" of famous Greek mathematicians. According to him, Euclid taught at Alexandria in the time of Ptolemy I Soter, who reigned over Egypt from 323 to 285 BCE. Medieval translators and editors often confused him with the philosopher Eukleides of Megara, a contemporary of Plato about a century before, and therefore called him

Megarensis. Proclus supported his date for Euclid by writing "Ptolemy once asked Euclid if there was not a shorter road to geometry than through the *Elements*, and Euclid replied that there was no royal road to geometry." Today few historians challenge the consensus that Euclid was older than Archimedes.

Euclid compiled his *Elements* from a number of works of earlier men. Among these are Hippocrates of Chios (flourished *c.* 460 BCE), not to be confused with the physician Hippocrates of Cos (*c.* 460–377 BCE). The latest compiler before Euclid was Theudius, whose textbook was used in the Academy and was probably the one used by Aristotle (384–322 BCE). The older elements were at once superseded by Euclid's and then forgotten. For his subject matter Euclid doubtless drew upon all his predecessors, but it is clear that the whole design of his work was his own, culminating in the construction of the five regular solids, now known as the Platonic solids.

A brief survey of the *Elements* belies a common belief that it concerns only geometry. This misconception may be caused by reading no further than Books I through IV, which cover elementary plane geometry. Euclid understood that building a logical and rigorous geometry (and mathematics) depends on the foundation—a foundation that Euclid began in Book I with 23 definitions (such as "a point is that which has no part" and "a line is a length without breadth"), five unproved assumptions that Euclid called postulates (now known as axioms), and five further unproved assumptions that he called common notions. Book I then proves elementary theorems about triangles and parallelograms and ends with the Pythagorean theorem.

The subject of Book II has been called geometric algebra because it states algebraic identities as theorems about equivalent geometric figures. Book II contains a construction of "the section," the division of a line into two parts such that the ratio of the larger to the smaller segment is equal to the ratio of the original line to the larger segment. (This division was renamed the golden section in the Renaissance after artists and architects rediscovered its pleasing proportions.) Book II also generalizes the Pythagorean theorem to arbitrary triangles, a result that is equivalent to the law of cosines. Book III deals with properties of circles and Book IV with the construction of regular polygons, in particular the pentagon.

Book V shifts from plane geometry to expound a general theory of ratios and proportions that is attributed by Proclus (along with Book XII) to Eudoxus of Cnidus. While Book V can be read independently of the rest of the *Elements*, its solution to the problem of incommensurables (irrational numbers) is essential to later books. In addition, it formed the foundation for a geometric theory of numbers until an analytic theory developed in the late 19th century. Book VI applies this theory of ratios to plane geometry, mainly triangles and parallelograms, culminating in the "application of areas," a procedure for solving quadratic problems by geometric means.

Books VII–IX contain elements of number theory, where number (*arithmos*) means positive integers greater than 1. Beginning with 22 new definitions—such as unity, even, odd, and prime—these books develop various properties of the positive integers. For instance, Book VII describes a method, *antanaresis* (now known as the Euclidean algorithm), for finding the greatest common divisor of two or more numbers; Book VIII examines numbers in continued proportions, now known as geometric sequences (such as ax, ax^2, ax^3, ax^4...); and Book IX proves that there are an infinite number of primes.

Books XI–XIII examine three-dimensional figures, in Greek *stereometria*. Book XI concerns the intersections of planes, lines, and parallelepipeds (solids with parallel parallelograms as opposite faces). Book XII applies Eudoxus' method of exhaustion to prove that the areas of circles are to one another as the squares of their diameters and that the volumes of spheres are to one another as the cubes of their diameters. Book XIII culminates with the construction of the five regular Platonic solids (pyramid, cube, octahedron, dodecahedron, icosahedron) in a given sphere.

The unevenness of the several books and the varied mathematical levels may give the impression that Euclid was but an editor of treatises written by other mathematicians. To some extent this is certainly true, although it is probably impossible to figure out which parts are his own and which were adaptations from his predecessors. Euclid's contemporaries considered his work final and authoritative. If more was to be said, it had to be as commentaries to the *Elements*.

Almost from the time of its writing, the *Elements* exerted a continuous and major influence on human affairs. It was the primary source of geometric reasoning, theorems, and methods at least until the advent of non-Euclidean geometry in the 19th century. It is sometimes said that, other than the Bible, the *Elements* is the most translated, published, and studied of all the books produced in the Western world. Euclid may not have been a first-class mathematician, but he set a standard for deductive reasoning and geometric instruction that persisted, practically unchanged, for more than 2,000 years.

EUDOXUS OF CNIDUS

(b. c. 395–390, Cnidus, Asia Minor [now in Turkey]—d. 342–337 BCE, Cnidus)

Eudoxus was a Greek mathematician and astronomer who substantially advanced proportion theory, contributed to the identification of constellations and thus to the development of observational astronomy in the Greek world, and established the first sophisticated, geometrical model of celestial motion. He also wrote on geography and contributed to philosophical discussions in Plato's Academy. Although none of his writings survive, his contributions are known from many discussions throughout antiquity.

According to the 3rd century CE historian Diogenes Laërtius (the source for most biographical details), Eudoxus studied mathematics with Archytas of Tarentum and medicine with Philistion of Locri. At age 23 he attended lectures in Athens, possibly at Plato's Academy (opened *c.* 387 BCE). After two months he left for Egypt, where he studied with priests for 16 months. Earning his living as a teacher, Eudoxus then returned to Asia Minor, in particular to Cyzicus on the southern shore of the Sea of Marmara, before returning to Athens where he associated with Plato's Academy.

Aristotle preserved Eudoxus's views on metaphysics and ethics. Unlike Plato, Eudoxus held that forms are in perceptible things. He also defined the good as what all things aim for, which he identified with pleasure. He eventually returned to his native Cnidus where he became a legislator and continued his research until his death at age 53. Followers of Eudoxus, including Menaechmus and Callippus, flourished in both Athens and in Cyzicus.

Eudoxus's contributions to the early theory of proportions (equal ratios) forms the basis for the general account of proportions found in Book V of Euclid's *Elements*. Where previous proofs of proportion required separate treatments for lines, surfaces, and solids, Eudoxus provided general proofs. It is unknown, however, how much later mathematicians may have contributed to the form found in the *Elements*. He certainly formulated the bisection principle that given two magnitudes of the same sort one can continuously divide the larger magnitude by at least halves so as to construct a part that is smaller than the smaller magnitude.

Similarly, Eudoxus's theory of incommensurable magnitudes (magnitudes lacking a common measure) and the method of exhaustion (its modern name) influenced Books X and XII of the *Elements*, respectively. Archimedes, in *On the Sphere and Cylinder* and in the *Method*, singled out for praise two of Eudoxus's proofs based on the method of exhaustion: that the volumes of pyramids and cones are one-third the volumes of prisms and cylinders, respectively, with the same bases and heights. Various traces suggest that Eudoxus's proof of the latter began by assuming that the cone and cylinder are commensurable, before reducing the case of the cone and cylinder being incommensurable to the commensurable case. Since the modern notion of a real number is analogous to the ancient notion of ratio, this approach may be compared with 19th-century definitions of the real numbers in terms of rational numbers. Eudoxus also proved that the areas of circles are proportional to the squares of their diameters.

Eudoxus is also probably largely responsible for the theory of irrational magnitudes of the form $a \pm b$ (found in the *Elements*, Book X), based on his discovery that the ratios of the side and diagonal of a regular pentagon inscribed in a circle to the diameter of the circle do not fall into the classifications of Theaetetus of Athens (c. 417–369 BCE). According to Eratosthenes of Cyrene, Eudoxus also contributed a solution to the problem of doubling the cube — that is, the construction of a cube with twice the volume of a given cube.

Eudoxus is the most innovative Greek mathematician before Archimedes. His work forms the foundation for the most advanced discussions in Euclid's *Elements* and set the stage for Archimedes' study of volumes and surfaces. The theory of proportions is the first completely articulated theory of magnitudes.

IBN AL-HAYTHAM

(b. *c.* 965, Basra, Iraq—d. *c.* 1040 CE, Cairo, Egypt)

Abū 'Alī al-Ḥasan ibn al-Haytham was an Arab mathematician and astronomer who made significant contributions to the principles of optics and the use of scientific experiments.

Conflicting stories are told about the life of Ibn al-Haytham, particularly concerning his scheme to regulate the Nile. In one version, told by the historian Ibn al-Qiftī (d. 1248), Ibn al-Haytham was invited by al-Ḥakim (reigned 996–1021; also known as "The Mad Caliph") to Egypt to demonstrate his claim that he could regulate the Nile. However, after personally reconnoitering near the southern border of Egypt, Ibn al-Haytham confessed his inability to engineer such a project. Although still given an official position by the caliph, Ibn al-Haytham began to fear for his life, so he feigned madness and was confined to his own home until the end of al-Ḥakim's caliphate. Ibn al-Qiftī also reports that Ibn al-Haytham then earned a living in Egypt largely by copying manuscripts. In fact, he claimed to possess a manuscript in Ibn al-Haytham's handwriting from 1040.

There are three lists of Ibn al-Haytham's writings, the first of which comes with his autobiography (1027), that collectively enumerate almost 100 works. It has recently been plausibly argued that there were two Ibn al-Haythams: al-Ḥasan ibn al-Ḥasan, the mathematician who wrote on optics, and Muḥammad ibn al-Ḥasan, the astronomer-philosopher who wrote the autobiography and the works in the first and second lists.

In his *Ḥall shukūk fī Kitāb Uqlīdis* ("Solution of the Difficulties of Euclid's *Elements*") Ibn al-Haytham investigated particular cases of Euclid's theorems, offered alternative constructions, and replaced some indirect proofs with direct proofs. He made an extended study of parallel lines in *Sharz muṣādarāt Kitāb Uqlīdis* ("Commentary on the Premises of Euclid's *Elements*") and based his treatment of parallels on equidistant lines rather than Euclid's definition of lines that never meet. His *Maqāla fī tamām Kitāb al-Makhrūṭāt* ("Completion of the Conics") is an attempt to reconstruct the lost eighth book of Apollonius's *Conics* (c. 200 BCE). Among his other mathematical works are treatises on the area of crescent-shaped figures and on the volume of a paraboloid of revolution (formed by rotating a parabola about its axis).

NICHOLAS ORESME

(b. *c.* 1320, Normandy, France—d. July 11, 1382 CE, Lisieux)

The work of the French Roman Catholic bishop, scholastic philosopher, economist, and mathematician Nicholas Oresme provided some basis for the development of modern mathematics and science and of French prose, particularly its scientific vocabulary.

It is known that Oresme was of Norman origin, although the exact place and year of his birth are uncertain. Similarly, the details of his early education are unknown. In 1348 his name appears on a list of graduate scholarship holders in theology at the College of Navarre at the University of Paris. As Oresme became grand master of the college in 1356, he must have completed his doctorate in theology before this date. Oresme was appointed canon (1362) and dean (1364) of the Cathedral of Rouen and also canon at the Sainte-Chapelle in Paris (1363). From about

1370, at the behest of King Charles V of France, Oresme translated Aristotle's *Ethics*, *Politics*, and *On the Heavens*, as well as the pseudo-Aristotelian *Economics*, from Latin into French. His effect on the French language can be discerned through his creation of French equivalents for many Latin scientific and philosophical terms. Oresme was elected bishop of Lisieux in 1377 and was consecrated in 1378.

Oresme presented his economic ideas in commentaries on the *Ethics*, *Politics*, and *Economics*, as well as an earlier treatise, *De origine, natura, jure et mutationibus monetarum* (c. 1360; "On the Origin, Nature, Juridical Status and Variations of Coinage"). Oresme argued that coinage belongs to the public, not to the prince, who has no right to vary arbitrarily the content or weight. His abhorrence of the effects of debasing the currency influenced Charles's monetary and tax policies. Oresme is generally considered the greatest medieval economist.

Oresme is also considered one of the most eminent scholastic philosophers, famous for his independent thinking and his critique of several Aristotelian tenets. He rejected Aristotle's definition of a body's place as the inner boundary of the surrounding medium in favour of a definition of place as the space occupied by the body. Similarly, he rejected Aristotle's definition of time as the measure of motion, arguing instead for a definition of time as the successive duration of things, independent of motion.

Oresme was a determined opponent of astrology, which he attacked on religious and scientific grounds. In *De proportionibus proportionum* ("On Ratios of Ratios") Oresme first examined raising rational numbers to rational powers before extending his work to include irrational powers. The results of both operations he termed *irrational ratios*, although he considered the first type commensurable with rational numbers, and the latter not. His motivation for this study was a suggestion of the theologian-mathematician Thomas Bradwardine (*c.* 1290–1349) that the relationship between forces (*F*), resistances (*R*), and velocities (*V*) is exponential. In modern terms: $F_2/R_2 = (F_1/R_1)^{V_2/V_1}$.

Oresme then asserted that the ratio of any two celestial motions is probably incommensurable. This excludes precise predictions of successively repeating conjunctions, oppositions, and other astronomical aspects, and he subsequently claimed, in *Ad pauca respicientes* (its name derives from the opening sentence "Concerning some matters..."), that astrology was thereby refuted. As with astrology, he fought against the widespread belief in occult and "marvelous" phenomena by explaining them in terms of natural causes in *Livre de divinacions* ("Book of Divinations").

Oresme's main contributions to mathematics are contained in his *Tractatus de configurationibus qualitatum et motuum* ("Treatise on the Configurations of Qualities and Motions"). In this work Oresme conceived of the idea of using rectangular coordinates (*latitudo* and *longitudo*) and the resulting geometric figures to distinguish between uniform and nonuniform distributions of various quantities, even extending his definition to include three-dimensional figures. Thus, Oresme helped lay the foundation that later led to the discovery of analytic geometry by René Descartes (1596–1650). Furthermore, he used his figures to give the first proof of the Merton theorem: the distance traveled in any given period by a body moving under uniform acceleration is the same as if the body moved at a uniform speed equal to its speed at the midpoint of the period. Some scholars believe that Oresme's graphical representation of velocities was of great influence in the further development of kinematics, affecting in particular the work of Galileo (1564–1642).

PYTHAGORAS

(b. *c.* 580, Samos, Ionia [now in Greece]—d. *c.* 500 BCE,
Metapontum, Lucania [now in Italy])

Greek philosopher, mathematician, and founder of the
Pythagorean brotherhood that, although religious in
nature, formulated principles that influenced the thought
of Plato and Aristotle and contributed to the development
of mathematics and Western rational philosophy.

Pythagoras. Hulton Archive/Getty Images

Pythagoras migrated to southern Italy about 532 BCE, apparently to escape Samos's tyrannical rule, and established his ethico-political academy at Croton (now Crotone, Italy).

It is difficult to distinguish Pythagoras's teachings from those of his disciples. None of his writings have survived, and Pythagoreans invariably supported their doctrines by indiscriminately citing their master's authority. Pythagoras, however, is generally credited with the theory of the functional significance of numbers in the objective world and in music. Other discoveries often attributed to him (e.g., the incommensurability of the side and diagonal of a square, and the Pythagorean theorem for right triangles) were probably developed only later by the Pythagorean school. More probably the bulk of the intellectual tradition originating with Pythagoras himself belongs to mystical wisdom rather than to scientific scholarship.

ZENO OF ELEA
(b. c. 495–d. c. 430 BCE)

Zeno of Elea was a Greek philosopher and mathematician, whom Aristotle called the inventor of dialectic. He is especially known for his paradoxes that contributed to the development of logical and mathematical rigour and that were insoluble until the development of precise concepts of continuity and infinity.

Zeno was famous for the paradoxes whereby, in order to recommend the Parmenidean doctrine of the existence of "the one" (i.e., indivisible reality), he sought to controvert the common-sense belief in the existence of "the many" (i.e., distinguishable qualities and things capable of motion). Zeno was the son of a certain Teleutagoras and the pupil and friend of Parmenides. In Plato's *Parmenides*,

Socrates, "then very young," converses with Parmenides and Zeno, "a man of about forty." But it may be doubted whether such a meeting was chronologically possible. Plato's account of Zeno's purpose, however, is presumably accurate. In reply to those who thought that Parmenides' theory of the existence of "the one" involved inconsistencies, Zeno tried to show that the assumption of the existence of a plurality of things in time and space carried with it more serious inconsistencies. In early youth he collected his arguments in a book, which, according to Plato, was put into circulation without his knowledge.

Zeno made use of three premises: first, that any unit has magnitude; second, that it is infinitely divisible; and third, that it is indivisible. Yet he incorporated arguments for each: for the first premise, he argued that that which, added to or subtracted from something else, does not increase or decrease the second unit, is nothing. For the second, he postulated that a unit, being one, is homogeneous and that therefore, if divisible, it cannot be divisible at one point rather than another. And for the third, he said that a unit, if divisible, is divisible either into extended minima, which contradicts the second premise or, because of the first premise, into nothing. He had in his hands a very powerful complex argument in the form of a dilemma, one horn of which supposed indivisibility, the other infinite divisibility, both leading to a contradiction of the original hypothesis. His method had great influence and may be summarized as follows: he continued Parmenides' abstract, analytic manner but started from his opponents' theses and refuted them by *reductio ad absurdum*. It was probably the two latter characteristics which Aristotle had in mind when he called him the inventor of dialectic.

That Zeno was arguing against actual opponents, Pythagoreans who believed in a plurality composed of numbers that were thought of as extended units, is a matter of controversy. It is not likely that any mathematical implications received attention in his lifetime. But in fact the logical problems which his paradoxes raise about a mathematical continuum are serious, fundamental, and inadequately solved by Aristotle.

THE 17TH AND 18TH CENTURIES

The 17th and 18th centuries saw the invention of calculus by Isaac Newton and Gottfried Leibniz. Mathematicians like Laplace and the Bernoulli family applied the insights gleaned from analysis to the scientific problems of the day.

JEAN LE ROND D'ALEMBERT
(b. Nov. 17, 1717, Paris, France—d. Oct. 29, 1783, Paris)

The French mathematician, philosopher, and writer Jean Le Rond d'Alembert achieved fame as a mathematician and scientist before acquiring a considerable reputation as a contributor to and editor of the famous *Encyclopédie*.

The illegitimate son of a famous hostess, Mme de Tencin, and one of her lovers, the chevalier Destouches-Canon, d'Alembert was abandoned on the steps of the Parisian church of Saint-Jean-le-Rond, from which he derived his Christian name. Although Mme de Tencin never recognized her son, Destouches eventually sought out the child and entrusted him to a glazier's wife, whom d'Alembert always treated as his mother. Through his father's influence, he was admitted to a prestigious Jansenist school, enrolling first as Jean-Baptiste Daremberg and subsequently changing his name, perhaps for reasons of euphony, to d'Alembert. Although Destouches never disclosed his identity as father of the child, he left his son an annuity of

Jean Le Rond d'Alembert was a mathematician, a philosopher, and a scientific editor who worked with Diderot on the Encyclopédie. Kean Collection/ Hulton Archive/Getty Images

1,200 livres. D'Alembert's teachers at first hoped to train him for theology, being perhaps encouraged by a commentary he wrote on St. Paul's Letter to the Romans, but they inspired in him only a lifelong aversion to the subject. He spent two years studying law and became an advocate in 1738, although he never practiced. After taking up medicine for a year, he finally devoted himself to mathematics — "the only occupation," he said later, "which really interested me." Apart from some private lessons, d'Alembert was almost entirely self-taught.

In 1739 he read his first paper to the Academy of Sciences, of which he became a member in 1741. In 1743, at the age of 26, he published his important *Traité de dynamique,* a fundamental treatise on dynamics containing the famous "d'Alembert's principle," which states that Newton's third law of motion (for every action there is an equal and opposite reaction) is true for bodies that are free to move as well as for bodies rigidly fixed. Other mathematical works followed very rapidly. In 1744 he applied his principle to the theory of equilibrium and motion of fluids, in his *Traité de l'équilibre et du mouvement des fluides.* This discovery was followed by the development of partial differential equations, a branch of the theory of calculus, the first papers on which were published in his *Réflexions sur la cause générale des vents* (1747). It won him a prize at the Berlin Academy, to which he was elected the same year. In 1747 he applied his new calculus to the problem of vibrating strings, in his *Recherches sur les cordes vibrantes*. In 1749 he furnished a method of applying his principles to the motion of any body of a given shape. And in 1749 he found an explanation of the precession of the equinoxes (a gradual change in the position of the Earth's orbit), determined its characteristics, and explained the phenomenon of the nutation (nodding) of the Earth's axis, in *Recherches sur la précession des équinoxes et sur la nutation de l'axe de la terre*. In 1752 he published *Essai d'une nouvelle théorie de la résistance des fluides,* an essay containing various original ideas and new observations. In it he considered air as an incompressible elastic fluid composed of small particles and, carrying over from the principles of solid body mechanics the view that resistance is related to loss of momentum on impact of moving bodies, he produced the surprising result that the resistance of the particles was zero. D'Alembert was himself dissatisfied with the result; the conclusion is known as "d'Alembert's paradox" and is not accepted by modern physicists. In the *Memoirs* of the Berlin Academy he published findings of his research on integral calculus—which devises relationships of variables by means of rates of change of their numerical value—a branch of mathematical science that is greatly indebted to him. In his *Recherches sur différents points importants du système du monde* (1754–56) he perfected the solution of the problem of the perturbations (variations of orbit) of the planets that he had presented to the academy some years before. From 1761 to 1780 he published eight volumes of his *Opuscules mathématiques*.

Meanwhile, d'Alembert began an active social life and frequented well-known salons, where he acquired a considerable reputation as a witty conversationalist and mimic. Like his fellow Philosophes—those thinkers, writers, and scientists who believed in the sovereignty of reason and nature (as opposed to authority and revelation) and rebelled against old dogmas and institutions—he turned to the improvement of society. A rationalist thinker in the free-thinking tradition, he opposed religion and stood for tolerance and free discussion. In politics the Philosophes sought a liberal monarchy with an "enlightened" king who would supplant the old aristocracy with a new, intellectual aristocracy. Believing in man's need to rely on his own powers, they promulgated a new social morality to replace Christian ethics. Science, the only real source of knowledge, had to be popularized for the benefit of the people, and it was in this tradition that he became associated with the *Encyclopédie* about 1746. When the original idea of a translation into French of Ephraim Chambers' English *Cyclopædia* was replaced by that of a new work under the general editorship of the Philosophe Denis Diderot, d'Alembert was made editor of the mathematical and scientific articles. In fact, he not only helped with the general editorship and contributed articles on other subjects but also tried to secure support for the enterprise in influential circles. He wrote the *Discours préliminaire* that introduced the first volume of the work in 1751. This was a remarkable attempt to present a unified view of contemporary knowledge, tracing the development and interrelationship of its various branches and showing how they formed coherent parts of a single structure. The second section of the *Discours* was devoted to the intellectual history of Europe from the time of the Renaissance. In 1752 d'Alembert wrote a preface to Volume III, which was a vigorous rejoinder to the *Encyclopédie*'s critics. Gradually discouraged by the growing difficulties of the enterprise, d'Alembert gave up his share of the editorship at the beginning of 1758, thereafter limiting his commitment to the production of mathematical and scientific articles.

In 1765 a serious illness compelled him to leave his foster-mother's house, and he eventually went to live in the house of Julie de Lespinasse, with whom he fell in love. He was the leading intellectual figure in her salon, which became an important recruiting centre for the French Academy. Although they may have been intimate for a short time, d'Alembert soon had to be satisfied with the role of steadfast friend. He discovered the extent of her passionate involvement with other men only after Julie's death in 1776. He transferred his home to an apartment at the Louvre—to which he was entitled as permanent secretary to the French Academy—where he died.

ISAAC BARROW
(b. October 1630, London, Eng.—d. May 4, 1677, London)

The English classical scholar, theologian, and mathematician Isaac Barrow was the teacher of Isaac Newton. He developed a method of determining tangents that closely approached the methods of calculus, and he first recognized that what became known as the processes of integration and differentiation in calculus are inverse operations.

Barrow entered Trinity College, Cambridge, in 1643. There he distinguished himself as a classical scholar as well as a mathematician, earning his bachelor's degree in 1648. He was elected a fellow of the college in 1649 and received his master's degree in 1652.

Isaac Barrow, pencil drawing by David Loggan, 1676; in the National Portrait Gallery, London. Courtesy of the National Portrait Gallery, London

Such precociousness helped to shield him from Puritan rule, for Barrow was an outspoken Royalist and Anglican. By the mid-1650s he contemplated the publication of a full and accurate Latin edition of the Greek mathematicians, yet in a concise manner that utilized symbols for brevity. However, only Euclid's *Elements* and *Data* appeared in 1656 and 1657, respectively, while other texts that Barrow prepared at the time—by Archimedes, Apollonius of Perga, and Theodosius of Bythnia—were not published until 1675. Barrow embarked on a European tour before the *Elements* was published, as the political climate in England deteriorated and the Regius professorship of Greek at the University of Oxford, to which he had been elected, was given to another. He spent four years in France, Italy, and Constantinople, returning to England with the restoration of the Stuart monarchy in 1660. On his return to England, Barrow was ordained in the Anglican Church and appointed to a Greek professorship at Cambridge. In 1662 he was also elected professor of geometry, but he resigned both positions after his election as Lucasian Professor of Mathematics at Cambridge in 1663.

Barrow was instrumental in institutionalizing the study of mathematics at Cambridge. From 1664 to 1666, he delivered a set of mathematical lectures—predominantly on the foundations of mathematics—that were published posthumously as *Lectiones mathematicae* (1683). These lectures treated such basic concepts as number, magnitude, and proportion; delved into the relationship between the various branches of mathematics; and considered the relation between mathematics and natural philosophy—most notably the concept of space. Barrow followed these with a series of lectures on geometry, *Lectiones geometricae* (1669), that were far more technical and novel. In investigating the generation of curves by motion, Barrow recognized the inverse relationship between integration and differentiation and came close to enunciating the fundamental theorem of calculus. His last series of lectures, on optics, *Lectiones opticae* (1670), built on the work of Johannes Kepler, René Descartes, and Thomas Hobbes, among others. In these lectures Barrow made major contributions to determining image location after reflection or refraction; opened new vistas for the study of astigmatism and caustics (a collection of rays that, emanating from a single point, are reflected or refracted by a curved surface); and made suggestions toward a theory of light and colours.

Barrow's tenure as mathematics professor coincided with the maturation of Newton's mathematical studies, and scholars often debate the exact nature of their relationship. Barrow was not Newton's official tutor, though they were both members of Trinity College. Newton attended Barrow's lectures, and it is clear that Barrow encouraged and furthered Newton's studies. Fully cognizant of the young man's talents, Barrow resigned his professorship in 1669 in Newton's favour and accepted a position as royal chaplain in London. In 1673 Barrow was appointed master of Trinity College by King Charles II.

Although Barrow was regarded by his mathematical contemporaries in England as second only to Newton, he was more widely esteemed for his sermons and other writings on behalf of the Church of England, and these were often reprinted well into the 19th century.

DANIEL BERNOULLI
(b. Feb. 8 [Jan. 29, Old Style], 1700, Groningen, Neth.—d. March 17, 1782, Basel, Switz.)

Daniel Bernoulli was the most distinguished of the second generation of the Bernoulli family of Swiss mathematicians. He investigated not only mathematics but also such fields as medicine, biology, physiology, mechanics, physics, astronomy, and oceanography. Bernoulli's theorem, which he derived, is named after him.

Daniel Bernoulli was the second son of Johann Bernoulli, who first taught him mathematics. After studying philosophy, logic, and medicine at the universities of Heidelberg, Strasbourg, and Basel, he received an M.D. degree (1721). In 1723–24 he wrote *Exercitationes quaedam Mathematicae* on differential equations and the physics of flowing water, which won him a position at the influential Academy of Sciences in St. Petersburg, Russia. Bernoulli lectured there until 1732 in medicine, mechanics, and physics, and he researched the properties of vibrating and rotating bodies and contributed to probability theory. In that same year he returned to the University of Basel to accept the post in anatomy and botany. By then he was widely esteemed by scholars and also admired by the public throughout Europe.

Daniel's reputation was established in 1738 with *Hydrodynamica,* in which he considered the properties of basic importance in fluid flow, particularly pressure, density, and velocity, and set forth their fundamental relationship. He put forward what is called Bernoulli's principle, which states that the pressure in a fluid decreases as its velocity increases. He also established the basis for the kinetic theory of gases and heat by demonstrating that the impact of molecules on a surface would explain pressure and that, assuming the constant, random motion of molecules, pressure and motion increase with temperature. About 1738 his father published *Hydraulica.* This attempt by Johann to obtain priority for himself was another instance of his antagonism toward his son.

Between 1725 and 1749 Daniel won 10 prizes from the Paris Academy of Sciences for work on astronomy, gravity, tides, magnetism, ocean currents, and the behaviour of ships at sea. He also made substantial contributions in probability. He shared the 1735 prize for work on planetary orbits with his father, who, it is said, threw him out of the house for thus obtaining a prize he felt should be his alone. Daniel's prizewinning papers reflected his success on the research frontiers of science and his ability to set forth clearly before an interested public the scientific problems of the day. In 1732 he accepted a post in botany and anatomy at Basel; in 1743, one in physiology; and in 1750, one in physics.

Jakob Bernoulli

(b. Jan. 6, 1655 [Dec. 27, 1654, Old Style], Basel, Switz.—d. Aug. 16, 1705, Basel)

Jakob Bernoulli was the first of the Bernoulli family of Swiss mathematicians. He introduced the first principles of the calculus of variation. Bernoulli numbers, a concept that he developed, were named for him.

The scion of a family of drug merchants, Jakob Bernoulli was compelled to study theology but became interested in mathematics despite his father's opposition. His travels led to a wide correspondence with mathematicians. Refusing a church appointment, he accepted a professorial chair of mathematics at the University of Basel in 1687. And, following his mastery of the mathematical works of John Wallis, Isaac Barrow (both English), René Descartes (French), and G.W. Leibniz, who first drew his attention to calculus, he embarked upon original contributions. In 1690 Bernoulli became the first to use the term *integral* in analyzing a curve of descent. His 1691 study of the catenary, or the curve formed by a chain suspended between its two extremities, was soon applied in the building of suspension bridges. In 1695 he also applied calculus to the design of bridges. During these years, he often engaged in disputes with his brother Johann Bernoulli over mathematical issues.

Jakob Bernoulli's pioneering work *Ars Conjectandi* (published posthumously, 1713; "The Art of Conjecturing") contained many of his finest concepts: his theory of permutations and combinations; the so-called Bernoulli numbers, by which he derived the exponential series; his treatment of mathematical and moral predictability; and the subject of probability—containing what is now called the Bernoulli law of large numbers, basic to all modern sampling theory. His works were published as *Opera Jacobi Bernoullii*, 2 vol. (1744).

JOHANN BERNOULLI

(b. Aug. 6 [July 27, Old Style], 1667, Basel, Switz.—d. Jan. 1, 1748, Basel)

Johann Bernoulli was a major member of the Bernoulli family of Swiss mathematicians. He investigated the then new mathematical calculus, which he applied to the measurement of curves, to differential equations, and to mechanical problems.

The son of a pharmacist, Johann studied medicine and obtained his doctor's degree in Basel in 1694, with a thesis on muscular contraction. However, he turned to mathematics despite his father's opposition. In 1691–92 he wrote two texts, not published until later, on differential and integral calculus. In 1692 he taught calculus to the mathematician Guillaume-François-Antoine de L'Hôpital, who agreed to pay him for mathematical discoveries. From 1695 to 1705 he taught mathematics at Groningen, Neth., and, on the death of his elder brother, Jakob, assumed a professorship at Basel.

Johann exceeded his brother in the number of contributions he made to mathematics. He applied calculus to the determination of lengths and areas of curves, such as the isochrone, along which a body will fall at constant speed, and the tautochrone, which was found to be important in clock construction. He also made contributions to the theory of differential equations, the mathematics of ship sails, and optics. Johann sent to L'Hôpital in Paris a method or rule for solving problems involving limits that would apparently be expressed by the ratio of zero to zero, now called L'Hôpital's rule on indeterminate forms because it was included in L'Hôpital's influential textbook of 1696, *Analyse des infiniment petits* ("Analysis of the Infinitely Small").

The Bernoulli brothers often worked on the same problems, but not without friction. Their most bitter dispute concerned finding the equation for the path followed by a particle from one point to another in the shortest time, if the particle is acted upon by gravity alone, a problem originally discussed by Galileo. In 1697 Jakob offered a reward for its solution. Accepting the challenge, Johann proposed the cycloid, the path of a point on

Johann Bernoulli and Jakob Bernoulli working on mathematical problems. © Photos.com/Jupiterimages

a moving wheel, pointing out at the same time the relation this curve bears to the path described by a ray of light passing through strata of variable density. A protracted, bitter dispute then arose when Jakob challenged the solution and proposed his own. The dispute marked the origin of a new discipline, the calculus of variations.

Ardent in his friendships and keen in his resentments, Johann zealously defended the cause of G.W. Leibniz in the dispute with Isaac Newton over who had originated calculus. His text in integral calculus appeared in 1742 and his differential calculus shortly afterward. During his last years he worked mainly on the principles of mechanics. His works were published in *Opera Johannis Bernoullii*, 4 vol. (1742).

BONAVENTURA CAVALIERI
(b. 1598, Milan [Italy]—d. Nov. 30, 1647, Bologna, Papal States)

Francesco Bonaventura Cavalieri was an Italian mathematician who made developments in geometry that were precursors to integral calculus.

As a boy Cavalieri joined the Jesuati, a religious order that followed the rule of St. Augustine and was suppressed in 1668 by Pope Clement IX. Euclid's works stimulated his interest in mathematics, and, after he met Galileo, Cavalieri considered himself a disciple of that great astronomer.

By 1629, when he was appointed professor of mathematics of the University of Bologna, Cavalieri had completely developed his method of indivisibles, a means of determining the size of geometric figures similar to the methods of integral calculus. He delayed publishing his results for six years out of deference to Galileo, who planned a similar work. Cavalieri's work appeared in 1635 and was entitled *Geometria Indivi si bilibus Continuorum*

Nova Quadam Ratione Promota ("A Certain Method for the Development of a New Geometry of Continuous Indivisibles"). As stated in his *Geometria,* the method of indivisibles was unsatisfactory and fell under heavy criticism, notably from the contemporary Swiss mathematician Paul Guldin. In reply to this criticism, Cavalieri wrote *Exercitationes Geometricae Sex* (1647; "Six Geometrical Exercises"), stating the principle in the more satisfactory form that was widely employed by mathematicians during the 17th century.

Cavalieri was largely responsible for introducing the use of logarithms as a computational tool in Italy through his book *Directorium Generale Uranometricum* (1632; "A General Directory of Uranometry"). His other works include *Lo specchio ustorio ouero trattato delle settioni coniche* (1632; "The Burning Glass; or, A Treatise on Conic Sections") and *Trigonometria plana et sphaerica, linearis et logarithmica* (1643; "Plane, Spherical, Linear, and Logarithmic Trigonometry").

LEONHARD EULER
(b. April 15, 1707, Basel, Switz. — d. Sept. 18, 1783, St. Petersburg, Russia)

The Swiss mathematician and physicist Leonhard Euler was one of the founders of pure mathematics. He not only made decisive and formative contributions to the subjects of geometry, calculus, mechanics, and number theory but also developed methods for solving problems in observational astronomy and demonstrated useful applications of mathematics in technology and public affairs.

Euler's mathematical ability earned him the esteem of Johann Bernoulli, one of the first mathematicians in Europe at that time, and of his sons Daniel and Nicolas. In 1727 he moved to St. Petersburg, where he became an associate of the St. Petersburg Academy of Sciences and in 1733 succeeded Daniel Bernoulli to the chair of mathematics.

By means of his numerous books and memoirs that he submitted to the academy, Euler carried integral calculus to a higher degree of perfection, developed the theory of trigonometric and logarithmic functions, reduced analytical operations to a greater simplicity, and threw new light on nearly all parts of pure mathematics. Overtaxing himself, Euler in 1735 lost the sight of one eye. Then, invited by Frederick the Great in 1741, he became a member of the Berlin Academy, where for 25 years he produced a steady stream of publications, many of which he contributed to the St. Petersburg Academy, which granted him a pension. In 1748, in his *Introductio in analysin infinitorum,* he developed the concept of function in mathematical analysis, through which variables are related to each other and in which he advanced the use of infinitesimals and infinite quantities. He did for modern analytic geometry and trigonometry what the *Elements* of Euclid had done for ancient geometry, and the resulting tendency to render mathematics and physics in arithmetical terms has continued ever since. He is known for familiar results in elementary geometry; for example, the Euler line through the orthocentre (the intersection of the altitudes in a triangle), the circumcentre (the centre of the circumscribed circle of a triangle), and the barycentre (the "centre of gravity," or centroid) of a triangle. He was responsible for treating trigonometric functions—i.e., the relationship of an angle to two sides of a triangle—as numerical ratios rather than as lengths of geometric lines and for relating them, through the so-called Euler identity ($e^{i\theta} = \cos\theta + i\sin\theta$), with complex numbers (e.g., $3 + 2\sqrt{-1}$). He discovered the imaginary logarithms of negative numbers and showed that each complex number has an infinite number of logarithms.

Euler's textbooks in calculus, *Institutiones calculi differentialis* in 1755 and *Institutiones calculi integralis* in 1768–70, have served as prototypes to the present because they contain formulas of differentiation and numerous methods of indefinite integration, many of which he invented himself, for determining the work done by a force and for solving geometric problems. And he made advances in the theory of linear differential equations, which are useful in solving problems in physics. Thus, he enriched mathematics with substantial new concepts and techniques. He introduced many current notations, such as Σ for the sum, $\int n$ for the sum of divisors of n, and the symbol e for the base of natural logarithms. He also introduced a, b, and c for the sides of a triangle and A, B, and C for the opposite angles. He was the first to use the letter "f" and parentheses for a function, the symbol π for the ratio of circumference to diameter in a circle, and i for $\sqrt{-1}$ as well.

After Frederick the Great became less cordial toward him, Euler in 1766 accepted the invitation of Catherine II to return to Russia. Soon after his arrival at St. Petersburg, a cataract formed in his remaining good eye, and he spent the last years of his life in total blindness. Despite this tragedy, his productivity continued undiminished, sustained by an uncommon memory and a remarkable facility in mental computations. His interests were broad, and his *Lettres à une princesse d'Allemagne* in 1768–72 were an admirably clear exposition of the basic principles of mechanics, optics, acoustics, and physical astronomy. Not a classroom teacher, Euler nevertheless had a more pervasive pedagogical influence than any modern mathematician. He had few disciples, but he helped to establish mathematical education in Russia.

Euler devoted considerable attention to developing a more perfect theory of lunar motion, which was particularly troublesome, since it involved the so-called three-body problem—the interactions of Sun, Moon, and Earth. His partial solution, published in 1753, assisted the British Admiralty in calculating lunar tables, of importance then in attempting to determine longitude at sea. One of the feats of his blind years was to perform all the elaborate calculations in his head for his second theory of lunar motion in 1772. Throughout his life Euler was much absorbed by problems dealing with the theory of numbers, which treats of the properties and relationships of integers, or whole numbers (0, ±1, ±2, etc.). In this, his greatest discovery, in 1783, was the law of quadratic reciprocity, which has become an essential part of modern number theory.

PIERRE DE FERMAT

(b. Aug. 17, 1601, Beaumont-de-Lomagne, France—d. Jan. 12, 1665, Castres)

French mathematician Pierre de Fermat was one of the leading mathematicians of the first half of the 17th century. Independently of French philosopher René Descartes, Fermat discovered the fundamental principle of analytic geometry. His methods for finding tangents to curves and their maximum and minimum points led him to be regarded as the inventor of the differential calculus. Through his correspondence with Blaise Pascal he was a co-founder of the theory of probability.

Little is known of Fermat's early life and education. He was of Basque origin and received his primary education in a local Franciscan school. He studied law, probably at Toulouse and perhaps also at Bordeaux. Having developed tastes for foreign languages, classical literature, and ancient science and mathematics, Fermat followed the custom of his day in composing conjectural "restorations" of lost works of antiquity. By 1629 he had begun a reconstruction of the long-lost *Plane Loci* of Apollonius, the Greek geometer of the 3rd century BCE. He soon found that the study of loci, or sets of points with certain characteristics, could be facilitated by the application of algebra to geometry through a coordinate system. Meanwhile, Descartes had observed the same basic principle of analytic geometry, that equations in two variable quantities define plane curves. Because Fermat's *Introduction to Loci* was published posthumously in 1679, the exploitation of their discovery, initiated in Descartes's *Géométrie* of 1637, has since been known as Cartesian geometry.

In 1631 Fermat received the baccalaureate in law from the University of Orléans. He served in the local parliament at Toulouse, becoming councillor in 1634. Sometime before 1638 he became known as Pierre de Fermat, though the authority for this designation is uncertain. In 1638 he was named to the Criminal Court.

Fermat's study of curves and equations prompted him to generalize the equation for the ordinary parabola $ay = x^2$, and that for the rectangular hyperbola $xy = a^2$, to the form $a^{n-1}y = x^n$. The curves determined by this equation are known as the parabolas or hyperbolas of Fermat according as n is positive or negative. He similarly generalized the Archimedean spiral $r = a\theta$. These curves in turn directed him in the middle 1630s to an algorithm, or rule of mathematical procedure, that was equivalent to differentiation. This procedure enabled him to find equations of tangents to curves and to locate maximum, minimum, and inflection points of polynomial curves, which are graphs of linear combinations of powers of the independent variable. During the same years, he found formulas for areas bounded by these curves through a summation process that is equivalent to the formula now used for the same purpose in the integral calculus. Such a formula is:

$$A = \int_0^a x^n dx = a^{n+1}/(n+1).$$

It is not known whether or not Fermat noticed that differentiation of x^n, leading to na^{n-1}, is the inverse of integrating x^n. Through ingenious transformations he handled problems involving more general algebraic curves, and he applied his analysis of infinitesimal quantities to a variety of other problems, including the calculation of centres of gravity and finding the lengths of curves. Descartes in the *Géométrie* had reiterated the widely held view, stemming from Aristotle, that the precise rectification or determination of the length of algebraic curves was impossible. But Fermat was one of several mathematicians who, in the years 1657–59, disproved the dogma. In a paper entitled "De Linearum Curvarum cum Lineis Rectis Comparatione" ("Concerning the Comparison of Curved Lines with Straight Lines"), he showed that the semicubical parabola and certain other algebraic curves were strictly rectifiable. He also solved the related problem of finding the surface area of a segment of a paraboloid of revolution. This paper appeared in a supplement to the *Veterum Geometria Promota,* issued by the mathematician Antoine de La Loubère in 1660. It was Fermat's only mathematical work published in his lifetime.

Fermat differed also with Cartesian views concerning the law of refraction (the sines of the angles of incidence and refraction of light passing through media of different densities are in a constant ratio), published by Descartes in 1637 in *La Dioptrique*. Like *La Géométrie,* it was an appendix to his celebrated *Discours de la méthode.* Descartes had sought to justify the sine law through a premise that light travels more rapidly in the denser of the two media involved in the refraction. Twenty years later Fermat noted that this appeared to be in conflict with the view espoused by Aristotelians that nature always chooses the shortest path. Applying his method of maxima and minima and making the assumption that light travels less rapidly in the denser medium, Fermat showed that the law of refraction is consonant with his "principle of least time." His argument concerning the speed of light was found later to be in agreement with the wave theory of the 17th-century Dutch scientist Christiaan Huygens, and in 1849 it was verified experimentally by A.-H.-L. Fizeau.

Through the mathematician and theologian Marin Mersenne, who, as a friend of Descartes, often acted as an intermediary with other scholars, Fermat in 1638 maintained a controversy with Descartes on the validity of their respective methods for tangents to curves. Fermat's views were fully justified some 30 years later in the calculus of Sir Isaac Newton. Recognition of the significance of Fermat's work in analysis was tardy, in part because he adhered to the system of mathematical symbols devised by François Viète, notations that Descartes's *Géométrie* had rendered largely obsolete. The handicap imposed by the awkward notations operated less severely in Fermat's favourite field of study, the theory of numbers. But here, unfortunately, he found no correspondent to share his enthusiasm. In 1654 he had enjoyed an exchange of letters with his fellow mathematician Blaise Pascal on problems in probability concerning games of chance, the results of which were extended and published by Huygens in his *De Ratiociniis in Ludo Aleae* (1657).

JAMES GREGORY

(b. November 1638, Drumoak [near Aberdeen], Scot.—d. October 1675, Edinburgh)

James Gregory was a Scottish mathematician and astronomer who discovered infinite series representations for a number of trigonometry functions, although he is mostly remembered for his description of the first practical reflecting telescope, now known as the Gregorian telescope.

James Gregory. © Photos.com/Jupiterimages

The son of an Anglican priest, Gregory received his early education from his mother. After his father's death in 1650, he was sent to Aberdeen, first to grammar school and then to Marischal College, graduating from the latter in 1657. (This Protestant college was combined with the Roman Catholic King's College in 1860 to form the University of Aberdeen.)

Following graduation, Gregory traveled to London where he published *Optica Promota* (1663; "The Advance of Optics"). This work analyzed the refractive and reflective properties of lens and mirrors based on various conic sections and substantially developed Johannes Kepler's theory of the telescope. In the epilogue, Gregory proposed a new telescope design with a secondary mirror in the shape of a concave ellipsoid that would collect the reflection from a primary parabolic mirror and refocus the image back through a small hole in the centre of the primary mirror to an eyepiece. In this work Gregory also

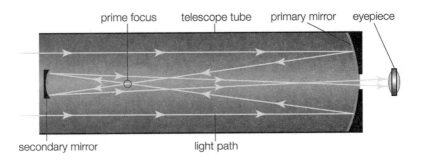

James Gregory's telescope design (1663) uses two concave mirrors—a primary parabolic-shaped mirror and a secondary elliptic-shaped mirror—to focus images in a short telescope tube. As indicated by the yellow rays in the figure: (1) light enters the open end of the telescope; (2) light rays travel to the primary mirror, where they are reflected and concentrated at the prime focus; (3) a secondary mirror slightly beyond the prime focus reflects and concentrates the rays near a small aperture in the primary mirror; and (4) the image is viewed through an eyepiece. Encyclopædia Britannica, Inc.

introduced estimation of stellar distances by photometric methods.

In 1663 Gregory visited The Hague and Paris before settling in Padua, Italy, to study geometry, mechanics, and astronomy. While in Italy he wrote *Vera Circuli et Hyperbolae Quadratura* (1667; "The True Squaring of the Circle and of the Hyperbola") and *Geometriae Pars Universalis* (1668; "The Universal Part of Geometry"). In the former work he used a modification of the method of exhaustion of Archimedes (c. 285–212/211 BCE) to find the areas of the circle and sections of the hyperbola. In his construction of an infinite sequence of inscribed and circumscribed geometric figures, Gregory was one of the first to distinguish between convergent and divergent infinite series. In the latter work Gregory collected the main results then known about transforming a very general class of curves into sections of known curves (hence the designation "universal"), finding the areas bounded by such curves, and calculating the volumes of their solids of revolution.

On the strength of his Italian treatises, Gregory was elected to the Royal Society on his return to London in 1668 and appointed to the University of St. Andrews, Scotland. In 1669, shortly after his return to Scotland, he married a young widow and started his own family. He visited London only once again, in 1673, to purchase supplies for what would have been Britain's first public astronomical observatory. In 1674, however, he became dissatisfied with the University of St. Andrews and left for the University of Edinburgh.

Although Gregory did not publish any more mathematical papers after his return to Scotland, his mathematical research continued. In 1670 and 1671 he communicated to the English mathematician John Collins a number of important results on infinite series expansions of various trigonometry functions, including what is now known as

Gregory's series for the arctangent function: arctan $x = x - x^3/_3 + x^5/_5 - x^7/_7 + \ldots$ Knowing that the arctangent of 1 is equal to $^\pi/_4$ led to the immediate substitution of 1 for x in this equation to produce the first infinite series expansion for π. Unfortunately, this series converges too slowly to π for the practical generation of digits in its decimal expansion. Nevertheless, it encouraged the discovery of other, more rapidly convergent infinite series for π.

The extent of Gregory's work has only been known and appreciated since the publication of *James Gregory: Tercentenary Memorial Volume* (ed. by H.W. Turnbull; 1939), which contains most of his letters and posthumous manuscripts.

Joseph-Louis Lagrange, comte de l'Empire

(b. Jan. 25, 1736, Turin, Sardinia-Piedmont [Italy]—d. April 10, 1813, Paris, France)

The Italian-French mathematician Joseph-Louis Lagrange, comte de l'Empire, made great contributions to number theory and to analytic and celestial mechanics. His most important book, *Mécanique analytique* (1788; "Analytic Mechanics"), was the basis for all later work in this field.

Lagrange was from a well-to-do family of French origin on his father's side. His father was treasurer to the king of Sardinia and lost his fortune in speculation. Lagrange later said, "If I had been rich, I probably would not have devoted myself to mathematics." His interest in mathematics was aroused by the chance reading of a memoir by the English astronomer Edmond Halley. At 19 (some say 16) he was teaching mathematics at the artillery school of Turin (he would later be instrumental in founding the Turin Academy of Sciences). His early publications, on the propagation of sound and on the concept of maxima and minima, were well received. The Swiss mathematician

Leonhard Euler praised Lagrange's version of his theory of variations.

By 1761 Lagrange was already recognized as one of the greatest living mathematicians. In 1764 he was awarded a prize offered by the French Academy of Sciences for an essay on the libration of the Moon (i.e., the apparent oscillation that causes slight changes in position of lunar features on the face that the Moon presents to the Earth). In this essay he used the equations that now bear his name. His success encouraged the academy in 1766 to propose, as a problem, the theory of the motions of the satellites of Jupiter. The prize was again awarded to Lagrange, and he won the same distinction in 1772, 1774, and 1778. In 1766, on the recommendation of Euler and the French mathematician Jean d'Alembert, Lagrange went to Berlin to fill a post at the academy vacated by Euler. This post had been offered at the invitation of Frederick the Great, who expressed the wish of "the greatest king in Europe" to have "the greatest mathematician in Europe" at his court.

Lagrange stayed in Berlin until 1787. His productivity in those years was prodigious: he published papers on the three-body problem, which concerns the evolution of three particles mutually attracted according to Sir Isaac Newton's law of gravity; differential equations; prime number theory; the fundamentally important number-theoretic equation that has been identified (incorrectly by Euler) with John Pell's name; probability; mechanics; and the stability of the solar system. In his long paper "Réflexions sur la résolution algébrique des équations" (1770; "Reflections on the Algebraic Resolution of Equations"), he inaugurated a new period in algebra and inspired Évariste Galois to his group theory.

A kind and quiet man, living only for science, Lagrange had little to do with the factions and intrigues around the king. When Frederick died, Lagrange preferred to accept

Louis XVI's invitation to Paris. He was given apartments in the Louvre, was continually honoured, and was treated with respect throughout the French Revolution. From the Louvre he published his classic *Mécanique analytique*, a lucid synthesis of the hundred years of research in mechanics since Newton, based on his own calculus of variations, in which certain properties of a mechanistic system are inferred by considering the changes in a sum (or integral) that are due to conceptually possible (or virtual) displacements from the path that describes the actual history of the system. This led to independent coordinates that are necessary for the specifications of a system of a finite number of particles, or "generalized coordinates." It also led to the so-called Lagrangian equations for a classical mechanical system in which the kinetic energy of the system is related to the generalized coordinates, the corresponding generalized forces, and the time. The book was typically analytic. He stated in his preface that "one cannot find any figures in this work."

The Revolution, which began in 1789, pressed Lagrange into work on the committee to reform the metric system. When the great chemist Antoine-Laurent Lavoisier was guillotined, Lagrange commented, "It took them only an instant to cut off that head, and a hundred years may not produce another like it." When the École Centrale des Travaux Publics (later renamed the École Polytechnique) was opened in 1794, he became, with Gaspard Monge, its leading professor of mathematics. His lectures were published as *Théorie des fonctions analytiques* (1797; "Theory of Analytic Functions") and *Leçons sur le calcul des fonctions* (1804; "Lessons on the Calculus of Functions") and were the first textbooks on real analytic functions. In them Lagrange tried to substitute an algebraic foundation for the existing and problematic analytic foundation of calculus—although ultimately unsuccessful, his criticisms spurred others to develop the modern analytic foundation. Lagrange also continued to work on his *Mécanique analytique*, but the new edition appeared only after his death.

Napoleon honoured the aging mathematician, making him a senator and a count of the empire, but he remained the quiet, unobtrusive academician, a venerable figure wrapped in his thoughts.

PIERRE-SIMON, MARQUIS DE LAPLACE

(b. March 23, 1749, Beaumount-en-Auge, Normandy, France—d. March 5, 1827, Paris)

The French mathematician, astronomer, and physicist Pierre-Simon, marquis de Laplace, is best known for his investigations into the stability of the solar system.

Laplace successfully accounted for all the observed deviations of the planets from their theoretical orbits by applying Sir Isaac Newton's theory of gravitation to the solar system, and he developed a conceptual view of evolutionary change in the structure of the solar system. He also demonstrated the usefulness of probability for interpreting scientific data.

Laplace was the son of a peasant farmer. Little is known of his early life except that he quickly showed his mathematical ability at the military academy at Beaumont. In 1766 Laplace entered the University of Caen, but he left for Paris the next year, apparently without taking a degree. He arrived with a letter of recommendation to the mathematician Jean d'Alembert, who helped him secure a professorship at the École Militaire, where he taught from 1769 to 1776.

In 1773 he began his major lifework—applying Newtonian gravitation to the entire solar system—by taking up a particularly troublesome problem: why Jupiter's orbit appeared to be continuously shrinking while Saturn's continually expanded. The mutual gravitational interactions within the solar system were so complex that mathematical solution seemed impossible. Indeed, Newton had concluded that divine intervention was periodically required to preserve the system in equilibrium. Laplace announced the invariability of planetary mean motions (average angular velocity). This discovery in 1773, the first and most important step in establishing the stability of the solar system, was the most important advance in physical astronomy since Newton. It won him associate membership in the French Academy of Sciences the same year.

During 1784–85 Laplace worked on the subject of attraction between spheroids. In this work the potential function of later physics can be recognized for the first time. Laplace explored the problem of the attraction of any spheroid upon a particle situated outside or upon its surface. Through his discovery that the attractive force of a mass upon a particle, regardless of direction, can be obtained directly by differentiating a single function, Laplace laid the mathematical foundation for the scientific study of heat, magnetism, and electricity.

In 1786 Laplace proved that the eccentricities and inclinations of planetary orbits to each other will always remain small, constant, and self-correcting. The effects of perturbations were therefore conservative and periodic, not cumulative and disruptive. Laplace removed the last apparent anomaly from the theoretical description of the solar system in 1787 with the announcement that lunar acceleration depends on the eccentricity of Earth's orbit. Although the mean motion of the Moon around Earth depends mainly on the gravitational attraction between them, it is slightly diminished by the pull of the Sun on the Moon. This solar action depends, however, on changes in the eccentricity of Earth's orbit resulting from perturbations by the other planets. As a result, the Moon's mean motion is accelerated as long as Earth's orbit tends to become more circular. But, when the reverse occurs, this motion is retarded. The inequality is therefore not truly cumulative, Laplace concluded, but is of a period running into millions of years. The last threat of instability thus disappeared from the theoretical description of the solar system.

In 1796 Laplace published *Exposition du système du monde* (*The System of the World*), a semipopular treatment of his work in celestial mechanics and a model of French prose. The book included his "nebular hypothesis"—attributing the origin of the solar system to cooling and contracting of a gaseous nebula—which strongly influenced future thought on planetary origin. His *Traité de mécanique céleste* (*Celestial Mechanics*), appearing in five volumes between 1798 and 1827, summarized the results obtained by his mathematical development and application of the law of gravitation. He offered a complete mechanical interpretation of the solar system by devising methods for calculating the motions of the planets and their satellites and their perturbations, including the resolution of tidal problems. The book made him a celebrity.

In 1814 Laplace published a popular work for the general reader, *Essai philosophique sur les probabilités* (*A Philosophical Essay on Probability*). This work was the introduction to the second edition of his comprehensive and important *Théorie analytique des probabilités* (*Analytic Theory of Probability*), first published in 1812, in which he described many of the tools he invented for mathematically predicting the probabilities that particular events will occur in nature. He applied his theory not only to the ordinary problems of chance but also to the inquiry into the causes of phenomena, vital statistics, and future events, while emphasizing its importance for physics and astronomy. The book is notable also for including a special case of what became known as the central limit theorem. Laplace proved that the distibution of errors in large data samples from astronomical observations can be approximated by a Gaussian or normal distribution.

Probably because he did not hold strong political views and was not a member of the aristocracy, he escaped imprisonment and execution during the French Revolution. Laplace was president of the Board of Longitude, aided in the organization of the metric system, helped found the scientific Society of Arcueil, and was created a marquis. He served for six weeks as minister of the interior under Napoleon, who famously reminisced that Laplace "carried the spirit of the infinitesimal into administration."

GOTTFRIED WILHELM LEIBNIZ
(b. July 1 [June 21, Old Style], 1646, Leipzig, Ger.—d. Nov. 14, 1716, Hannover, Hanover)

The German philosopher, mathematician, and political adviser Gottfried Wilhelm Leibniz was important both as a metaphysician and as a logician and distinguished also for his independent invention of the differential and integral calculus.

Leibniz was born into a pious Lutheran family near the end of the Thirty Years' War, which had laid Germany in ruins. As a child, he was educated in the Nicolai School but was largely self-taught in the library of his father, who had died in 1652. At Easter time in 1661, he entered the University of Leipzig as a law student. There he came into contact with the thought of men who had revolutionized science and philosophy—men such as Galileo, Francis Bacon, Thomas Hobbes, and René Descartes. Leibniz dreamed of reconciling—a verb that he did not hesitate to use time and again throughout his career—these modern thinkers with the Aristotle of the Scholastics. In 1666 he wrote *De Arte Combinatoria* ("On the Art of Combination"), in which he formulated a model that is the theoretical ancestor of some modern computers: all reasoning, all discovery, verbal or not, is reducible to an ordered combination of elements, such as numbers, words, sounds, or colours.

After completing his legal studies in 1666, Leibniz applied for the degree of doctor of law. He was refused because of his age and consequently left his native city forever. At Altdorf—the university town of the free city of Nürnberg—his dissertation *De Casibus Perplexis* ("On Perplexing Cases") procured him the doctor's degree at once, as well as the immediate offer of a professor's chair, which, however, he declined. During his stay in Nürnberg, he met Johann Christian, Freiherr von Boyneburg, one of the most distinguished German statesmen of the day. Boyneburg took him into his service and introduced him to the court of the prince elector, the archbishop of Mainz, Johann Philipp von Schönborn, where he was concerned with questions of law and politics.

King Louis XIV of France was a growing threat to the German Holy Roman Empire. To ward off this danger and divert the king's interests elsewhere, the archbishop hoped to propose to Louis a project for an expedition into Egypt. Because he was using religion as a pretext, he expressed the hope that the project would promote the reunion of the church. Leibniz, with a view toward this reunion, worked on the *Demonstrationes Catholicae*. His research led him to situate the soul in a point—this was new progress toward the monad—and to develop the principle of sufficient reason (nothing occurs without a reason). His meditations on the difficult theory of the point were related to problems encountered in optics, space, and movement. They were published in 1671 under the general title *Hypothesis Physica Nova* ("New Physical Hypothesis"). He asserted that movement depends, as in the theory of the German astronomer Johannes Kepler, on the action of a spirit (God).

In 1672 the Elector sent the young jurist on a mission to Paris, where he arrived at the end of March. He was soon left without protectors by the deaths of Freiherr von Boyneburg in December 1672 and of the Elector of Mainz in February 1673. He was now, however, free to pursue his scientific studies. In search of financial support, he constructed a calculating machine and presented it to the Royal Society during his first journey to London, in 1673.

Late in 1675 Leibniz laid the foundations of both integral and differential calculus. With this discovery, he ceased to consider time and space as substances—another step closer to monadology. He began to develop the notion that the concepts of extension and motion contained an element of the imaginary, so that the basic laws of motion could not be discovered merely from a study of their nature. Nevertheless, he continued to hold that extension and motion could provide a means for explaining and predicting the course of phenomena. Thus, contrary to Descartes, Leibniz held that it would not be contradictory to posit that this world is a well-related dream. If visible movement depends on the imaginary element found in the concept of extension, it can no longer be defined by simple local movement; it must be the result of a force. In criticizing the Cartesian formulation of the laws of motion, known as mechanics, Leibniz became, in 1676, the founder of a new formulation, known as dynamics, which substituted kinetic energy for the conservation of movement. At the same time, beginning with the principle that light follows the path of least resistance, he believed that he could demonstrate the ordering of nature toward a final goal or cause.

Leibniz continued his work but was still without an income-producing position. By October 1676, however, he had accepted a position in the employment of John Frederick, the duke of Braunschweig-Lüneburg. John Frederick, a convert to Catholicism from Lutheranism in 1651, had become duke of Hanover in 1665. He appointed Leibniz librarian, but, beginning in February 1677, Leibniz solicited the post of councillor, which he was finally granted in 1678. It should be noted that, among the great philosophers of his time, he was the only one who had to earn a living. As a result, he was always a jack-of-all-trades to royalty.

Trying to make himself useful in all ways, Leibniz proposed that education be made more practical, that academies be founded. He worked on hydraulic presses, windmills, lamps, submarines, clocks, and a wide variety of mechanical devices. He devised a means of perfecting carriages and experimented with phosphorus. He also developed a water pump run by windmills, which ameliorated the exploitation of the mines of the Harz Mountains, and he worked in these mines as an engineer frequently from 1680 to 1685. Leibniz is considered to be among the creators of geology because of the observations he compiled there, including the hypothesis that the Earth was at first molten. These many occupations did not stop his work in mathematics: In March 1679 he perfected the binary system of numeration (i.e., using two as a base), and at the end of the same year he proposed the basis for analysis situs, now known as general topology, a branch of mathematics that deals with selected properties of collections of related physical or abstract elements. He was also working on his dynamics and his philosophy, which was becoming increasingly anti-Cartesian. At this point, Duke John Frederick died on Jan. 7, 1680, and his brother, Ernest Augustus I, succeeded him.

Leibniz continued his developments in mathematics. In 1681 he was concerned with the proportion between a circle and a circumscribed square and, in 1684, with the resistance of solids. In the latter year he published *Nova Methodus pro Maximis et Minimis* ("New Method for the Greatest and the Least"), which was an exposition of his differential calculus.

In 1685 Leibniz was named historian for the House of Brunswick and, on this occasion, *Hofrat* ("court adviser"). His job was to prove, by means of genealogy, that the princely house had its origins in the House of Este, an Italian princely family, which would allow Hanover to lay claim to a ninth electorate. In search of these documents, Leibniz began travelling in November 1687. Going by way of southern Germany, he arrived in Austria, where he learned that Louis XIV had once again declared a state of war. In Vienna, he was well received by the Emperor. He then went to Italy. Everywhere he went, he met scientists and continued his scholarly work, publishing essays on the movement of celestial bodies and on the duration of things. He returned to Hanover in mid-July 1690. His efforts had not been in vain. In October 1692 Ernest Augustus obtained the electoral investiture.

Until the end of his life, Leibniz continued his duties as historian. He did not, however, restrict himself to a genealogy of the House of Brunswick. He enlarged his goal to a history of Earth, which included such matters as geological events and descriptions of fossils. He searched by way of monuments and linguistics for the origins and migrations of peoples; then for the birth and progress of the sciences, ethics, and politics; and, finally, for the elements of a *historia sacra*. In this project of a universal history, Leibniz never lost sight of the fact that everything interlocks. Even though he did not succeed in writing this history, his effort was influential because he devised new combinations of old ideas and invented totally new ones.

COLIN MACLAURIN

(b. February 1698, Kilmodan, Argyllshire, Scot.—d. June 14, 1746, Edinburgh)

The Scottish mathematician Colin Maclaurin developed and extended Sir Isaac Newton's work in calculus, geometry, and gravitation.

A child prodigy, he entered the University of Glasgow at age 11. At the age of 19 he was elected a professor of mathematics at Marischal College, Aberdeen, and two years later he became a fellow of the Royal Society of London. At this time he became acquainted with Newton. In his first work, *Geometrica Organica; Sive Descriptio Linearum Curvarum Universalis* (1720; "Organic Geometry, with the Description of the Universal Linear Curves"), Maclaurin developed several theorems similar to some in Newton's *Principia*, introduced the method of generating conic sections (the circle, ellipse, hyperbola, and parabola) that bears his name, and showed that certain types of curves (of the third and fourth degree) can be described by the intersection of two movable angles.

On the recommendation of Newton, he was made a professor of mathematics at the University of Edinburgh in 1725. In 1740 he shared, with the Swiss mathematicians Leonhard Euler and Daniel Bernoulli, the prize offered by the French Academy of Sciences for an essay on tides.

Maclaurin, engraving by S. Freeman; in the British Museum. Courtesy of the trustees of the British Museum; photograph, J.R. Freeman & Co. Ltd.

His two-volume *Treatise of Fluxions* (1742), a defense of the Newtonian method, was written in reply to criticisms by Bishop George Berkeley of England that Newton's calculus was based on faulty reasoning. Apart from providing a geometric framework for Newton's method of fluxions, the treatise is notable on several counts. It contains solutions to a number of geometric problems, shows that stable figures for a homogeneous rotating fluid mass are the ellipsoids of revolution, and gives for the first time the correct theory for distinguishing between maxima and minima in general, pointing out the importance of the distinction in the theory of the multiple points of curves. It also contains a detailed discussion of infinite series, including the special case of Taylor series now named in his honour.

In 1745, when Jacobites (supporters of the Stuart king James II and his descendants) were marching on Edinburgh, Maclaurin took a prominent part in preparing trenches and barricades for the city's defense. As soon as the rebel army captured Edinburgh, Maclaurin fled to England until it was safe to return. The ordeal of his escape ruined his health, and he died at age 48.

Maclaurin's *Account of Sir Isaac Newton's Philosophical Discoveries* was published posthumously, as was his *Treatise of Algebra* (1748). "De Linearum Geometricarum Proprietatibus Generalibus Tractatus" ("A Tract on the General Properties of Geometrical Lines"), noted for its elegant geometric demonstrations, was appended to his *Algebra*.

SIR ISAAC NEWTON

(b. Dec. 25, 1642 [Jan. 4, 1643, New Style], Woolsthorpe, Lincolnshire, Eng.—d. March 20 [March 31], 1727, London)

The English physicist and mathematician Sir Isaac Newton was the culminating figure of the scientific revolution of the 17th century. In mechanics, his three laws of motion, the basic principles of modern physics, resulted in the formulation of the law of universal gravitation. In mathematics, he was the original discoverer of the infinitesimal calculus. Newton's *Philosophiae Naturalis Principia Mathematica (Mathematical Principles of Natural*

Sir Isaac Newton is arguably one of the most recognizable names in science and mathematics. He discovered the laws of motion, calculus (an honour shared with Leibniz), and gravity, and developed a theory of colour based on the light spectrum of white light, among other accomplishments. Archive Photos/Getty Images

Philosophy), 1687, was one of the most important single works in the history of modern science.

Born in the hamlet of Woolsthorpe, Newton was the only son of a local yeoman, also Isaac Newton, who had died three months before, and of Hannah Ayscough. That same year, at Arcetri near Florence, Galileo Galilei had died. Newton would eventually pick up his idea of a mathematical science of motion and bring his work to full fruition. A tiny and weak baby, Newton was not expected to survive his first day of life, much less 84 years. Deprived of a father before birth, he soon lost his mother as well, for within two years she married a second time. Her husband, the well-to-do minister Barnabas Smith, left young Isaac with his grandmother and moved to a neighbouring village to raise a son and two daughters. For nine years, until the death of Barnabas Smith in 1653, Isaac was effectively separated from his mother, and his pronounced psychotic tendencies have been ascribed to this traumatic event. He hated his stepfather. When he examined the state of his soul in 1662 and compiled a catalog of sins in shorthand, he remembered "Threatning my father and mother Smith to burne them and the house over them." The acute sense of insecurity that rendered him obsessively anxious when his work was published and irrationally violent when he defended it accompanied Newton throughout his life and can plausibly be traced to his early years.

After his mother was widowed a second time, she determined that her first-born son should manage her now considerable property. It quickly became apparent, however, that this would be a disaster, both for the estate and for Newton. He could not bring himself to concentrate on rural affairs—set to watch the cattle, he would curl up under a tree with a book. Fortunately, the mistake was recognized, and Newton was sent back to the grammar school in Grantham, where he had already studied, to prepare for the university. As with many of the leading scientists of the age, he left behind in Grantham anecdotes about his mechanical ability and his skill in building models of machines, such as clocks and windmills. At the school he apparently gained a firm command of Latin but probably received no more than a smattering of arithmetic. By June 1661, he was ready to matriculate at Trinity College, Cambridge, somewhat older than the other undergraduates because of his interrupted education.

When Newton arrived in Cambridge in 1661, the movement now known as the scientific revolution was well advanced, and many of the works basic to modern science had appeared. Astronomers from Copernicus to Kepler had elaborated the heliocentric system of the universe. Galileo had proposed the foundations of a new mechanics built on the principle of inertia. Led by Descartes, philosophers had begun to formulate a new conception of nature as an intricate, impersonal, and inert machine. Yet as far as the universities of Europe, including Cambridge, were concerned, all this might well have never happened. They continued to be the strongholds of outmoded Aristotelianism, which rested on a geocentric view of the universe and dealt with nature in qualitative rather than quantitative terms.

Like thousands of other undergraduates, Newton began his higher education by immersing himself in Aristotle's work. Even though the new philosophy was not in the curriculum, it was in the air. Some time during his undergraduate career, Newton discovered the works of the French natural philosopher René Descartes and the other mechanical philosophers, who, in contrast to Aristotle, viewed physical reality as composed entirely of particles of matter in motion and who held that all the phenomena of nature result from their mechanical interaction. A new set of notes, which he entitled "Quaestiones Quaedam Philosophicae"

("Certain Philosophical Questions"), begun sometime in 1664, usurped the unused pages of a notebook intended for traditional scholastic exercises. Under the title he entered the slogan "Amicus Plato amicus Aristoteles magis amica veritas" ("Plato is my friend, Aristotle is my friend, but my best friend is truth"). Newton's scientific career had begun.

The "Quaestiones" reveal that Newton had discovered the new conception of nature that provided the framework of the scientific revolution. He had thoroughly mastered the works of Descartes and had also discovered that the French philosopher Pierre Gassendi had revived atomism, an alternative mechanical system to explain nature. The "Quaestiones" also reveal that Newton already was inclined to find the latter a more attractive philosophy than Cartesian natural philosophy, which rejected the existence of ultimate indivisible particles. The works of the 17th-century chemist Robert Boyle provided the foundation for Newton's considerable work in chemistry.

Although he did not record it in the "Quaestiones," Newton had also begun his mathematical studies. He again started with Descartes, from whose *La Géometrie* he branched out into the other literature of modern analysis with its application of algebraic techniques to problems of geometry. He then reached back for the support of classical geometry. Within little more than a year, he had mastered the literature. Pursuing his own line of analysis, he began to move into new territory. He discovered the binomial theorem, and he developed the calculus, a more powerful form of analysis that employs infinitesimal considerations in finding the slopes of curves and areas under curves.

By 1669 Newton was ready to write a tract summarizing his progress, *De Analysi per Aequationes Numeri Terminorum Infinitas* ("On Analysis by Infinite Series"), which circulated in manuscript through a limited circle and made his name known. During the next two years he revised it as *De methodis serierum et fluxionum* ("On the Methods of Series and Fluxions"). The word fluxions, Newton's private rubric, indicates that the calculus had been born. Despite the fact that only a handful of savants were even aware of Newton's existence, he had arrived at the point where he had become the leading mathematician in Europe.

When Newton received the bachelor's degree in April 1665, the most remarkable undergraduate career in the history of university education had passed unrecognized. On his own, without formal guidance, he had sought out the new philosophy and the new mathematics and made them his own, but he had confined the progress of his studies to his notebooks. Then, in 1665, the plague closed the university, and for most of the following two years he was forced to stay at his home, contemplating at leisure what he had learned. During the plague years Newton laid the foundations of the calculus and extended an earlier insight into an essay, "Of Colours," which contains most of the ideas elaborated in his *Opticks*. It was during this time that he examined the elements of circular motion and, applying his analysis to the Moon and the planets, derived the inverse square relation that the radially directed force acting on a planet decreases with the square of its distance from the Sun—which was later crucial to the law of universal gravitation. The world heard nothing of these discoveries.

In August 1684, Newton was visited by the British astronomer Edmond Halley, who was also troubled by the problem of orbital dynamics. Upon learning that Newton had solved the problem, he extracted Newton's promise to send the demonstration. Three months later he received a short tract entitled *De Motu* ("On Motion"). Already Newton was at work improving and expanding it. In two and a half years, the tract *De Motu* grew into *Philosophiae Naturalis Principia Mathematica*, which is not only Newton's masterpiece but also the fundamental work for the whole of modern science.

Significantly, *De Motu* did not state the law of universal gravitation. For that matter, even though it was a treatise on planetary dynamics, it did not contain any of the three Newtonian laws of motion. Only when revising *De Motu* did Newton embrace the principle of inertia (the first law) and arrive at the second law of motion. The second law, the force law, proved to be a precise quantitative statement of the action of the forces between bodies that had become the central members of his system of nature. By quantifying the concept of force, the second law completed the exact quantitative mechanics that has been the paradigm of natural science ever since.

The quantitative mechanics of the *Principia* is not to be confused with the mechanical philosophy. The latter was a philosophy of nature that attempted to explain natural phenomena by means of imagined mechanisms among invisible particles of matter. The mechanics of the *Principia* was an exact quantitative description of the motions of visible bodies. It rested on Newton's three laws of motion: (1) that a body remains in its state of rest unless it is compelled to change that state by a force impressed on it. (2) that the change of motion (the change of velocity times the mass of the body) is proportional to the force impressed. (3) that to every action there is an equal and opposite reaction. The analysis of circular motion in terms of these laws yielded a formula of the quantitative measure, in terms of a body's velocity and mass, of the centripetal force necessary to divert a body from its rectilinear path into a given circle. When Newton substituted this formula into Kepler's third law, he found that the centripetal force holding the planets in their given orbits about the Sun must decrease with the square of the planets' distances from the Sun. He applied the ancient Latin word *gravitas* (literally, "heaviness" or "weight") to this force.

The *Principia* immediately raised Newton to international prominence. In their continuing loyalty to the mechanical ideal, Continental scientists rejected the idea of action at a distance for a generation, but even in their rejection they could not withhold their admiration for the technical expertise revealed by the work. Young British scientists spontaneously recognized him as their model.

With the publication of the *Principia* the great bulk of his creative work had been completed. He was never again satisfied with the academic cloister, and he sought a place in London. Finally, in 1696, he was appointed warden of the mint. Although he did not resign his Cambridge appointments until 1701, he moved to London and henceforth centred his life there. The move to London was the effective conclusion of his creative activity.

In London, Newton assumed the role of patriarch of English science. In 1703 he was elected President of the Royal Society. Four years earlier, the French Académie des Sciences (Academy of Sciences) had named him one of eight foreign associates. In 1705 Queen Anne knighted him, the first occasion on which a scientist was so honoured.

In Gottfried Wilhelm Leibniz, the German philosopher and mathematician, Newton met a contestant more of his own calibre. It is now well established that Newton developed the calculus before Leibniz seriously pursued mathematics. It is almost universally agreed that Leibniz later arrived at the calculus independently. There has never been any question that Newton did not publish his method of fluxions. Thus, it was Leibniz's paper in 1684 that first made the calculus a matter of public knowledge. In the *Principia* Newton hinted at his method, but he did not really publish it until he appended two papers to the *Opticks* in 1704. By then the priority controversy was already smouldering. If, indeed, it mattered, it would be impossible finally to assess responsibility for the ensuing fracas. What began as mild innuendoes rapidly escalated into blunt charges of plagiarism on both sides. Egged on by followers anxious to win a reputation under his auspices, Newton allowed himself to be drawn into the centre of the fray. And, once his temper was aroused by accusations of dishonesty, his anger was beyond constraint. Leibniz's conduct of the controversy was not pleasant, and yet it paled beside that of Newton. As president of the Royal Society, he appointed an "impartial" committee to investigate the issue, secretly wrote the report officially published by the society, and reviewed it anonymously in the *Philosophical Transactions*. Even Leibniz's death could not allay Newton's wrath, and he continued to pursue the enemy beyond the grave. The battle with Leibniz, the irrepressible need to efface the charge of dishonesty, dominated the final 25 years of Newton's life. It obtruded itself continually upon his consciousness. Almost any paper on any subject from those years is apt to be interrupted by a furious paragraph against the German philosopher, as he honed the instruments of his fury ever more keenly. In the end, only Newton's death ended his wrath.

GILLES PERSONNE DE ROBERVAL

(b. Aug. 8, 1602, Roberval, France—d. Oct. 27, 1675, Paris)

Gilles Personne de Roberval was a French mathematician who made important advances in the geometry of curves.

In 1632 Roberval became professor of mathematics at the Collège de France, Paris, a position he held until his death. He studied the methods of determination of surface area and volume of solids, developing and improving the method of indivisibles used by the Italian mathematician Bonaventura Cavalieri for computing some of the simpler cases. He discovered a general method of drawing tangents, by treating a curve as the result of the motion of a moving point and by resolving the motion of the point into two simpler components. He also discovered a method for obtaining one curve from another, by means of which planar regions of finite dimensions can be found that are equal in area to the regions between certain curves and their asymptotes (lines that the curves approach but never intersect). To these curves, which were also used to determine areas, the Italian mathematician Evangelista Torricelli gave the name of Robervallian lines.

BROOK TAYLOR
(b. Aug. 18, 1685, Edmonton, Middlesex, Eng.—d. Dec. 29, 1731, London)

The British mathematician Brook Taylor was a proponent of Newtonian mechanics and noted for his contributions to the development of calculus.

Taylor was born into a prosperous and educated family who encouraged the development of his musical and artistic talents, both of which found mathematical expression in his later life. He was tutored at home before he entered St. John's College, Cambridge, in 1701 to study law. He completed his LL.B. in 1709 and his doctorate in 1714, but it is doubtful that he ever practiced as a lawyer.

Taylor's first important mathematical paper, which provided a solution to the problem of the centre of oscillation of a body, was published in 1714, although he had actually written it by 1708. His delay in publishing led to a priority dispute with the noted Swiss mathematician Johann Bernoulli. Taylor's famous investigation of the vibrating string, a topic that played a large role in clarifying what mathematicians meant by a function, was also published in 1714.

Taylor's *Methodus Incrementorum Directa et Inversa* (1715; "Direct and Indirect Methods of Incrementation") added to higher mathematics a new branch now called the calculus of finite differences. Using this new development, Taylor studied a number of special problems, including the vibrating string, the determination of the centres of oscillation and percussion, and the path of a light ray refracted in the atmosphere. The *Methodus* also contained the celebrated formula known as Taylor's theorem, which Taylor had first stated in 1712 and the full significance of which began to be recognized only in 1772 when the French mathematician Joseph-Louis Lagrange proclaimed it the basic principle of differential calculus.

A gifted artist, Taylor set forth in *Linear Perspective* (1715) the basic principles of perspective. This work and his *New Principles of Linear Perspective* (1719) contained the first general treatment of the principle of vanishing points. Taylor was elected a fellow of the Royal Society of London in 1712 and in the same year sat on the committee for adjudicating Sir Isaac Newton's and Gottfried Wilhelm Leibniz's conflicting claims of priority in the invention of calculus.

EVANGELISTA TORRICELLI

(b. Oct. 15, 1608, Faenza, Romagna—d. Oct. 25, 1647, Florence)

The Italian physicist and mathematician Evangelista Torricelli invented the barometer, and his work in geometry aided in the eventual development of integral calculus. Inspired by Galileo's writings, he wrote a treatise on mechanics, *De Motu* ("Concerning Movement"), which impressed Galileo. In 1641 Torricelli was invited to Florence, where he served the elderly astronomer as secretary and assistant during the last three months of Galileo's life. Torricelli was then appointed to succeed him as professor of mathematics at the Florentine Academy.

Two years later, pursuing a suggestion by Galileo, he filled a glass tube 1.2 metres (4 feet) long with mercury and inverted the tube into a dish. He observed that some of the mercury did not flow out and that the space above the mercury in the tube was a vacuum. Torricelli became the first man to create a sustained vacuum. After much observation, he concluded that the variation of the height of the mercury from day to day was caused by changes in atmospheric pressure. He never published his findings, however, because he was too deeply involved in the study of pure mathematics—including calculations of the cycloid, a geometric curve described by a point on the rim of a turning wheel. In his *Opera Geometrica* (1644; "Geometric Works"), Torricelli included his findings on fluid motion and projectile motion.

JOHN WALLIS

(b. Nov. 23, 1616, Ashford, Kent, Eng. —d. Oct. 28, 1703, Oxford, Oxfordshire)

The English mathematician John Wallis contributed substantially to the origins of the calculus and was the most influential English mathematician before Isaac Newton.

Wallis learned Latin, Greek, Hebrew, logic, and arithmetic during his early school years. In 1632 he entered the University of Cambridge, where he received B.A. and M.A. degrees in 1637 and 1640, respectively. He was ordained a priest in 1640 and shortly afterward exhibited his skill in mathematics by deciphering a number of cryptic messages from Royalist partisans that had fallen into the hands of the Parliamentarians. In 1645, the year of his marriage, Wallis moved to London, where in 1647 his serious interest in mathematics began when he read William Oughtred's *Clavis Mathematicae* ("The Keys to Mathematics").

Wallis's appointment in 1649 as Savilian professor of geometry at the University of Oxford marked the beginning of intense mathematical activity that lasted almost uninterruptedly to his death. A chance perusal of the works of the Italian physicist Evangelista Torricelli, who developed a method of indivisibles to

John Wallis, oil painting after a portrait by Sir Godfrey Kneller; in the National Portrait Gallery, London. Courtesy of the National Portrait Gallery, London

effect the quadrature of curves, derived from the Italian mathematician Bonaventura Cavalieri, stimulated Wallis's interest in the age-old problem of the quadrature of the circle, that is, finding a square that has an area equal to that of a given circle. In his *Arithmetica Infinitorum* ("The Arithmetic of Infinitesimals") of 1655, the result of his interest in Torricelli's work, Wallis extended Cavalieri's law of quadrature by devising a way to include negative and fractional exponents. Thus he did not follow Cavalieri's geometric approach and instead assigned numerical values to spatial indivisibles. By means of a complex logical sequence, he established the following relationship:

$$\frac{4}{\pi} = \frac{3 \cdot 3 \cdot 5 \cdot 5 \cdot 7 \cdot 7 \cdot 9 \cdot 9 \cdot 11 \cdot 11 \ldots}{2 \cdot 4 \cdot 4 \cdot 6 \cdot 6 \cdot 8 \cdot 8 \cdot 10 \cdot 10 \cdot 12 \ldots}$$

Isaac Newton reported that his work on the binomial theorem and on the calculus arose from a thorough study of the *Arithmetica Infinitorum* during his undergraduate years at Cambridge. The book promptly brought fame to Wallis, who was then recognized as one of the leading mathematicians in England.

In 1657 Wallis published the *Mathesis Universalis* ("Universal Mathematics"), on algebra, arithmetic, and geometry, in which he further developed notation. He invented and introduced the symbol ∞ for infinity. This symbol found use in treating a series of squares of indivisibles. His introduction of negative and fractional exponential notation was an important advance. The idea of the power of a number is very old. The application of the exponent dates from the 14th century. The French mathematician René Descartes in 1632 first used the symbol a^3. However Wallis was the first to demonstrate the utility of the exponent, particularly by his negative and fractional exponents.

Wallis was active in the weekly scientific meetings that, beginning as early as 1645, led to the formation of the Royal Society of London by charter of King Charles II in 1662. In his *Tractatus de Sectionibus Conicis* (1659; "Tract on Conic Sections"), he described the curves that are obtained as cross sections by cutting a cone with a plane as properties of algebraic coordinates. His *Mechanica, sive Tractatus de Motu* ("Mechanics, or Tract on Motion") in 1669–71 (three parts) refuted many of the errors regarding motion that had persisted since the time of Archimedes. He gave a more rigorous meaning to such terms as force and momentum, and he assumed that the gravity of the Earth may be regarded as localized at its centre.

Wallis's life was embittered by quarrels with his contemporaries, including the political philosopher Thomas Hobbes, who characterized his *Arithmetica Infinitorum* as a "scab of symbols," and the Dutch mathematician Christiaan Huygens, whom he once tricked with an anagram concerning a possible satellite of Saturn. Against the French philosopher and mathematician René Descartes he was particularly severe. Approaching his 70th year, Wallis published, in 1685, his *Treatise on Algebra,* an important study of equations that he applied to the properties of conoids, which are shaped almost like a cone. Moreover, in this work he anticipated the concept of complex numbers (e.g., $a + b\sqrt{-1}$, in which a and b are real).

By applying algebraic techniques rather than those of traditional geometry, Wallis contributed substantially to solving problems involving infinitesimals—that is, those quantities that are incalculably small. Thereby mathematics, eventually through the differential and integral calculus, became the most powerful tool of research in astronomy and theoretical physics. Wallis's many mathematical and scientific works were collected and published together as the *Opera Mathematica* in three folio volumes in 1693–99.

THE 19TH AND 20TH CENTURIES

In the 19th and 20th centuries, the foundations of analysis were examined in detail by mathematicians such as Richard Dedekind and David Hilbert. New avenues of inquiry were opened, such as functional analysis by Stefan Banach and measure theory by Henri-Léon Lebesgue.

STEFAN BANACH

(b. March 30, 1892, Kraków, Austria Hungary [now in Poland]—
d. Aug. 31, 1945, Lvov, Ukrainian S.S.R. [now Lviv, Ukraine])

The Polish mathematician Stefan Banach founded modern functional analysis and helped develop the theory of topological vector spaces.

Banach was given the surname of his mother, who was identified as Katarzyna Banach on his birth certificate, and the first name of his father, Stefan Greczek. He never knew his mother, and when still a young boy he was sent by his father to be raised by a family in Kraków. Banach apparently worked his way through the engineering school at the Lvov Technical University from 1910 to 1914. Unfit for military service because of poor eyesight, he worked on road constructions and taught at local schools during World War I.

At the end of the war several mathematical papers that Banach had worked on in his spare time were published and resulted in his being offered an assistantship at Lvov Technical University in 1920. Awarded a doctorate by the University of Lvov (now Ivan Franco National University of Lviv) in 1922, Banach began his lifelong affiliation with the university, building a school of mathematics and founding an important new mathematics journal, *Studia Mathematica*, in 1929. He was elected president of the Polish Mathematical Society in 1939, but his life changed with the Nazi occupation from 1941 to 1944. Under the occupation, Banach was compelled to feed lice for a German study of infectious diseases. He died of lung cancer in 1945 before he could resume his academic life with an appointment at Jagiellonian University, Kraków.

Banach contributed to the theory of orthogonal series and made innovations in the theory of measure and integration, but his most important contribution was in functional analysis. Of his published works, his *Théorie des opérations linéaires* (1932; "Theory of Linear Operations") is the most important. Banach and his coworkers summarized the previously developed concepts and theorems of functional analysis and integrated them into a comprehensive system. Banach himself introduced the concept of normed linear spaces, which are now known as Banach spaces. He also proved several fundamental theorems in the field, and his applications of theory inspired much of the work in functional analysis for the next few decades.

His two-volume collected works with commentaries, *Oeuvres avec des commentaires*, was published in 1979.

BERNHARD BOLZANO

(b. Oct. 5, 1781, Prague, Bohemia, Austrian Habsburg domain [now in Czech Republic]—d. Dec. 18, 1848, Prague)

The Bohemian mathematician and theologian Bernhard Bolzano provided a more detailed proof for the binomial theorem in 1816 and suggested the means of distinguishing between finite and infinite classes.

Bolzano graduated from the University of Prague as an ordained priest in 1805 and was immediately appointed professor of philosophy and religion at the university. Within a matter of years, however, Bolzano alienated many faculty and church leaders with his teachings of the social waste of militarism and the needlessness of war. He urged a total reform of the educational, social, and economic systems that would direct the nation's interests toward peace rather than toward armed conflict between nations. Upon his refusal to recant his beliefs, Bolzano was dismissed from the university in 1819 and at that point devoted his energies to his writings on social, religious, philosophical, and mathematical matters.

Bolzano held advanced views on logic, mathematical variables, limits, and continuity. In his studies of the physical aspects of force, space, and time he proposed theories counter to those suggested by the German philosopher Immanuel Kant. Much of his work remained unpublished during his lifetime and did not have wide impact until the late 19th and early 20th centuries, when a number of his conclusions were arrived at independently.

Bolzano's published works include *Der binomische Lehrsatz* (1816; "The Binomial Theorem"), *Rein analytischer Beweis* (1817; "Pure Analytic Proof"), *Functionenlehre* (1834; "Functions Model"), *Wissenschaftslehre,* 4 vol. (1834; "Scientific Model"), *Versuch einer neuen Darstellung der Logik,* 4 vol. (1837; "An Attempt at a New Presentation of Logic"), and *Paradoxien des Unendlichen* (1851; "Paradoxes of Infinity").

LUITZEN EGBERTUS JAN BROUWER
(b. Feb. 27, 1881, Overschie, Neth.—d. Dec. 2, 1966, Blaricum)

Luitzen Egbertus Jan Brouwer was a Dutch mathematician who founded mathematical intuitionism (a doctrine that views the nature of mathematics as mental constructions governed by self-evident laws) and whose work completely transformed topology, the study of the most basic properties of geometric surfaces and configurations.

Brouwer studied mathematics at the University of Amsterdam from 1897 to 1904. Even then he was interested in philosophical matters, as evidenced by his *Leven, Kunst, en Mystiek* (1905; "Life, Art, and Mysticism"). In his doctoral thesis, "Over de grondslagen der wiskunde" (1907; "On the Foundations of Mathematics"), Brouwer attacked the logical foundations of mathematics, as represented by the efforts of the German mathematician David Hilbert and the English philosopher Bertrand Russell, and shaped the beginnings of the intuitionist school. The following year, in "Over de onbetrouwbaarheid der logische principes" ("On the Untrustworthiness of the Logical Principles"), he rejected as invalid the use in mathematical proofs of the principle of the excluded middle (or excluded third). According to this principle, every mathematical statement is either true or false. No other possibility is allowed. Brouwer denied that this dichotomy applied to infinite sets.

Brouwer taught at the University of Amsterdam from 1909 to 1951. He did most of his important work in topology between 1909 and 1913. In connection with his studies of the work of Hilbert, he discovered the plane translation theorem, which characterizes topological mappings of the Cartesian plane, and the first of his fixed-point theorems, which later became important in the establishment of some fundamental theorems in branches of mathematics such as differential equations and game theory. In 1911 he established his theorems on the invariance of the dimension of a manifold under continuous invertible transformations. In addition, he merged the methods developed by the German mathematician Georg Cantor with the methods of analysis situs, an early stage of topology. In view of his remarkable contributions, many mathematicians consider Brouwer the founder of topology.

In 1918 he published a set theory, the following year a theory of measure, and by 1923 a theory of functions, all developed without using the principle of the excluded middle. He continued his studies until 1954, and, although he did not gain widespread acceptance for his precepts, intuitionism enjoyed a resurgence of interest after World War II, primarily because of contributions by the American mathematician Stephen Cole Kleene. His *Collected Works*, in two volumes, was published in 1975–76.

AUGUSTIN-LOUIS, BARON CAUCHY
(b. Aug. 21, 1789, Paris, France—d. May 23, 1857, Sceaux)

The French mathematician Augustin-Louis, Baron Cauchy, pioneered in analysis and the theory of substitution groups (groups whose elements are ordered sequences of a set of things). He was one of the greatest of modern mathematicians.

At the onset of the Reign of Terror (1793–94) during the French Revolution, Cauchy's family fled from Paris to the village of Arcueil, where Cauchy first became acquainted with the mathematician Pierre-Simon Laplace and the chemist Claude-Louis Berthollet.

Cauchy became a military engineer and in 1810 went to Cherbourg to work on the harbours and fortifications for Napoleon's English invasion fleet. In spite of his work load he produced several mathematical papers of note, including the solution of a problem sent to him by Joseph-Louis Lagrange that established a relationship between the number of edges, the number of vertices, and the number of faces of a convex polyhedron, and the solution of Pierre de Fermat's problem on polygonal numbers.

Cauchy returned to Paris in 1813, and Lagrange and Laplace persuaded him to devote himself entirely to mathematics. The following year he published the memoir on definite integrals that became the basis of the theory of complex functions. From 1816 he held professorships in the Faculty of Sciences, the Collège de France, and the École Polytechnique, all in Paris. When Gaspard Monge was expelled for political reasons from the Academy of Sciences (1816), Cauchy was appointed to fill the vacancy. The same year he won the grand prix of the Institute of France for a paper on wave propagation, now accepted as a classic in hydrodynamics. In 1822 he laid the foundations of the mathematical theory of elasticity.

Cauchy's greatest contributions to mathematics, characterized by the clear and rigorous methods that he introduced, are embodied predominantly in his three great treatises: *Cours d'analyse de l'École Royale Polytechnique* (1821; "Courses on Analysis from the École Royale Polytechnique"); *Résumé des leçons sur le calcul infinitésimal* (1823; "Résumé of Lessons on Infinitesimal Calculus"); and *Leçons sur les applications du calcul infinitésimal à la géométrie* (1826–28; "Lessons on the

Applications of Infinitesimal Calculus to Geometry"). The first phase of modern rigour in mathematics originated in his lectures and researches in analysis during the 1820s. He clarified the principles of calculus and put them on a satisfactory basis by developing them with the aid of limits and continuity, concepts now considered vital to analysis. To the same period belongs his development of the theory of functions of a complex variable (a variable involving a multiple of the square root of minus one), today indispensable in applied mathematics from physics to aeronautics.

Although acting only from the highest motives, Cauchy often offended his colleagues by his self-righteous obstinacy and aggressive religious bigotry. Upon the exile of Charles X in 1830 and the ascension of Louis-Philippe to the throne, Cauchy went into exile, too, rather than take the oath of allegiance. A chair of mathematical physics was created for him at the University of Turin, but in 1833 he left to tutor the Duke de Bordeaux, grandson of Charles X. In 1838, with the suspension of the oath, he returned to France, resuming his chair at the École Polytechnique.

Cauchy made substantial contributions to the theory of numbers and wrote three important papers on error theory. His work in optics provided a mathematical basis for the workable but somewhat unsatisfactory theory of the properties of the ether, a hypothetical, omnipresent medium once thought to be the conductor of light. His collected works, *Oeuvres complètes d'Augustin Cauchy* (1882–1970), were published in 27 volumes.

RICHARD DEDEKIND

(b. Oct. 6, 1831, Braunschweig, duchy of Braunschweig [Germany]—d. Feb. 12, 1916, Braunschweig)

German mathematician Julius Wilhelm Richard Dedekind developed a major redefinition of irrational numbers in terms of arithmetic concepts. Although not fully recognized in his lifetime, his treatment of the ideas of the infinite and of what constitutes a real number continues to influence modern mathematics.

Dedekind was the son of a lawyer. While attending the Gymnasium Martino-Catharineum in 1838–47 in Braunschweig, he was at first interested primarily in chemistry and physics. At the Caroline College in 1848–50, however, he turned to calculus, algebra, and analytic geometry, which helped qualify him to study advanced mathematics at the University of Göttingen under the mathematician Carl Friedrich Gauss.

After two years of independent study of algebra, geometry, and elliptic functions, Dedekind served as *Privatdozent* ("unsalaried lecturer") in 1854–58 at the University of Göttingen, where, in his lectures, he introduced, probably for the first time, the Galois theory of equations and attended the lectures of the mathematician Peter Gustav Lejeune Dirichlet. These experiences led Dedekind to see the need for a redefinition of irrational numbers in terms of arithmetic properties. The geometric approach had led Eudoxus in the 4th century BCE to define them as approximations by rational numbers (e.g., a series of nonrepeating decimals, as $\sqrt{2} = 1.414213 \ldots$).

In 1858 Dedekind joined the faculty of the Zürich Polytechnic, where he remained for five years. In 1862 he accepted a position in the Technical High School in Braunschweig, where he remained in comparative isolation for the rest of his life.

While teaching there, Dedekind developed the idea that both rational and irrational numbers could form a continuum (with no gaps) of real numbers, provided that the real numbers have a one-to-one relationship with points on a line. He said that an irrational number would then be that boundary value that separates two especially constructed collections of rational numbers.

Dedekind perceived that the character of the continuum need not depend on the quantity of points on a line segment (or continuum) but rather on how the line submits to being divided. His method, now called the Dedekind cut, consisted in separating all the real numbers in a series into two parts such that each real number in one part is less than every real number in the other. Such a cut, which corresponds to a given value, defines an irrational number if no largest or no smallest is present in either part. Whereas a rational number is defined as a cut in which one part contains a smallest or a largest. Dedekind would therefore define the square root of 2 as the unique number dividing the continuum into two collections of numbers such that all the members of one collection are greater than those of the other, or that cut, or division, separating a series of numbers into two parts such that one collection contains all the numbers whose squares are larger than 2 and the other contains all the numbers whose squares are less than 2.

Dedekind developed his arithmetical rendering of irrational numbers in 1872 in his *Stetigkeit und Irrationale Zahlen* (Eng. trans., "Continuity and Irrational Numbers," published in *Essays on the Theory of Numbers*). He also proposed, as did the German mathematician Georg Cantor, two years later, that a set—a collection of objects or components—is infinite if its components may be arranged in a one-to-one relationship with the components of one of its subsets. By supplementing the geometric method in analysis, Dedekind contributed substantially to the modern treatment of the infinitely large and the infinitely small.

While vacationing in Interlaken, Switz., in 1874, Dedekind met Cantor. Dedekind gave a sympathetic hearing to an exposition of the revolutionary idea of sets that Cantor had just published, which later became prominent in the teaching of modern mathematics. Because both mathematicians were developing highly original concepts, such as in number theory and analysis, which were not readily accepted by their contemporaries, and because both lacked adequate professional recognition, a lasting friendship developed.

Continuing his investigations into the properties and relationships of integers—that is, the idea of number—Dedekind published *Über die Theorie der ganzen algebraischen Zahlen* (1879; "On the Theory of Algebraic Whole Numbers"). There he proposed the "ideal" as a collection of numbers that may be separated out of a larger collection, composed of algebraic integers that satisfy polynomial equations with ordinary integers as coefficients. The ideal is a collection of all algebraic integer multiples of a given algebraic integer. For example, the notation (2) represents such a particular collection, as . . . -8, -6, -4, -2, 0, 2, 4, 6, 8 . . . . The sum of two ideals is an ideal that is composed of all the sums of all their individual members. The product of two ideals is similarly defined. Ideals, considered as integers, can then be added, multiplied, and hence factored. By means of this theory of ideals, he allowed the process of unique factorization—that is, expressing a number as the product of only one set of primes, or 1 and itself—to be applied to many algebraic structures that hitherto had eluded analysis.

JOSEPH, BARON FOURIER
(b. March 21, 1768, Auxerre, France—d. May 16, 1830, Paris)

The French mathematician Jean-Baptiste-Joseph, Baron Fourier, known also as an Egyptologist and administrator, exerted strong influence on mathematical physics through his *Théorie analytique de la chaleur* (1822; *The Analytical Theory of Heat*). He showed how the conduction of heat in solid bodies may be analyzed in terms of infinite mathematical series now called by his name, the Fourier series. Far transcending the particular subject of heat conduction, his work stimulated research in mathematical physics, which has since been often identified with the solution of boundary-

Joseph Fourier, lithograph by Jules Boilly, 1823; in the Academy of Sciences, Paris. Giraudon/Art Resource, New York

value problems, encompassing many natural occurrences such as sunspots, tides, and the weather. His work also had a great influence on the theory of functions of a real variable, one of the main branches of modern mathematics.

Fourier, the son of a tailor, first attended the local military school conducted by Benedictine monks. He showed such proficiency in mathematics in his early years that he later became a teacher in mathematics at the same school. The ideals of the French Revolution then swept him into politics, and more than once his life was in danger. When the École Normale was founded in 1794 in Paris, he was among its first students, and, in 1795, he became a teacher there. The same year, after the École Polytechnique was opened, he joined its faculty and became a colleague of Gaspard Monge and other mathematicians.

In 1798, with Monge and others, Fourier accompanied Napoleon on his expedition to Egypt. Until 1801 he was engaged in extensive research on Egyptian antiquities, gave advice on engineering and diplomatic undertakings, and served for three years as the secretary of the Institut d'Égypte, which Napoleon established in Cairo in 1798.

After his return to France, Fourier was charged with the publication of the enormous mass of Egyptian materials. This became the *Description de l'Égypte,* to which he also wrote a lengthy historical preface on the ancient civilization of Egypt. He was also appointed prefect (administrator for the national government and *département*) of the Isère *département,* a position he held from 1802 to 1814, with his headquarters at Grenoble. He showed great administrative ability, as in directing the drainage of swamps, while continuing his Egyptological and mathematical work. In 1809 Napoleon made him a baron. Following Napoleon's fall from power in 1815, Fourier was appointed director of the Statistical Bureau of the Seine, allowing him a period of quiet academic life in Paris. In 1817 he was elected to the Académie des Sciences, of which, in 1822, he became perpetual secretary. Because of his work in Egyptology he was elected in 1826 to the Académie Française and the Académie de Médecine.

Fourier began his work on the *Théorie analytique de la chaleur* in Grenoble in 1807 and completed it in Paris in 1822. His work enabled him to express the conduction of heat in two-dimensional objects (i.e., very thin sheets of material) in terms of the differential equation

$$\frac{\partial u}{\partial t} = k \left[\frac{\partial^2 u}{\partial x^2} + \frac{\partial^2 u}{\partial y^2} \right]$$

in which u is the temperature at any time t at a point (x, y) of the plane and k is a constant of proportionality called the diffusivity of the material. The problem is to find the temperature, for example, in a conducting plate, if at time $t = 0$, the temperature is given at the boundary and at the points of the plane. For the solution of such problems in one dimension, Fourier introduced series with sines and cosines as terms:

$$y = \tfrac{1}{2}a_0 + (a_1 \cos x + b_1 \sin x)$$
$$+ (a_2 \cos 2x + b_2 \sin 2x) + \cdots \cdot$$

Such Fourier series, already occasionally used by Leonhard Euler and other 18th-century mathematicians, but somewhat distrusted, received through Fourier their important position in modern mathematics. He also extended this concept into the so-called Fourier integral. Doubts of the validity of the Fourier series, which led later mathematicians to a fundamental renewal of the concept of real function, were resolved by P.G.L. Dirichlet, Bernhard Riemann, Henri Lebesgue, and others.

Fourier worked on the theory almost his entire life. He was also interested in the determination of roots of algebraic equations (the so-called theorem of Fourier).

CARL FRIEDRICH GAUSS
(b. April 30, 1777, Brunswick [Germany]—d. Feb. 23, 1855, Göttingen, Hanover)

The German mathematician Carl Friedrich Gauss is generally regarded as one of the greatest mathematicians of all time for his contributions to number theory, geometry, probability theory, geodesy, planetary astronomy, the theory of functions, and potential theory (including electromagnetism).

Gauss was the only child of poor parents. He was rare among mathematicians in that he was a calculating prodigy, and he retained the ability to do elaborate calculations in his head most of his life. Impressed by this ability and by his gift for languages, his teachers and his devoted mother recommended him to the duke of Brunswick in 1791, who granted him financial assistance to continue his education locally and then to study mathematics at the University of Göttingen from 1795 to 1798. Gauss's pioneering work gradually established him as the era's preeminent mathematician, first in the German-speaking world and then farther afield, although he remained a remote and aloof figure.

Gauss's first significant discovery, in 1792, was that a regular polygon of 17 sides can be constructed by ruler and compass alone. Its significance lies not in the result but in the proof, which rested on a profound analysis of the factorization of polynomial equations and opened the door to later ideas of Galois theory. His doctoral thesis of 1797 gave a proof of the fundamental theorem of algebra: every polynomial equation with real or complex coefficients has as many roots (solutions) as its degree (the highest power of the variable). Gauss's proof, though not wholly convincing, was remarkable for its critique of earlier attempts. Gauss later gave three more proofs of this major result, the last on the 50th anniversary of the first, which shows the importance he attached to the topic.

Gauss's recognition as a truly remarkable talent, though, resulted from two major publications in 1801. Foremost was his publication of the first systematic textbook on algebraic number theory, *Disquisitiones Arithmeticae*. This book begins with the first account of modular arithmetic, gives a thorough account of the solutions of quadratic polynomials in two variables in integers, and ends with the theory of factorization mentioned above. This choice of topics and its natural generalizations set the agenda in number theory for much of the 19th century, and Gauss's continuing interest in the subject spurred much research, especially in German universities.

The second publication was his rediscovery of the asteroid Ceres. Its original discovery, by the Italian astronomer

Giuseppe Piazzi in 1800, had caused a sensation, but it vanished behind the Sun before enough observations could be taken to calculate its orbit with sufficient accuracy to know where it would reappear. Many astronomers competed for the honour of finding it again, but Gauss won. His success rested on a novel method for dealing with errors in observations, today called the method of least squares. Thereafter Gauss worked for many years as an astronomer and published a major work on the computation of orbits—the numerical side of such work was much less onerous for him than for most people. As an intensely loyal subject of the duke of Brunswick and, after 1807 when he returned to Göttingen as an astronomer, of the duke of Hanover, Gauss felt that the work was socially valuable.

Gauss also wrote on cartography, the theory of map projections. For his study of angle-preserving maps, he was awarded the prize of the Danish Academy of Sciences in 1823. This work came close to suggesting that complex functions of a complex variable are generally angle-preserving, but Gauss stopped short of making that fundamental insight explicit, leaving it for Bernhard Riemann, who had a deep appreciation of Gauss's work. Gauss also had other unpublished insights into the nature of complex functions and their integrals, some of which he divulged to friends.

In fact, Gauss often withheld publication of his discoveries. As a student at Göttingen, he began to doubt the a priori truth of Euclidean geometry and suspected that its truth might be empirical. For this to be the case, there must exist an alternative geometric description of space. Rather than publish such a description, Gauss confined himself to criticizing various a priori defenses of Euclidean geometry. It would seem that he was gradually convinced that there exists a logical alternative to Euclidean geometry. However, when the Hungarian János Bolyai and the Russian Nikolay Lobachevsky published their accounts of a new, non-Euclidean geometry about 1830, Gauss failed to give a coherent account of his own ideas. It is possible to draw these ideas together into an impressive whole, in which his concept of intrinsic curvature plays a central role, but Gauss never did this. Some have attributed this failure to his innate conservatism, others to his incessant inventiveness that always drew him on to the next new idea, still others to his failure to find a central idea that would govern geometry once Euclidean geometry was no longer unique. All these explanations have some merit, though none has enough to be the whole explanation.

Another topic on which Gauss largely concealed his ideas from his contemporaries was elliptic functions. He published an account in 1812 of an interesting infinite series, and he wrote but did not publish an account of the differential equation that the infinite series satisfies. He showed that the series, called the hypergeometric series, can be used to define many familiar and many new functions. But by then he knew how to use the differential equation to produce a very general theory of elliptic functions and to free the theory entirely from its origins in the theory of elliptic integrals. This was a major breakthrough, because, as Gauss had discovered in the 1790s, the theory of elliptic functions naturally treats them as complex-valued functions of a complex variable, but the contemporary theory of complex integrals was utterly inadequate for the task. When some of this theory was published by the Norwegian Niels Abel and the German Carl Jacobi about 1830, Gauss commented to a friend that Abel had come one-third of the way. This was accurate, but it is a sad measure of Gauss's personality in that he still withheld publication. After Gauss's death in 1855, the discovery of many novel ideas among his unpublished papers extended his influence well into the remainder of the century.

DAVID HILBERT

(b. Jan. 23, 1862, Königsberg, Prussia [now Kaliningrad, Russia]—d. Feb. 14, 1943, Göttingen, Ger.)

German mathematician David Hilbert reduced geometry to a series of axioms and contributed substantially to the establishment of the formalistic foundations of mathematics. His work in 1909 on integral equations led to 20th-century research in functional analysis.

The first steps of Hilbert's career occurred at the University of Königsberg, at which, in 1884, he finished his *Inaugurel-dissertation* (Ph.D.). He remained at Königsberg as a *Privatdozent* (lecturer, or assistant professor) in 1886–92, as an *Extraordinarius* (associate professor) in 1892–93, and as an *Ordinarius* in 1893–95. In 1892 he married Käthe Jerosch, and they had one child, Franz. In 1895 Hilbert accepted a professorship in mathematics at the University of Göttingen, at which he remained for the rest of his life.

The University of Göttingen had a flourishing tradition in mathematics, primarily as the result of the contributions of Carl Friedrich Gauss, Peter Gustav Lejeune Dirichlet, and Bernhard Riemann in the 19th century. During the first three decades of the 20th century this mathematical tradition achieved even greater eminence, largely because of Hilbert. The Mathematical Institute at Göttingen drew students and visitors from all over the world.

Hilbert's intense interest in mathematical physics also contributed to the university's reputation in physics. His colleague and friend, the mathematician Hermann Minkowski, aided in the new application of mathematics to physics until his untimely death in 1909. Three winners of the Nobel Prize for Physics—Max von Laue in 1914, James Franck in 1925, and Werner Heisenberg in 1932—spent significant parts of their careers at the University of Göttingen during Hilbert's lifetime.

In a highly original way, Hilbert extensively modified the mathematics of invariants—the entities that are not altered during such geometric changes as rotation, dilation, and reflection. Hilbert proved the theorem of invariants—that all invariants can be expressed in terms of a finite number. In his *Zahlbericht* ("Commentary on Numbers"), a report on algebraic number theory published in 1897, he consolidated what was known in this subject and pointed the way to the developments that followed. In 1899 he published the *Grundlagen der Geometrie* (*The Foundations of Geometry*, 1902), which contained his definitive set of axioms for Euclidean geometry and a keen analysis of their significance. This popular book, which appeared in 10 editions, marked a turning point in the axiomatic treatment of geometry.

A substantial part of Hilbert's fame rests on a list of 23 research problems he enunciated in 1900 at the International Mathematical Congress in Paris. In his address, "The Problems of Mathematics," he surveyed nearly all the mathematics of his day and endeavoured to set forth the problems he thought would be significant for mathematicians in the 20th century. Many of the problems have since been solved, and each solution was a noted event. Of those that remain, however, one, in part, requires a solution to the Riemann hypothesis, which is usually considered to be the most important unsolved problem in mathematics.

In 1905 (and again from 1918) Hilbert attempted to lay a firm foundation for mathematics by proving consistency— that is, that finite steps of reasoning in logic could not lead to a contradiction. But in 1931 the Austrian–U.S. mathematician Kurt Gödel showed this goal to be unattainable: propositions may be formulated that are undecidable. Thus, it cannot be known with certainty that mathematical axioms do not lead to contradictions. Nevertheless, the development of logic after Hilbert was different, for he established the formalistic foundations of mathematics.

Hilbert's work in integral equations in about 1909 led directly to 20th-century research in functional analysis (the branch of mathematics in which functions are studied collectively). His work also established the basis for his work on infinite-dimensional space, later called Hilbert space, a concept that is useful in mathematical analysis and quantum mechanics. Making use of his results on integral equations, Hilbert contributed to the development of mathematical physics by his important memoirs on kinetic gas theory and the theory of radiations. In 1909 he proved the conjecture in number theory that for any n, all positive integers are sums of a certain fixed number of nth powers. For example, $5 = 2^2 + 1^2$, in which $n = 2$. In 1910 the second Bolyai award went to Hilbert alone and, appropriately, Henri Poincaré wrote the glowing tribute.

The city of Königsberg in 1930, the year of his retirement from the University of Göttingen, made Hilbert an honorary citizen. For this occasion he prepared an address entitled "*Naturerkennen und Logik*" ("The Understanding of Nature and Logic"). The last six words of Hilbert's address sum up his enthusiasm for mathematics and the devoted life he spent raising it to a new level: "*Wir müssen wissen, wir werden wissen*" ("We must know, we shall know"). The last decade of Hilbert's life was darkened by the tragedy brought to himself and to so many of his students and colleagues by the Nazi regime.

ANDREY KOLMOGOROV

(b. April 25 [April 12, Old Style], 1903, Tambov, Russia—d. Oct. 20, 1987, Moscow)

The work of the Russian mathematician Andrey Nikolayevich Kolmogorov influenced many branches of modern mathematics, especially harmonic analysis, probability, set theory, information theory, and number theory. A man of broad culture, with interests in technology, history, and education, he played an active role in the reform of education in the Soviet Union. He is best remembered for a brilliant series of papers on the theory of probability.

Kolmogorov's mother died giving him birth. He was raised by her sister and took his maternal grandfather's family name. His aunt moved with him to Moscow when he was seven years old, where he demonstrated an early interest in biology and history. In 1920, as yet undecided over a career, he enrolled simultaneously at Moscow State University to study history and mathematics and at the Mendeleev Chemical Engineering Institute to study metallurgy. However, he soon revealed a remarkable talent for mathematics and specialized in that subject. As a 19-year-old student he was entrusted with teaching mathematics and physics courses in the Potylikhin Experimental School, and by the time he graduated in 1925 he had published 10 mathematical papers, most of them on trigonometric series—an extraordinary output for a student. This astonishing outburst of mathematical creativity continued as a graduate student with eight more papers written through 1928. He later expanded the most important of these papers, "General Theory of Measure and Probability Theory"—which aimed to develop a rigorous, axiomatic foundation for probability—into an influential monograph *Grundbegriffe der Wahrscheinlichkeitsrechnung* (1933; *Foundations of the Theory of Probability*, 1950). In 1929, having completed his doctorate, Kolmogorov was elected a member of the Institute of Mathematics and Mechanics at Moscow State University, with which he remained associated for the rest of his life. In 1931, following a radical restructuring of the Moscow mathematical community, he was elected a professor. Two years later he was appointed director of the Mathematical Research Institute at the university, a position he held until 1939 and again from 1951 to 1953. In 1938 he was chosen to head the new department of probability and statistics at the Steklov Mathematical Institute of the U.S.S.R. Academy of Sciences in Moscow (now the Russian Academy of Sciences), a position that he held until 1958. He was elected to the Academy of Sciences in 1939, and between 1946 and 1949 he was also the head of the Turbulence Laboratory of the U.S.S.R. Academy of Sciences Institute of Theoretical Geophysics in Moscow.

Of the many areas of pure and applied mathematical research to which Kolmogorov contributed, probability theory is unquestionably the most important, in terms of both the depth and breadth of his contributions. In addition to his work on the foundations of probability, he contributed profound papers on stochastic processes, especially Markov processes. In Markov processes only the present state has any bearing upon the probability of future states. States are therefore said to retain no "memory" of past events. Kolmogorov invented a pair of functions to characterize the transition probabilities for a Markov process and showed that they amount to what he called an "instantaneous mean" and an "instantaneous variance." Using these functions, he was able to write a set of partial differential equations to determine the probabilities of transition from one state to another. These equations provided an entirely new approach to the application of probability theory in physics, chemistry, civil engineering, and biology. To note just two examples, in 1937 Kolmogorov published a paper on the use of statistical theory to study the process of crystallization, and the following year he published a paper on mathematical biology using a branching stochastic process to describe the asymptotic probability of extinction of a species over a large number of generations.

Kolmogorov's interest in problems of turbulence in fluids (turbulent flow) arose in the late 1930s, when he realized that the recently developed stochastic field theory would be relevant to these problems. In 1941 and 1942 he contributed four papers to this area, in which his contributions were multiplied by a talented group of collaborators working under his direction.

During the 1930s, while continuing a prolific output of papers on particular mathematical topics, Kolmogorov began to write articles on methodological questions involving the theories of real analysis and probability. He also began to write expository articles for encyclopedias and journals aimed at a popular audience. After the end of World War II, established as one of the leading Soviet mathematicians, he began writing articles of historical and philosophical content. During the 1950s he contributed more than 80 articles to the second edition of the *Great Soviet Encyclopedia*.

In the mid-1950s Kolmogorov began to work on problems of information theory. He was inspired, in part, by the earlier nonrigorous work of the American engineer Claude Shannon. Working with Israil Gelfand and Akiva Yaglom, he was able to give a mathematical definition of the notion of quantity of information. In the 1960s he began writing articles on automata theory and theory of algorithms. The breadth of his culture and interests is shown by articles that he wrote at this time on the metrical structure of some of the masterpieces of Russian poetry.

The late 1960s marked Kolmogorov's entrance into the theory of pedagogy, in which he was enormously influential through his textbooks and his service as a member of the U.S.S.R. Academy of Pedagogical Sciences. He cowrote and reviewed school textbooks and actively participated in reforming the mathematics curriculum in Soviet schools. Though suffering from Parkinson's disease and nearly blind during the last few years of his life, he continued to take an active interest in the mathematical world until he died.

HENRI-LÉON LEBESGUE
(b. June 28, 1875, Beauvais, France — d. July 26, 1941, Paris),

Henri-Léon Lebesgue was a French mathematician whose generalization of the Riemann integral revolutionized the field of integration.

Lebesgue was *maître de conférences* (lecture master) at the University of Rennes from 1902 until 1906, when he went to Poitiers, first as *chargé de cours* (assistant lecturer) of the faculty of sciences and later as professor. In 1910 he went to the Sorbonne in Paris as *maître de conférences* in mathematical analysis, and in 1921 he became a professor at the Collège de France. In 1917 he was awarded the Prix Saintour, and in 1922 he was elected to the French Academy of Sciences. He was made an honorary member of the London Mathematical Society in 1924 and a foreign member of the Royal Society of London in 1930.

One of the greatest mathematicians of his day, Lebesgue made an important contribution to topology with his covering theorem (which helps define the dimension of a set). He also worked on Fourier series and potential theory, but his main work was on integration theory.

Toward the close of the 19th century, mathematical analysis was limited effectively to continuous functions, and artificial restrictions were necessary to cope with discontinuities that cropped up with greater frequency as more exotic functions were encountered. The Riemann method of integration was applicable only to continuous and a few discontinuous functions. Influenced by the work of Émile Borel, Camille Jordan, and others, Lebesgue formulated a new theory of measure and framed a new definition of the definite integral, which he presented in his doctoral thesis at the Sorbonne in 1902. The Lebesgue integral is one of the great achievements of modern real analysis, and Lebesgue integration was instrumental in greatly expanding the scope of Fourier analysis.

In addition to about 50 papers, Lebesgue wrote two major books, *Leçons sur l'intégration et la recherche des fonctions primitives* (1904; "Lessons on Integration and Analysis of Primitive Functions") and *Leçons sur les séries trigonométriques* (1906; "Lessons on the Trigonometric Series").

HENRI POINCARÉ

(b. April 29, 1854, Nancy, France—d. July 17, 1912, Paris)

French mathematician Jules Henri Poincaré was one of the greatest mathematicians and mathematical physicists at the end of the 19th century. He made a series of profound innovations in geometry, the theory of differential equations, electromagnetism, topology, and the philosophy of mathematics.

Poincaré grew up in Nancy and studied mathematics from 1873 to 1875 at the École Polytechnique in Paris.

He continued his studies at the Mining School in Caen before receiving his doctorate from the École Polytechnique in 1879. While a student, he discovered new types of complex functions that solved a wide variety of differential equations. This major work involved one of the first "mainstream" applications

Henri Poincaré, 1909. H. Roger-Viollet

of non-Euclidean geometry, a subject discovered by the Hungarian János Bolyai and the Russian Nikolay Lobachevsky about 1830 but not generally accepted by mathematicians until the 1860s and '70s. Poincaré published a long series of papers on this work in 1880–84 that effectively made his name internationally. The prominent German mathematician Felix Klein, only five years his senior, was already working in the area, and it was widely agreed that Poincaré came out the better from the comparison.

In the 1880s Poincaré also began work on curves defined by a particular type of differential equation, in which he was the first to consider the global nature of the solution curves and their possible singular points (points where the differential equation is not properly defined). He investigated such questions as: Do the solutions spiral into or away from a point? Do they, like the hyperbola, at first approach a point and then swing past and recede from it? Do some solutions form closed loops? If so, do nearby curves spiral toward or away from these closed loops? He showed that the number and types of singular points are determined purely by the topological nature of the surface. In particular, it is only on the torus that the differential equations he was considering have no singular points.

Poincaré intended this preliminary work to lead to the study of the more complicated differential equations that describe the motion of the solar system. In 1885 an added inducement to take the next step presented itself when King Oscar II of Sweden offered a prize for anyone who could establish the stability of the solar system. This would require showing that equations of motion for the planets could be solved and the orbits of the planets shown to be curves that stay in a bounded region of space for all time. Some of the greatest mathematicians since Isaac Newton had attempted to solve this problem, and Poincaré soon realized that he could not make any headway unless he concentrated on a simpler, special case, in which two massive bodies orbit one another in circles around their common centre of gravity while a minute third body orbits them both. The third body is taken to be so small that it does not affect the orbits of the larger ones. Poincaré could establish that the orbit is stable, in the sense that the small body returns infinitely often arbitrarily close to any position it has occupied. This does not mean, however, that it does not also move very far away at times, which would have disastrous consequences for life on Earth. For this and other achievements in his essay, Poincaré was awarded the prize in 1889. But, on writing the essay for publication, Poincaré discovered that another result in it was wrong, and in putting that right he discovered that the motion could be chaotic. He had hoped to show that if the small body could be started off in such a way that it traveled in a closed orbit, then starting it off in almost the same way would result in an orbit that at least stayed close to the original orbit. Instead, he discovered that even small changes in the initial conditions could produce large, unpredictable changes in the resulting orbit. (This phenomenon is now known as pathological sensitivity to initial positions, and it is one of the characteristic signs of a chaotic system.) Poincaré summarized his new mathematical methods in astronomy in *Les Méthodes nouvelles de la mécanique céleste*, 3 vol. (1892, 1893, 1899; "The New Methods of Celestial Mechanics").

Poincaré was led by this work to contemplate mathematical spaces (now called manifolds) in which the position of a point is determined by several coordinates. Very little was known about such manifolds, and, although the German mathematician Bernhard Riemann had hinted at them a generation or more earlier, few had taken the hint. Poincaré took up the task and looked for ways in which such manifolds could be distinguished, thus opening up the whole subject of topology, then known as analysis situs. Riemann had shown that in two dimensions surfaces can be distinguished by their genus (the number of holes in the surface), and Enrico Betti in Italy and Walther von Dyck in Germany had extended this work to three dimensions, but much remained to be done. Poincaré singled out the idea of considering closed curves in the manifold that cannot be deformed into one another. For example, any curve on the surface of a sphere can be continuously shrunk to a point, but there are curves on a torus (curves wrapped around a hole, for instance) that cannot. Poincaré asked if a three-dimensional manifold in which every curve can be shrunk to a point is topologically equivalent to a three-dimensional sphere. This problem (now known as the Poincaré conjecture) became one of the most important unsolved problems in algebraic topology. Ironically, the conjecture was first proved for dimensions greater than three: in dimensions five and above by Stephen Smale in the 1960s and in dimension four as a consequence of work by Simon Donaldson and Michael Freedman in the 1980s. Finally, Grigori Perelman proved the conjecture for three dimensions in 2006. All of these achievements were marked with the award of a Fields Medal. Poincaré's *Analysis Situs* (1895) was an early systematic treatment of topology, and he is often called the father of algebraic topology.

Poincaré felt that our understanding of the natural numbers was innate and therefore fundamental, so he was critical of attempts to reduce all of mathematics to symbolic logic (as advocated by Bertrand Russell in England and Louis Couturat in France) and of attempts to reduce mathematics to axiomatic set theory. In these beliefs he turned out to be right, as shown by Kurt Gödel in 1931.

Bernhard Riemann

(b. Sept. 17, 1826, Breselenz, Hanover [Germany]—d. July 20, 1866, Selasca, Italy)

German mathematician Georg Friedrich Bernhard Riemann's profound and novel approaches to the study of geometry laid the mathematical foundation for Albert Einstein's theory of relativity. He also made important contributions to the theory of functions, complex analysis, and number theory.

Riemann was born into a poor Lutheran pastor's family, and all his life he was a shy and introverted person. He was fortunate to have a schoolteacher who recognized his rare mathematical ability and lent him advanced books to read, including Adrien-Marie Legendre's *Number Theory* (1830). Riemann read the book in a week and then claimed to know it by heart. He went on to study mathematics at the University of Göttingen in 1846–47 and 1849–51 and at the University of Berlin (now the Humboldt University of Berlin) in 1847–49. He then gradually worked his way up the academic profession, through a succession of poorly paid jobs, until he became a full professor in 1859 and gained, for the first time in his life, a measure of financial security. However, in 1862, shortly after his marriage to Elise Koch, Riemann fell seriously ill with tuberculosis. Repeated trips to Italy failed to stem the progress of the disease, and he died in Italy in 1866.

Riemann's visits to Italy were important for the growth of modern mathematics there. Enrico Betti in particular took up the study of Riemannian ideas. Ill health prevented Riemann from publishing all his work, and some of his best was published only posthumously—e.g., the first edition of Riemann's *Gesammelte mathematische Werke* (1876; "Collected Mathematical Works"), edited by Richard Dedekind and Heinrich Weber.

Riemann's influence was initially less than it might have been. Göttingen was a small university, Riemann was a poor lecturer, and, to make matters worse, several of his best students died young. His few papers are also difficult to read, but his work won the respect of some of the best mathematicians in Germany, including his friend Dedekind and his rival in Berlin, Karl Weierstrass. Other mathematicians were gradually drawn to his papers by their intellectual depth, and in this way he set an agenda for conceptual thinking over ingenious calculation. This emphasis was taken up by Felix Klein and David Hilbert, who later established Göttingen as a world centre for mathematics research, with Carl Gauss and Riemann as its iconic figures.

In his doctoral thesis (1851), Riemann introduced a way of generalizing the study of polynomial equations in two real variables to the case of two complex variables. In the real case a polynomial equation defines a curve in the plane. Because a complex variable z can be thought of as a pair of real variables $x + iy$ (where $i = \sqrt{-1}$), an equation involving two complex variables defines a real surface—now known as a Riemann surface—spread out over the plane. In 1851 and in his more widely available paper of 1857, Riemann showed how such surfaces can be classified by a number, later called the genus, that is determined by the maximal number of closed curves that can be drawn on the surface without splitting it into separate pieces. This is one of the first significant uses of topology in mathematics.

In 1854 Riemann presented his ideas on geometry for the official postdoctoral qualification at Göttingen; the elderly Gauss was an examiner and was greatly impressed. Riemann argued that the fundamental ingredients for geometry are a space of points (called today a manifold) and a way of measuring distances along curves in the space. He argued that the space need not be ordinary

Euclidean space and that it could have any dimension (he even contemplated spaces of infinite dimension). Nor is it necessary that the surface be drawn in its entirety in three-dimensional space. A few years later this inspired the Italian mathematician Eugenio Beltrami to produce just such a description of non-Euclidean geometry, the first physically plausible alternative to Euclidean geometry. Riemann's ideas went further and turned out to provide the mathematical foundation for the four-dimensional geometry of space-time in Einstein's theory of general relativity. It seems that Riemann was led to these ideas partly by his dislike of the concept of action at a distance in contemporary physics and by his wish to endow space with the ability to transmit forces such as electromagnetism and gravitation.

In 1859 Riemann also introduced complex function theory into number theory. He took the zeta function, which had been studied by many previous mathematicians because of its connection to the prime numbers, and showed how to think of it as a complex function. The Riemann zeta function then takes the value zero at the negative integers (the so-called trivial zeros) and also at points on a certain line (called the critical line). Standard methods in complex function theory, due to Augustin-Louis Cauchy in France and Riemann himself, would give much information about the distribution of prime numbers if it could be shown that all the nontrivial zeros lie on this line—a conjecture known as the Riemann hypothesis. All nontrivial zeros discovered thus far have been on the critical line. In fact, infinitely many zeros have been discovered to lie on this line. Such partial results have been enough to show that the number of prime numbers less than any number x is well approximated by $x/\ln x$. The Riemann hypothesis was one of the 23 problems that Hilbert challenged mathematicians to solve in his famous

1900 address, "The Problems of Mathematics." Over the years a growing body of mathematical ideas have built upon the assumption that the Riemann hypothesis is true. Its proof, or disproof, would have far-reaching consequences and confer instant renown.

Riemann took a novel view of what it means for mathematical objects to exist. He sought general existence proofs, rather than "constructive proofs" that actually produce the objects. He believed that this approach led to conceptual clarity and prevented the mathematician from getting lost in the details, but even some experts disagreed with such nonconstructive proofs. Riemann also studied how functions compare with their trigonometric or Fourier series representation, which led him to refine ideas about discontinuous functions. He showed how complex function theory illuminates the study of minimal surfaces (surfaces of least area that span a given boundary). He was one of the first to study differential equations involving complex variables, and his work led to a profound connection with group theory. He introduced new general methods in the study of partial differential equations and applied them to produce the first major study of shock waves.

STEPHEN SMALE
(b. July 15, 1930, Flint, Mich., U.S.)

American mathematician Stephen Smale was awarded the Fields Medal in 1966 for his work on topology in higher dimensions.

Smale grew up in a rural area near Flint. From 1948 to 1956 he attended the University of Michigan, obtaining B.S., M.S., and Ph.D. degrees in mathematics. As an instructor at the University of Chicago from 1956 to 1958, Smale achieved notoriety by proving that there exists an eversion of the sphere (meaning, in a precise theoretical sense, that it is possible to turn a sphere inside out).

In 1960 Smale obtained his two most famous mathematical results. First he constructed a function, now known as the horseshoe, that serves as a paradigm for chaos. Next Smale proved the generalized Poincaré conjecture for all dimensions greater than or equal to five. (The classical conjecture states that a simply connected closed three-dimensional manifold is a three-dimensional sphere, a set of points in four-dimensional space at the same distance from the origin.) The two-dimensional version of this theorem (the two-dimensional sphere is the surface of a common sphere in three-dimensional space) was established in the 19th century, and the three-dimensional version was established at the start of the 21st century. Smale's work was remarkable in that he bypassed dimensions three and four to resolve the problem for all higher dimensions. In 1961 he followed up with the *h*-cobordism theorem, which became the fundamental tool for classifying different manifolds in higher-dimensional topology.

In 1965 Smale took a six-month hiatus from mathematical research to join radical activist Jerry Rubin in establishing the first campaign of nonviolent civil disobedience directed at ending U.S. involvement in the Vietnam War. Smale's mathematical and political lives collided the following year at the International Congress of Mathematicians in Moscow, where he received the Fields Medal. There Smale held a controversial press conference in which he criticized the actions of both the U.S. and Soviet governments.

Smale's mathematical work is notable for both its breadth and depth, reaching the areas of topology, dynamical systems, economics, nonlinear analysis, mechanics, and computation. In 1994 Smale retired from the University of California at Berkeley and then joined the faculty of the City University of Hong Kong.

Smale's publications include *Differential Equations, Dynamical Systems, and Linear Algebra* (1974; with Morris W. Hirsch), *The Mathematics of Time: Essays on Dynamical Systems, Economic Processes, and Related Topics* (1980), and *The Collected Papers of Stephen Smale* (2000).

KARL WEIERSTRASS

(b. Oct. 31, 1815, Ostenfelde, Bavaria [Germany]—d. Feb. 19, 1897, Berlin)

German mathematician Theodor Wilhelm Karl Weierstrass was one of the founders of the modern theory of functions.

His domineering father sent him to the University of Bonn at age 19 to study law and finance in preparation for a position in the Prussian civil service. Weierstrass pursued four years of intensive fencing and drinking and returned home with no degree. He then entered the Academy of Münster in 1839 to prepare for a career as a secondary school teacher. At Münster he came under the influence of Cristof Gudermann, professor of mathematics, who was particularly interested in the theory of elliptic functions. Gudermann cultivated Weierstrass's interest in the theory of functions with emphasis on the expansion of functions by power series.

In 1841 Weierstrass obtained his teacher's certificate and began a 14-year career as a teacher of mathematics at the Pro-Gymnasium in Deutsche Krone (1842–48) and at the Collegium Hoseanum in Braunsberg (1848–56). During this time of isolation from other mathematicians—his salary was so small that he could not even correspond with his fellows—Weierstrass worked unceasingly on analysis. He conceived and in large part carried out a program known as the arithmetization of analysis, under which analysis is based on a rigorous development of the real number system. His preoccupation with rigour in mathematics is illustrated by his later development (1861) of a function that, though continuous, had no derivatives at any point. This idiosyncrasy of an apparently differentiable function caused consternation among the school of analysts who depended heavily upon intuition.

Weierstrass's work on the theory of functions was guided by his desire to complete the work begun by Niels Abel of Norway and Karl Jacobi of Germany, primarily Abel's theorem that the number of independent integrals of algebraic functions is finite and Jacobi's discovery of multiple periodic functions of many variables.

In 1854 Weierstrass burst from obscurity when his unexpected memoir on Abelian functions was published in *Crelle's Journal*. The University of Königsberg conferred upon him an honorary doctor's degree, and in 1856 a position was found for him at the Royal Polytechnic School in Berlin. Weierstrass contributed few papers to scholarly journals. His work was embodied in his lectures, which were collected in *Gesammelte Abhandlungen*, 8 vol. (1894–1927; "Collected Works").

Known as the father of modern analysis, Weierstrass devised tests for the convergence of series and contributed to the theory of periodic functions, functions of real variables, elliptic functions, Abelian functions, converging infinite products, and the calculus of variations. He also advanced the theory of bilinear and quadratic forms. His greatest influence was felt through his students (among them Sofya Kovalevskaya), many of whom became creative mathematicians.

CHAPTER 7
CONCEPTS IN ANALYSIS
AND CALCULUS

ALGEBRAIC VERSUS
TRANSCENDENTAL OBJECTS

One important difference between the differential calculus of Pierre de Fermat and René Descartes and the full calculus of Isaac Newton and Gottfried Wilhelm Leibniz is the difference between algebraic and transcendental objects. The rules of differential calculus are complete in the world of algebraic curves—those defined by equations of the form $p(x, y) = 0$, where p is a polynomial. (For example, the most basic parabola is given by the polynomial equation $y = x^2$.) In his *Geometry* of 1637, Descartes called these curves "geometric," because they "admit of precise and exact measurement." He contrasted them with "mechanical" curves obtained by processes such as rolling one curve along another or unwinding a thread from a curve. He believed that the properties of these curves could never be exactly known. In particular, he believed that the lengths of curved lines "cannot be discovered by human minds."

The distinction between geometric and mechanical is actually not clear-cut: the cardioid, obtained by rolling a circle on a circle of the same size, is algebraic, but the cycloid, obtained by rolling a circle along a line, is not. However, it is generally true that mechanical processes produce curves that are nonalgebraic or transcendental, as Leibniz called them. Where Descartes was really wrong was in thinking that transcendental curves could never be exactly known. It was precisely the integral calculus that enabled mathematicians to come to grips with the transcendental.

A good example is the catenary, the shape assumed by a hanging chain. The catenary looks like a parabola, and indeed Galileo conjectured that it actually was. However, in 1691 Johann Bernoulli, Christiaan Huygens, and Leibniz independently discovered that the catenary's true equation was not $y = x^2$ but $y = (e^x + e^{-x})/2$.

The above formula is given in modern notation. Admittedly, the exponential function e^x had not been given a name or notation by the 17th century. However, its power series had been found by Newton, so it was in a reasonable sense exactly known.

Newton was also the first to give a method for recognizing the transcendance of curves. Realizing that an algebraic curve $p(x, y) = 0$, where p is a polynomial of total degree n, meets a straight line at most n points, Newton remarked in his *Principia* that any curve meeting a line in infinitely many points must be transcendental. For example, the cycloid is transcendental, and so is any spiral curve. In fact, the catenary is also transcendental, though this did not become clear until the periodicity of the exponential function for complex arguments was discovered in the 18th century.

The distinction between algebraic and transcendental may also be applied to numbers. Numbers like $\sqrt{2}$ are called algebraic numbers because they satisfy polynomial equations with integer coefficients. (In this case, $\sqrt{2}$ satisfies the equation $x^2 = 2$.) All other numbers are called transcendental. As early as the 17th century, transcendental numbers were believed to exist, and π was the usual suspect. Perhaps Descartes had π in mind when he despaired of finding the relation between straight and curved lines. A brilliant, though flawed, attempt to prove that π is transcendental was made by James Gregory in 1667. However, the problem was too difficult for 17th-century methods. The transcendance of π was not successfully proved until

1882, when Carl Lindemann adapted a proof of the transcendance of *e* found by Charles Hermite in 1873.

ARGAND DIAGRAM

The Argand diagram is a graphic portrayal of complex numbers, those of the form $x + yi$, in which x and y are real numbers and i is the square root of -1. It was devised by the Swiss mathematician Jean Robert Argand about 1806. A similar representation had been proposed by the Danish surveyor Caspar Wessel in 1797, but this was not generally known until later. One axis represents the pure imaginary numbers (those consisting of the yi portion only). The second axis represents the real numbers (x-values only). This permits the complex numbers to be plotted as points in the plane defined by the two axes.

BESSEL FUNCTION

The Bessel functions (also called the Cylinder functions), are a set of mathematical functions systematically derived around 1817 by the German astronomer Friedrich Wilhelm Bessel during an investigation of solutions of one of Kepler's equations of planetary motion. Particular functions of the set had been formulated earlier by the Swiss mathematicians Daniel Bernoulli, who studied the oscillations of a chain suspended by one end, and Leonhard Euler, who analyzed the vibrations of a stretched membrane.

After Bessel published his findings, other scientists found that the functions appeared in mathematical descriptions of many physical phenomena, including the flow of heat or electricity in a solid cylinder, the propagation of electromagnetic waves along wires, the diffraction of light, the motions of fluids, and the deformations of elastic bodies. One of these investigators, Lord Rayleigh, also placed the Bessel functions in a larger context by showing that they arise in the solution of Laplace's equation when the latter is formulated in cylindrical (rather than Cartesian or spherical) coordinates.

Specifically, a Bessel function is a solution of the differential equation

$$x^2 \frac{d^2 y}{dx^2} + x \frac{dy}{dx} + (x^2 - n^2)\, y = 0,$$

which is called Bessel's equation. For integral values of n, the Bessel functions are

$$J_n(x) = \frac{x^n}{2^n n!}\left[1 - \frac{x^2}{2(2n+2)} \right.$$
$$\left. + \frac{x^4}{2 \cdot 4(2n+2)(2n+4)} - \cdots \right].$$

The graph of $J_0(x)$ looks like that of a damped cosine curve, and that of $J_1(x)$ looks like that of a damped sine curve.

Certain physical problems lead to differential equations analogous to Bessel's equation. Their solutions take the form of combinations of Bessel functions and are called Bessel functions of the second or third kind.

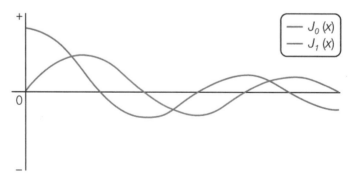

Bessel functions. Encyclopædia Britannica, Inc.

BOUNDARY VALUE

The boundary value is a condition accompanying a differential equation in the solution of physical problems. In mathematical problems arising from physical situations, there are two considerations involved when finding a solution: (1) the solution and its derivatives must satisfy a differential equation, which describes how the quantity behaves within the region. And (2) the solution and its derivatives must satisfy other auxiliary conditions either describing the influence from outside the region (boundary values) or giving information about the solution at a specified time (initial values), representing a compressed history of the system as it affects its future behaviour. A simple example of a boundary-value problem may be demonstrated by the assumption that a function satisfies the equation $f'(x) = 2x$ for any x between 0 and 1 and that it is known that the function has the boundary value of 2 when $x = 1$. The function $f(x) = x^2$ satisfies the differential equation but not the boundary condition. The function $f(x) = x^2 + 1$, on the other hand, satisfies both the differential equation and the boundary condition. The solutions of differential equations involve unspecified constants, or functions in the case of several variables, which are determined by the auxiliary conditions.

The relationship between physics and mathematics is important here, because it is not always possible for a solution of a differential equation to satisfy arbitrarily chosen conditions. But if the problem represents an actual physical situation, it is usually possible to prove that a solution exists, even if it cannot be explicitly found. For partial differential equations, there are three general classes of auxiliary conditions: (1) initial-value problems, as when the initial position and velocity of a traveling wave are known, (2) boundary-value problems, representing conditions on the boundary that do not change from moment to moment, and (3) initial- and boundary-value problems, in which the initial conditions and the successive values on the boundary of the region must be known to find a solution.

CALCULUS OF VARIATIONS

The calculus of variations is the branch of mathematics concerned with the problem of finding a function for which the value of a certain integral is either the largest or the smallest possible. Many problems of this kind are easy to state, but their solutions commonly involve difficult procedures of the differential calculus and differential equations.

The isoperimetric problem—that of finding, among all plane figures of a given perimeter, the one enclosing the greatest area—was known to Greek mathematicians of the 2nd century BCE. The term *isoperimetric problem* has been extended in the modern era to mean any problem in the calculus of variations in which a function is to be made a maximum or a minimum, subject to an auxiliary condition called the isoperimetric condition, although it may have nothing to do with perimeters. For example, the problem of finding a solid of given volume that has the least surface area is an isoperimetric problem, the given volume being the auxiliary, or isoperimetric, condition. An example of an isoperimetric problem from the field of aerodynamics is that of finding the shape of a solid having a given volume that will encounter minimum resistance as it travels through the atmosphere at a constant velocity.

Modern interest in the calculus of variations began in 1696 when Johann Bernoulli of Switzerland proposed a brachistochrone ("least-time") problem as a challenge to his peers. Suppose that a thin wire in the shape of a curve joins two points at different elevations. Further suppose that a bead is placed on the wire at the higher point and allowed to slide under gravity, starting from rest and assuming no friction. The question is: What should be the shape of the curve so that the bead will reach the lower point in the least time?

The problem was solved independently in 1696 by Johann Bernoulli, his brother Jakob Bernoulli, the German Gottfried Wilhelm Leibniz, the Frenchman Guillaume-François-Antoine, marquis de L'Hôpital, and the Englishman Isaac Newton. Their basic idea was to set up an integral for the total time of fall in terms of the unknown curve and then vary the curve so that a minimum time is obtained. This technique, typical of the calculus of variations, led to a differential equation whose solution is a curve called the cycloid.

It is possible to formulate various scientific laws in terms of general principles involving the calculus of variations. These are called variational principles and are usually expressed by stating that some given integral is a maximum or a minimum. One example is the French mathematician Pierre-Louis Moreau de Maupertuis's principle of least action (c. 1744), which sought to explain all processes as driven by a demand that some property be economized or minimized. In particular, minimizing an integral, called an action integral, led several mathematicians (most notably the Italian-French Joseph-Louis Lagrange in the 18th century and the Irish William Rowan Hamilton in the 19th century) to a teleological explanation of Newton's laws of motion. Nevertheless, a general appreciation of the principle of least resistance came only with its use in the 1940s as a foundation for quantum electrodynamics.

Applications of variational principles also occur in elasticity, electromagnetic theory, aerodynamics, the theory of vibrations, and other areas in engineering and science.

CHAOS THEORY

The study of apparently random or unpredictable behaviour in systems governed by deterministic laws is called chaos theory. A more accurate term, "deterministic chaos," suggests a paradox because it connects two notions that are familiar and commonly regarded as incompatible. The first is that of randomness or unpredictability, as in the trajectory of a molecule in a gas or in the voting choice of a particular individual from out of a population. In conventional analyses, randomness was considered more apparent than real, arising from ignorance of the many causes at work. In other words, it was commonly believed that the world is unpredictable because it is complicated. The second notion is that of deterministic motion, as that of a pendulum or a planet, which has been accepted since the time of Isaac Newton as exemplifying the success of science in rendering predictable that which is initially complex.

In recent decades, however, a diversity of systems have been studied that behave unpredictably despite their seeming simplicity and the fact that the forces involved are governed by well-understood physical laws. The common element in these systems is a very high degree of sensitivity to initial conditions and to the way in which they are set in motion. For example, the meteorologist Edward Lorenz discovered that a simple model of heat convection possesses intrinsic unpredictability, a circumstance he called the "butterfly effect," suggesting that the mere flapping of a butterfly's wing can change the weather.

A more homely example is the pinball machine: the ball's movements are precisely governed by laws of gravitational rolling and elastic collisions—both fully understood—yet the final outcome is unpredictable.

In classical mechanics the behaviour of a dynamical system can be described geometrically as motion on an "attractor." The mathematics of classical mechanics effectively recognized three types of attractor: single points (characterizing steady states), closed loops (periodic cycles), and tori (combinations of several cycles). In the 1960s a new class of "strange attractors" was discovered by the American mathematician Stephen Smale. On strange attractors the dynamics is chaotic. Later it was recognized that strange attractors have detailed structure on all scales of magnification. A direct result of this recognition was

Romanesco broccoli grows naturally in a fractal pattern. Each bud is made up of a series of smaller buds, which are all arranged in a logarithmic spiral. © www.istockphoto.com

the development of the concept of the fractal (a class of complex geometric shapes that commonly exhibit the property of self-similarity), which led in turn to remarkable developments in computer graphics.

Applications of the mathematics of chaos are highly diverse, including the study of turbulent flow of fluids, irregularities in heartbeat, population dynamics, chemical reactions, plasma physics, and the motion of groups and clusters of stars.

CONTINUITY

Continuity is the rigorous formulation of the intuitive concept of a function that varies with no abrupt breaks or jumps. A function is a relationship in which every value of an independent variable — say x — is associated with a value of a dependent variable — say y. Continuity of a function is sometimes expressed by saying that if the x-values are close together, then the y-values of the function will also be close. But if the question "How close?" is asked, difficulties arise.

For close x-values, the distance between the y-values can be large even if the function has no sudden jumps. For example, if $y = 1{,}000x$, then two values of x that differ by 0.01 will have corresponding y-values differing by 10. On the other hand, for any point x, points can be selected close enough to it so that the y-values of this function will be as close as desired, simply by choosing the x-values to be closer than 0.001 times the desired closeness of the y-values. Thus, continuity is defined precisely by saying that a function $f(x)$ is continuous at a point x_0 of its domain if and only if, for any degree of closeness ε desired for the y-values, there is a distance δ for the x-values (in the above example equal to 0.001ε) such that for any x of the domain within the distance δ from x_o, $f(x)$ will be within the distance ε from $f(x_o)$. In contrast, the function that equals 0 for x less than or equal to 1 and that equals 2 for x larger than 1 is not continuous at the point $x = 1$, because the difference between the value of the function at 1 and at any point ever so slightly greater than 1 is never less than 2.

A function is said to be continuous if and only if it is continuous at every point of its domain. A function is said to be continuous on an interval, or subset of its domain, if and only if it is continuous at each point of the interval. The sum, difference, and product of continuous functions with the same domain are also continuous, as is the quotient, except at points at which the denominator is zero. Continuity can also be defined in terms of limits by saying that $f(x)$ is continuous at x_o of its domain if and only if, for values of x in its domain,

$$\lim_{x \to x_0} f(x) = f(x_0).$$

A more abstract definition of continuity can be given in terms of sets, as is done in topology, by saying that for any open set of y-values, the corresponding set of x-values is also open. (A set is "open" if each of its elements has a "neighbourhood," or region enclosing it, that lies entirely within the set.) Continuous functions are the most basic and widely studied class of functions in mathematical analysis, as well as the most commonly occurring ones in physical situations.

CONVERGENCE

Convergence is the property (exhibited by certain infinite series and functions) of approaching a limit more and more closely as an argument (variable) of the function increases or decreases or as the number of terms of the series increases.

For example, the function $y = 1/x$ converges to zero as x increases. Although no finite value of x will cause the value of y to actually become zero, the limiting value of y is zero because y can be made as small as desired by choosing x large enough. The line $y = 0$ (the x-axis) is called an asymptote of the function.

Similarly, for any value of x between (but not including) -1 and +1, the series $1 + x + x^2 + \cdots + x^n$ converges toward the limit $1/(1 - x)$ as n, the number of terms, increases. The interval $-1 < x < 1$ is called the range of convergence of the series. For values of x outside this range, the series is said to diverge.

CURVATURE

Curvature is the rate of change of direction of a curve with respect to distance along the curve. At every point on a circle, the curvature is the reciprocal of the radius. For other curves (and straight lines, which can be regarded as circles of infinite radius), the curvature is the reciprocal of the radius of the circle that most closely conforms to the curve at the given point.

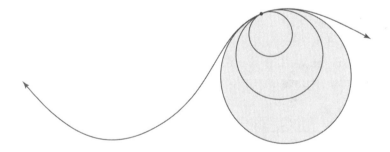

The curvature at each point of a line is defined to be $1/r$, where r is the radius of the osculating, or "kissing," circle that best approximates the line at the given point. Encyclopædia Britannica, Inc.

If the curve is a section of a surface (that is, the curve formed by the intersection of a plane with the surface), then the curvature of the surface at any given point can be determined by suitable sectioning planes. The most useful planes are two that both contain the normal (the line perpendicular to the tangent plane) to the surface at the point. One of these planes produces the section with the greatest curvature among all such sections. The other produces that with the least. These two planes define the two so-called principal directions on the surface at the point. These directions lie at right angles to one another. The curvatures in the principal directions are called the principal curvatures of the surface. The mean curvature of the surface at the point is either the sum of the principal curvatures or half that sum (usage varies among authorities). The total (or Gaussian) curvature is the product of the principal curvatures.

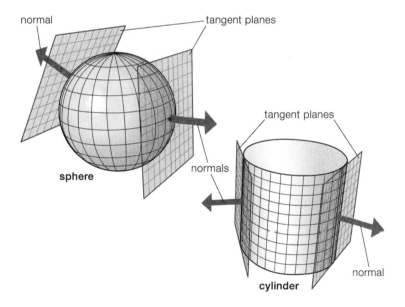

The normal, or perpendicular, at each point of a surface defines the corresponding tangent plane, and vice versa. Encyclopædia Britannica, Inc.

DERIVATIVE

The rate of change of a function with respect to a variable is called the derivative. Derivatives are fundamental to the solution of problems in calculus and differential equations. In general, scientists observe changing systems (dynamical systems) to obtain the rate of change of some variable of interest, incorporate this information into some differential equation, and use integration techniques to obtain a function that can be used to predict the behaviour of the original system under diverse conditions.

Geometrically, the derivative of a function can be interpreted as the slope of the graph of the function or, more precisely, as the slope of the tangent line at a point. Its calculation, in fact, derives from the slope formula for a straight line, except that a limiting process must be used for curves. The slope is often expressed as the "rise" over the "run," or, in Cartesian terms, the ratio of the change in y to the change in x. For a straight line, the formula for the slope is $(y_1 - y_0)/(x_1 - x_0)$. Another way to express this formula is $[f(x_0 + h) - f(x_0)]/h$, if h is used for $x_1 - x_0$ and $f(x)$ for y. This change in notation is useful for advancing from the idea of the slope of a line to the more general concept of the derivative of a function.

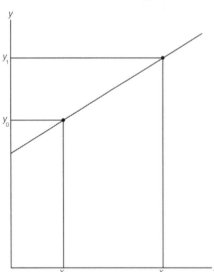

Two points, such as (x_0, y_0) and (x_1, y_1), determine the slope of a straight line.

For a curve, this ratio depends on where the points are chosen, reflecting the fact that curves do not have a constant slope. To find the slope at a desired point, the choice of the second point needed to calculate the ratio represents a difficulty because, in general, the ratio will represent only an average slope between the points, rather than the actual slope at either point. To get around this difficulty, a limiting process is used whereby the second point is not fixed but specified by a variable, as h in the ratio for the straight line above. Finding the limit in this case is a process of finding a number that the ratio approaches as h approaches o, so that the limiting ratio will represent the actual slope at the given point. Some manipulations must be done on the quotient $[f(x_0 + h) - f(x_0)]/h$ so that it can be rewritten in a form in which the limit as h approaches o can be seen more directly. Consider, for example, the parabola given by x^2. In finding the derivative of x^2 when x is 2, the quotient is $[(2 + h)^2 - 2^2]/h$. By expanding the numerator, the quotient becomes $(4 + 4h + h^2 - 4)/h$ $= (4h + h^2)/h$. Both numerator and denominator still approach o, but if h is not actually zero but only very close to it, then h can be divided out, giving $4 + h$, which is easily seen to approach 4 as h approaches o.

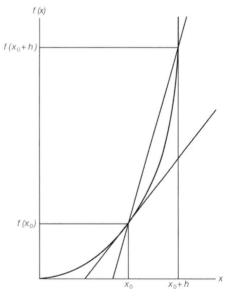

The slope, or instantaneous rate of change, for a curve at a particular point $(x_0, f(x_0))$ can be determined by observing the limit of the average rate of change as a second point $(x_0 + h, f(x_0 + h))$ approaches the original point.

To sum up, the derivative of $f(x)$ at x_o, written as $f'(x_o)$, $(df/dx)(x_o)$, or $Df(x_o)$, is defined as

$$\lim_{h \to 0} [f(x_0 + h) - f(x_0)]/h$$

if this limit exists.

Differentiation—i.e., calculating the derivative—seldom requires the use of the basic definition but can instead be accomplished through a knowledge of the three basic derivatives, the use of four rules of operation, and a knowledge of how to manipulate functions.

DIFFERENCE EQUATION

The mathematical equality involving the differences between successive values of a function of a discrete variable is called a difference equation. A discrete variable is one that is defined or of interest only for values that differ by some finite amount, usually a constant and often 1. For example, the discrete variable x may have the values $x_0 = a$, $x_1 = a + 1$, $x_2 = a + 2, \ldots, x_n = a + n$. The function y has the corresponding values $y_0, y_1, y_2, \ldots, y_n$, from which the differences can be found:

$$\Delta y_0 = y_1 - y_0$$
$$\Delta y_1 = y_2 - y_1$$
$$\cdots$$
$$\Delta y_n = y_{n+1} - y_n.$$

Any equation that relates the values of Δy_i to each other or to x_i is a difference equation. In general, such an equation takes the form

$$y_i - a_i y_{i-1} = b_i.$$

Systematic methods have been developed for the solution of these equations and for those in which, for example, second-order differences are involved. A second-order difference is defined as

$$\Delta^2 y_i = \Delta(\Delta y_i) = \Delta y_{i+1} - \Delta y_i$$
$$= (y_{i+2} - y_{i+1}) - (y_{i+1} - y_i)$$
$$= y_{i+2} - 2y_{i+1} + y_i.$$

DIFFERENTIAL

The differential is an expression based on the derivative of a function, useful for approximating certain values of the function. The derivative of a function at the point x_0, written as $f'(x_0)$, is defined as the limit as Δx approaches 0 of the quotient $\Delta y/\Delta x$, in which Δy is $f(x_0 + \Delta x) - f(x_0)$. Because the derivative is defined as the limit, the closer Δx is to 0, the closer will be the quotient to the derivative. Therefore, if Δx is small, then $\Delta y \approx f'(x_0)\Delta x$ (the wavy lines mean "is approximately equal to"). For example, to approximate $f(17)$ for $f(x) = \sqrt{x}$, first note that its derivative $f'(x)$ is equal to $(x^{-1/2})/2$. Choosing a computationally convenient value for x_0, in this case the perfect square 16, results in a simple calculation of $f'(x_0)$ as 1/8 and Δx as 1, giving an approximate value of 1/8 for Δy. Because $f(16)$ is 4, it follows that $f(17)$, or $\sqrt{17}$, is approximately 4.125, the actual value being 4.123 to three decimal places.

DIFFERENTIAL EQUATION

A differential equation is a mathematical statement containing one or more derivatives—that is, terms representing the rates of change of continuously varying quantities. Differential equations are very common in science and engineering, as well as in many other fields of quantitative study, because what can be directly observed and measured for systems undergoing changes are their rates of change. The solution of a differential equation is, in general, an equation expressing the functional dependence of one variable upon one or more others. It ordinarily contains constant terms that are not present in the original differential equation. Another way of saying this is that the solution of a differential equation produces a function that can be used to predict the behaviour of the original system, at least within certain constraints.

Differential equations are classified into several broad categories, and these are in turn further divided into many subcategories. The most important categories are ordinary differential equations and partial differential equations. When the function involved in the equation depends on only a single variable, its derivatives are ordinary derivatives and the differential equation is classed as an ordinary differential equation. On the other hand, if the function depends on several independent variables, so that its derivatives are partial derivatives, the differential equation is classed as a partial differential equation. The following are examples of ordinary differential equations:

$$\frac{dy}{dt} = -ky,$$

$$m\frac{d^2y}{dt^2} = -k^2y,$$

$$\left[1 + \left(\frac{dy}{dx}\right)^2\right]\frac{d^3y}{dx^3} - 3\frac{dy}{dx}\left(\frac{d^2y}{dx^2}\right)^2 = 0.$$

In these, y stands for the function, and either t or x is the independent variable. The symbols k and m are used here to stand for specific constants.

Whichever the type may be, a differential equation is said to be of the nth order if it involves a derivative of the nth order but no derivative of an order higher than this. The equation

$$\frac{\partial u}{\partial t} = k^2 \left[\frac{\partial^2 u}{\partial x^2} + \frac{\partial^2 u}{\partial y^2} + \frac{\partial^2 u}{\partial z^2} \right]$$

is an example of a partial differential equation of the second order. The theories of ordinary and partial differential equations are markedly different, and for this reason the two categories are treated separately.

Instead of a single differential equation, the object of study may be a simultaneous system of such equations. The formulation of the laws of dynamics frequently leads to such systems. In many cases, a single differential equation of the nth order is advantageously replaceable by a system of n simultaneous equations, each of which is of the first order, so that techniques from linear algebra can be applied.

An ordinary differential equation in which, for example, the function and the independent variable are denoted by y and x is in effect an implicit summary of the essential characteristics of y as a function of x. These characteristics would presumably be more accessible to analysis if an explicit formula for y could be produced. Such a formula, or at least an equation in x and y (involving no derivatives) that is deducible from the differential equation, is called a solution of the differential equation. The process of deducing a solution from the equation by the applications of algebra and calculus is called solving or integrating the equation. It should be noted, however, that the differential equations that can be explicitly solved form but a small minority. Thus, most functions must be studied by indirect methods. Even its existence must be proved when there is no possibility of producing it for inspection. In practice, methods from numerical analysis, involving computers, are employed to obtain useful approximate solutions.

DIFFERENTIATION

The process of finding the derivative, or rate of change, of a function is called differentiation. In contrast to the abstract nature of the theory behind it, the practical technique of differentiation can be carried out by purely algebraic manipulations, using three basic derivatives, four rules of operation, and a knowledge of how to manipulate functions.

The three basic derivatives (D) are: (1) for algebraic functions, $D(x^n) = nx^{n-1}$, in which n is any real number; (2) for trigonometric functions, $D(\sin x) = \cos x$; and (3) for exponential functions, $D(e^x) = e^x$.

For functions built up of combinations of these classes of functions, the theory provides the following basic rules for differentiating the sum, product, or quotient of any two functions $f(x)$ and $g(x)$ the derivatives of which are known (where a and b are constants): $D(af + bg) = aDf + bDg$ (sums); $D(fg) = fDg + gDf$ (products); and $D(f/g) = (gDf - fDg)/g^2$ (quotients).

The other basic rule, called the chain rule, provides a way to differentiate a composite function. If $f(x)$ and $g(x)$ are two functions, the composite function $f(g(x))$ is calculated for a value of x by first evaluating $g(x)$ and then evaluating the function f at this value of $g(x)$. For instance, if $f(x) = \sin x$ and $g(x) = x^2$, then $f(g(x)) = \sin x^2$, while $g(f(x)) = (\sin x)^2$. The chain rule states that the derivative of a composite function is given by a product, as $D(f(g(x))) = Df(g(x)) \cdot Dg(x)$. In words, the first factor on the right, $Df(g(x))$, indicates that the derivative of $Df(x)$ is first found as usual, and then x, wherever it occurs, is replaced by the function $g(x)$. In the example of sin x^2, the rule gives the result $D(\sin x^2) = D\sin(x^2) \cdot D(x^2) = (\cos x^2) \cdot 2x$.

In the German mathematician Gottfried Wilhelm Leibniz's notation, which uses d/dx in place of D and thus allows differentiation with respect to different variables to be made explicit, the chain rule takes the more memorable "symbolic cancellation" form: $d(f(g(x)))/dx = df/dg \cdot dg/dx$.

DIRECTION FIELD

A direction field is a way of graphically representing the solutions of a first-order differential equation without actually solving the equation. The equation $y' = f(x,y)$ gives a direction, y', associated with each point (x,y) in the plane that must be satisfied by any solution curve passing through that point. The direction field is defined as the collection of small line segments passing through various points having a slope that will satisfy the given differential equation at that point. The actual family of curves (solutions of the differential equation) must have a direction at each point that agrees with that of the line segment of the direction field at that point, so that this method is valuable for gaining some feeling for the behaviour of the solutions in cases in which the equation is difficult to solve or in which the solution is a complicated function. Often it is helpful when drawing the direction field to determine the lines or curves, called isoclines, on which the slope of the direction field segments is constant. For example, in the equation $y' = x + y$ the slope will have the constant value k when $k = x + y$, or when $y = -x + k$. That is, the isoclines are straight lines with a slope of -1. These lines can then be sketched in lightly to aid in constructing the direction field. The actual family of solutions in this case is $y = aex - x - 1$ for any constant a, as found by methods of differential equations.

DIRICHLET PROBLEM

The Dirichlet problem is that of formulating and solving certain partial differential equations that arise in studies of the flow of heat, electricity, and fluids. Initially, the problem was to determine the equilibrium temperature distribution on a disk from measurements taken along the boundary. The temperature at points inside the disk

Peter Gustav Lejeune Dirichlet (1805–1859) proved, among many other notable contributions to mathematics, that in any arithmetic progression in which the first term was coprime to the difference there are infinitely many primes. Hulton Archive/Getty Images

must satisfy a partial differential equation called Laplace's equation corresponding to the physical condition that the total heat energy contained in the disk shall be a minimum. A slight variation of this problem occurs when there are points inside the disk at which heat is added (sources) or removed (sinks) as long as the temperature still remains constant at each point (stationary flow), in which case Poisson's equation is satisfied. The Dirichlet problem can also be solved for any simply connected region—i.e., one containing no holes—if the temperature varies continuously along the boundary. The problem is named for the 19th-century German mathematician Peter Gustav Lejeune Dirichlet, who suggested the first general method of solving this class of problems.

ELLIPTIC EQUATION

The elliptic equations are a class of partial differential equations describing phenomena that do not change from moment to moment, as when a flow of heat or fluid takes place within a medium with no accumulations. The Laplace equation, $u_{xx} + u_{yy} = 0$, is the simplest such equation describing this condition in two dimensions. In addition to satisfying a differential equation within the region, the elliptic equation is also determined by its values (boundary values) along the boundary of the region, which represent the effect from outside the region. These conditions can be either those of a fixed temperature distribution at points of the boundary (Dirichlet problem) or those in which heat is being supplied or removed across the boundary in such a way as to maintain a constant temperature distribution throughout (Neumann problem).

If the highest-order terms of a second-order partial differential equation with constant coefficients are linear and if the coefficients a, b, c of the u_{xx}, u_{xy}, u_{yy} terms satisfy the inequality $b^2 - 4ac < 0$, then, by a change of coordinates, the principal part (highest-order terms) can be written as the Laplacian $u_{xx} + u_{yy}$. Because the properties of a physical system are independent of the coordinate system used to formulate the problem, it is expected that the properties of the solutions of these elliptic equations should be similar to the properties of the solutions of Laplace's equation. If the coefficients a, b, and c are not constant but depend on x and y, then the equation is called elliptic in a given region if $b^2 - 4ac < 0$ at all points in the region. The functions $x^2 - y^2$ and $e^x \cos y$ satisfy the Laplace equation, but the solutions to this equation are usually more complicated because of the boundary conditions that must be satisfied as well.

EXACT EQUATION

An exact equation is a type of differential equation that can be solved directly without the use of any of the special techniques in the subject. A first-order differential equation (of one variable) is called exact, or an exact differential, if it is the result of a simple differentiation. The equation $P(x, y)y' + Q(x, y) = 0$, or in the equivalent alternate notation $P(x, y)dy + Q(x, y)dx = 0$, is exact if $Px(x, y) = Qy(x, y)$. (The subscripts in this equation indicate which variable the partial derivative is taken with respect to.) In this case, there will be a function $R(x, y)$, the partial x-derivative of which is Q and the partial y-derivative of which is P, such that the equation $R(x, y) = c$ (where c is constant) will implicitly define a function y that will satisfy the original differential equation.

For example, in the equation $(x^2 + 2y)y' + 2xy + 1 = 0$, the x-derivative of $x^2 + 2y$ is $2x$ and the y-derivative of $2xy + 1$ is also $2x$, and the function $R = x^2y + x + y^2$ satisfies the conditions $R_x = Q$ and $R_y = P$. The function defined implicitly by

$x^2y + x + y^2 = c$ will solve the original equation. Sometimes if an equation is not exact, it can be made exact by multiplying each term by a suitable function called an integrating factor. For example, if the equation $3y + 2xy' = 0$ is multiplied by $1/xy$, it becomes $3/x + 2y'/y = 0$, which is the direct result of differentiating the equation in which the natural logarithmic function (ln) appears: $3 \ln x + 2 \ln y = c$, or equivalently $x^3y^2 = c$, which implicitly defines a function that will satisfy the original equation.

Higher-order equations are also called exact if they are the result of differentiating a lower-order equation. For example, the second-order equation $p(x)y'' + q(x)y' + r(x)y = 0$ is exact if there is a first-order expression $p(x)y' + s(x)y$ such that its derivative is the given equation. The given equation will be exact if, and only if, $p'' - q' + r = 0$, in which case s in the reduced equation will equal $q - p'$. If the equation is not exact, there may be a function $z(x)$, also called an integrating factor, such that when the equation is multiplied by the function z it becomes exact.

EXPONENTIAL FUNCTION

The exponential function is a relation of the form $y = a^x$, with the independent variable x ranging over the entire real number line as the exponent of a positive number a. Probably the most important of the exponential functions is $y = e^x$, sometimes written $y = \exp(x)$, in which e (2.7182818...) is the base of the natural system of logarithms (ln). By definition x is a logarithm, and there is thus a logarithmic function that is the inverse of the exponential function. Specifically, if $y = e^x$, then $x = \ln y$. The exponential function is also defined as the sum of the infinite series

$$e^{\pm x} = 1 \pm x + \frac{x^2}{2!} \pm \frac{x^3}{3!} + \frac{x^4}{4!} \pm \frac{x^5}{5!} + \cdots,$$

which converges for all x and in which $n!$ is a product of the first n positive integers. Thus in particular, the constant

$$e^1 = 2.7182818\cdots$$
$$= 1 + \frac{1}{1!} + \frac{1}{2!} + \frac{1}{3!} + \cdots + \frac{1}{n!} + \cdots$$

The exponential functions are examples of nonalgebraic, or transcendental, functions—i.e., functions that cannot be represented as the product, sum, and difference of variables raised to some nonnegative integer power. Other common transcendental functions are the logarithmic functions and the trigonometric functions. Exponential functions frequently arise and quantitatively describe a number of phenomena in physics, such as radioactive decay, in which the rate of change in a process or substance depends directly on its current value.

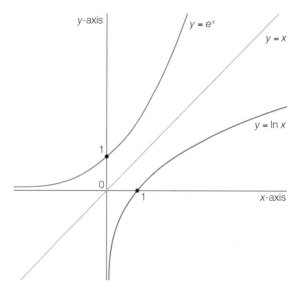

The exponential and natural logarithm functions are inverse functions. That is, applying one and then the other to some value returns the original value. This can be seen graphically by the functions' symmetry with respect to the line $x = y$. Encyclopædia Britannica, Inc.

EXTREMUM

Any point at which the value of a function is largest (a maximum) or smallest (a minimum) is an extremum (plural extrema). There are both absolute and relative (or local) maxima and minima. At a relative maximum the value of the function is larger than its value at immediately adjacent points, while at an absolute maximum the value of the function is larger than its value at any other point in the interval of interest. At relative maxima inside the interval, if the function is smooth rather than peaked, its rate of change, or derivative, is zero. The derivative may be zero, however, at a point where the function has neither a maximum nor a minimum, as in the case for the function x^3 at $x = 0$. One way to determine this is by going back to the original definition and finding the value of the function at immediately adjacent points. For example, the function $x^3 - 3x$ has the derivative $3x^2 - 3$, which equals 0 when x is ±1. By testing nearby points, such as 0.9 and 1.1, the function is seen to have a relative minimum when x is 1 and, similarly, a relative maximum when x is -1. There is also a second-derivative test: if the derivative of a function is zero at a point, then the function will have a relative maximum or minimum if the second derivative at that point is less than or greater than 0, respectively, the test failing if it equals 0. Relative maxima can also occur at points at which the derivative fails to exist, and these points must also be tested.

The theory of extrema applies to practical problems of optimization, such as finding the dimensions for a container that will hold the maximum volume for a given amount of material used in its construction. Locating the extreme points also aids in graphing functions.

FLUXION

Fluxion was the original term for derivative introduced by Isaac Newton in 1665. Newton referred to a varying (flowing) quantity as a fluent and to its instantaneous rate of change as a fluxion. Newton stated that the fundamental problems of the infinitesimal calculus were: (1) given a fluent (that would now be called a function), to find its fluxion (now called a derivative); and, (2) given a fluxion (a function), to find a corresponding fluent (an indefinite integral). Thus, if $y = x^3$, the fluxion of the quantity y equals $3x^2$ times the fluxion of x. In modern notation, $dy/dt = 3x^2(dx/dt)$. Newton's terminology and notations of fluxions were eventually discarded in favour of the derivatives and differentials that were developed by G.W. Leibniz.

FOURIER TRANSFORM

As a transform of an integrable complex-valued function f of one real variable, the Fourier transform is the complex-valued function $\hat{f}$ of a real variable defined by the following equation

$$\hat{f}(\xi) = (2\pi)^{-1/2} \int_{-\infty}^{\infty} e^{-ix\xi} f(x)\, dx.$$

In the integral equation

$$f(y) = \int_{-\infty}^{\infty} K(x, y)\, F(x)\, dx,$$

the function $f(y)$ is an integral transform of $F(x)$, and $K(x,y)$ is the kernel. Often the reciprocal relationship is valid:

$$F(y) = \int_{-\infty}^{\infty} K'(x, y)\, f(x)\, dx.$$

FUNCTION

A function is an expression, rule, or law that defines a relationship between one variable (the independent variable) and another variable (the dependent variable). Functions are ubiquitous in mathematics and are essential for formulating physical relationships in the sciences. The modern definition of function was first given in 1837 by the German mathematician Peter Dirichlet:

> *If a variable* y *is so related to a variable* x *that whenever a numerical value is assigned to* x, *there is a rule according to which a unique value of* y *is determined, then* y *is said to be a function of the independent variable* x.

This relationship is commonly symbolized as $y = f(x)$. In addition to $f(x)$, other abbreviated symbols such as $g(x)$ and $P(x)$ are often used to represent functions of the independent variable x, especially when the nature of the function is unknown or unspecified.

Many widely used mathematical formulas are expressions of known functions. For example, the formula for the area of a circle, $A = \pi r^2$, gives the dependent variable A (the area) as a function of the independent variable r (the radius). Functions involving more than two variables also are common in mathematics, as can be seen in the formula for the area of a triangle, $A = bh/2$, which defines A as a function of both b (base) and h (height). In these examples, physical constraints force the independent variables to be positive numbers. When the independent variables are also allowed to take on negative values — thus, any real number — the functions are known as real-valued functions.

The formula for the area of a circle is an example of a polynomial function. The general form for such functions is $P(x) = a_0 + a_1x + a_2x^2 + \cdots + a_nx^n$, where the coefficients $(a_0, a_1, a_2, ..., a_n)$ are given, x can be any real number, and all the powers of x are counting numbers (1, 2, 3, ...). (When the powers of x can be any real number, the result is known as an algebraic function.) Polynomial functions have been studied since the earliest times because of their versatility—practically any relationship involving real numbers can be closely approximated by a polynomial function. Polynomial functions are characterized by the highest power of the independent variable. Special names are commonly used for such powers from one to five—linear, quadratic, cubic, quartic, and quintic.

Polynomial functions may be given geometric representation by means of analytic geometry. The independent variable x is plotted along the x-axis (a horizontal line), and the dependent variable y is plotted along the y-axis (a vertical line). The graph of the function then consists of the points with coordinates (x, y) where $y = f(x)$.

Another common type of function that has been studied since antiquity is the trigonometric functions, such as sin x and cos x, where x is the measure of an angle. Because of their periodic nature, trigonometric functions are often used to model behaviour that repeats, or "cycles." Nonalgebraic functions, such as exponential and trigonometric functions, are also known as transcendental functions.

Practical applications of functions whose variables are complex numbers are not so easy to illustrate, but they are nevertheless very extensive. They occur, for example, in electrical engineering and aerodynamics. If the complex variable is represented in the form $z = x + iy$, where i is the imaginary unit (the square root of -1) and x and y are real variables, it is possible to split the complex function into real and imaginary parts: $f(z) = P(x, y) + iQ(x, y)$.

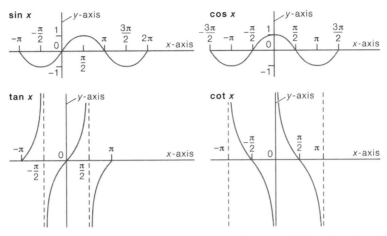

Graphs of some trigonometric functions. Note that each of these functions is periodic. Thus, the sine and cosine functions repeat every 2π, and the tangent and cotangent functions repeat every π. Encyclopædia Britannica, Inc.

By interchanging the roles of the independent and dependent variables in a given function, one can obtain an inverse function. Inverse functions do what their name implies: they undo the action of a function to return a variable to its original state. Thus, if for a given function $f(x)$ there exists a function $g(y)$ such that $g(f(x)) = x$ and $f(g(y)) = y$, then g is called the inverse function of f and given the notation f^{-1}, where by convention the variables are interchanged. For example, the function $f(x) = 2x$ has the inverse function $f^{-1}(x) = x/2$.

A function may be defined by means of a power series. For example, the infinite series

$$e^x = 1 + x + \frac{x^2}{2!} + \cdots + \frac{x^n}{n!} + \cdots$$

$$\sin x = x - \frac{x^3}{3!} + \frac{x^5}{5!} \cdots$$

$$\cos x = 1 - \frac{x^2}{2!} + \frac{x^4}{4!} \cdots$$

could be used to define these functions for all complex values of x. Other types of series and also infinite products may be used when convenient. An important case is the Fourier series, expressing a function in terms of sines and cosines:

$$f(x) = a_0 + a_1 \cos x + a_2 \cos 2x + \cdots$$
$$+ b_1 \sin x + b_2 \sin 2x + \cdots$$

Such representations are of great importance in physics, particularly in the study of wave motion and other oscillatory phenomena.

Sometimes functions are most conveniently defined by means of differential equations. For example, $y = \sin x$ is the solution of the differential equation $d^2y/dx^2 + y = 0$ having $y = 0$, $dy/dx = 1$ when $x = 0$. Similarly, $y = \cos x$ is the solution of the same equation having $y = 1$, $dy/dx = 0$ when $x = 0$.

HARMONIC ANALYSIS

Harmonic analysis is the mathematical procedure for describing and analyzing phenomena of a periodically recurrent nature. Many complex problems have been reduced to manageable terms by the technique of breaking complicated mathematical curves into sums of comparatively simple components.

Many physical phenomena, such as sound waves, alternating electric currents, tides, and machine motions and vibrations, may be periodic in character. Such motions can be measured at a number of successive values of the independent variable, usually the time, and these data or a curve plotted from them will represent a function of that independent variable. Generally, the mathematical expression for the function will be unknown. However, with the periodic functions found in nature, the function can be expressed as the sum of a number of sine and cosine terms. Such a sum is known as a Fourier series, after the French mathematician Joseph Fourier (1768–1830), and the determination of the coefficients of these terms is called harmonic analysis. One of the terms of a Fourier series has a period equal to that of the function, $f(x)$, and is called the fundamental. Other terms have shortened periods that are integral sub-multiples of the fundamental. These are called harmonics. The terminology derives from one of the earliest applications, the study of the sound waves created by a violin.

In 1822 Fourier stated that a function $y = f(x)$ could be expressed between the limits $x = 0$ and $x = 2\pi$ by the infinite series that is now given in the form

$$f(x) = \tfrac{1}{2}a_0 + \sum_{k=1}^{\infty} (a_k \cos kx + b_k \sin kx),\qquad (1)$$

provided the function is single-valued, finite, and continuous except for a finite number of discontinuities, and where

$$a_k = \frac{1}{\pi} \int_0^{2\pi} f(x) \cos kx\, dx$$

and

$$b_k = \frac{1}{\pi} \int_0^{2\pi} f(x) \sin kx\, dx$$

for $k \geq 0$. With the further restriction that there be only a finite number of extrema (local maxima and minima), the theorem was proved by the German mathematician Peter Lejeune Dirichlet in 1829.

The use of a larger number of terms will increase the accuracy of the approximation, and the large amounts of calculations needed are best done by machines called harmonic (or spectrum) analyzers. These measure the relative amplitudes of sinusoidal components of a periodically recurrent function. The first such instrument was invented by the British mathematician and physicist William Thomson (later Baron Kelvin) in 1873. This machine, used for the harmonic analysis of tidal observations, embodied 11 sets of mechanical integrators, one for each harmonic to be measured. A still more complicated machine, handling up to 80 coefficients, was designed in 1898 by the American physicists Albert Abraham Michelson and Samuel W. Stratton.

Early machines and methods made use of an experimentally determined curve or set of data. In the case of electric currents or voltages, an entirely different method is possible. Instead of making an oscillographic record of the voltage or current and analyzing it mathematically, the analysis is performed directly on the electric quantity by recording the response as the natural frequency of a tuned circuit is varied through a wide range. Thus, harmonic analyzers and synthesizers of the 20th century tended to be electromechanical rather than purely mechanical devices. Modern analyzers display the frequency-modulated signals visually by means of a cathode-ray tube, and digital or analog computer principles are used to carry out the Fourier analysis automatically, thereby achieving approximations of great accuracy.

HARMONIC FUNCTION

A mathematical function of two variables having the property that its value at any point is equal to the average of its values along any circle around that point, provided the function is defined within the circle, is a harmonic function. An infinite number of points are involved in this average, so that it must be found by means of an integral, which represents an infinite sum. In physical situations, harmonic functions describe those conditions of equilibrium such as the temperature or electrical charge distribution over a region in which the value at each point remains constant.

Harmonic functions can also be defined as functions that satisfy Laplace's equation, a condition that can be shown to be equivalent to the first definition. The surface defined by a harmonic function has zero convexity, and these functions thus have the important property that they have no maximum or minimum values inside the region in which they are defined. Harmonic functions are also analytic, which means that they possess all derivatives (are perfectly "smooth") and can be represented as polynomials with an infinite number of terms, called power series.

Spherical harmonic functions arise when the spherical coordinate system is used. (In this system, a point in space is located by three coordinates, one representing the distance from the origin and two others representing the angles of elevation and azimuth, as in astronomy.) Spherical harmonic functions are commonly used to describe three-dimensional fields, such as gravitational, magnetic, and electrical fields, and those arising from certain types of fluid motion.

INFINITE SERIES

An infinite series is a sum of infinitely many numbers related in a given way and listed in a given order. Infinite series are useful in mathematics and in such disciplines as physics, chemistry, biology, and engineering.

For an infinite series $a_1 + a_2 + a_3 + \cdots$, a quantity $s_n = a_1 + a_2 + \cdots + a_n$, which involves adding only the first n terms, is called a partial sum of the series. If s_n approaches a fixed number S as n becomes larger and larger, the series is said to converge. In this case, S is called the sum of the series. An infinite series that does not converge is said to diverge. In the case of divergence, no value of a sum is assigned. For example, the nth partial sum of the infinite series $1 + 1 + 1 + \cdots$ is n. As more terms are added, the partial sum fails to approach any finite value (it grows without bound). Thus, the series diverges. An example of a convergent series is

$$1 + \frac{1}{2} + \frac{1}{4} + \cdots + \frac{1}{2^n}$$

As n becomes larger, the partial sum approaches 2, which is the sum of this infinite series. In fact, the series $1 + r + r^2 + r^3 + \cdots$ (in the example above r equals 1/2) converges to the sum $1/(1 - r)$ if $0 < r < 1$ and diverges if $r \geq 1$. This series is called the geometric series with ratio r and was one of the first infinite series to be studied. Its solution goes back to Zeno of Elea's paradox involving a race between Achilles and a tortoise.

Certain standard tests can be applied to determine the convergence or divergence of a given series, but such a determination is not always possible. In general, if the series $a_1 + a_2 + \cdots$ converges, then it must be true that a_n approaches 0 as n becomes larger. Furthermore, adding or deleting a finite number of terms from a series never affects whether or not the series converges. Furthermore, if all the terms in a series are positive, its partial sums will increase, either approaching a finite quantity (converging) or growing without bound (diverging). This observation leads to what is called the comparison test: if $0 \leq a_n \leq b_n$ for all n and if $b_1 + b_2 + \cdots$ is a convergent infinite series, then $a_1 + a_2 + \cdots$ also converges. When the comparison test is applied to a geometric series, it is reformulated slightly and called the ratio test: if $a_n > 0$ and if $a_{n+1}/a_n \leq r$ for some $r < 1$ for every n, then $a_1 + a_2 + \cdots$ converges. For example, the ratio test proves the convergence of the series

$$1 + \frac{1}{2} + \frac{1}{3 \cdot 2} + \frac{1}{4 \cdot 3 \cdot 2} + \cdots$$

Many mathematical problems that involve a complicated function can be solved directly and easily when the function can be expressed as an infinite series involving trigonometric functions (sine and cosine). The process of breaking up a rather arbitrary function into an infinite trigonometric series is called Fourier analysis or harmonic analysis and has numerous applications in the study of various wave phenomena.

INFINITESIMALS

Infinitesimals were introduced by Isaac Newton as a means of "explaining" his procedures in calculus. Before the concept of a limit had been formally introduced and understood, it was not clear how to explain why calculus worked. In essence, Newton treated an infinitesimal as a positive number that was smaller, somehow, than any positive real number. In fact, it was the unease of mathematicians with such a nebulous idea that led them to develop the concept of the limit.

The status of infinitesimals decreased further as a result of Richard Dedekind's definition of real numbers as "cuts." A cut splits the real number line into two sets. If there exists a greatest element of one set or a least element of the other set, then the cut defines a rational number. Otherwise the cut defines an irrational number. As a logical consequence of this definition, it follows that there is a rational number between zero and any nonzero number. Hence, infinitesimals do not exist among the real numbers.

This does not prevent other mathematical objects from behaving like infinitesimals, and mathematical logicians of the 1920s and '30s actually showed how such objects could be constructed. One way to do this is to use a theorem about predicate logic proved by Kurt Gödel in 1930. All of mathematics can be expressed in predicate logic, and Gödel showed that this logic has the following remarkable property:

A set Σ of sentences has a model [that is, an interpretation that makes it true] if any finite subset of Σ has a model.

This theorem may be used to construct infinitesimals as follows. First, consider the axioms of arithmetic, together with the following infinite set of sentences (expressible in predicate logic) that say "ι is an infinitesimal": $\iota > 0$, $\iota < \frac{1}{2}$, $\iota < \frac{1}{3}$, $\iota < \frac{1}{4}$, $\iota < \frac{1}{5}$, ...

Any finite subset of these sentences has a model. For example, say the last sentence in the subset is "$\iota < 1/n$". Then the subset can be satisfied by interpreting ι as $1/(n + 1)$. It then follows from Gödel's property that the whole set has a model. That is, ι is an actual mathematical object.

The infinitesimal ι cannot be a real number, of course, but it can be something like an infinite decreasing sequence. In 1934 the Norwegian Thoralf Skolem gave an explicit construction of what is now called a nonstandard model of arithmetic, containing "infinite numbers" and infinitesimals, each of which is a certain class of infinite sequences.

In the 1960s the German-born American Abraham Robinson similarly used nonstandard models of analysis to create a setting where the nonrigorous infinitesimal arguments of early calculus could be rehabilitated. He found that the old arguments could always be justified, usually with less trouble than the standard justifications with limits. He also found infinitesimals useful in modern analysis and proved some new results with their help. Quite a few mathematicians have converted to Robinson's infinitesimals, but for the majority they remain "nonstandard." Their advantages are offset by their entanglement with mathematical logic, which discourages many analysts.

INFINITY

Infinity is the concept of something that is unlimited, endless, without bound. The common symbol for infinity, ∞, was invented by the English mathematician John Wallis in 1657. Three main types of infinity may be distinguished: the mathematical, the physical, and the metaphysical. Mathematical infinities occur, for instance, as the number of points on a continuous line or as the size of the endless sequence of counting numbers: 1, 2, 3,.... Spatial and temporal concepts of infinity occur in physics when one asks if there are infinitely many stars or if the universe will last forever. In a metaphysical discussion of God or the Absolute, there are questions of whether an ultimate entity must be infinite and whether lesser things could be infinite as well.

The ancient Greeks expressed infinity by the word *apeiron*, which had connotations of being unbounded, indefinite, undefined, and formless. One of the earliest appearances of infinity in mathematics regards the ratio between the diagonal and the side of a square. Pythagoras (*c.* 580–500 BCE) and his followers initially believed that any aspect of the world could be expressed by an arrangement involving just the whole numbers (0, 1, 2, 3,...), but they were surprised to discover that the diagonal and the side of a square are incommensurable—that is, their lengths cannot both be expressed as whole-number multiples of any shared unit (or measuring stick). In modern mathematics this discovery is expressed by saying that the ratio is irrational and that it is the limit of an endless, non-repeating decimal series. In the case of a square with sides of length 1, the diagonal is $\sqrt{2}$, written as 1.414213562..., where the ellipsis (...) indicates an endless sequence of digits with no pattern.

Both Plato (428/427–348/347 BCE) and Aristotle (384–322 BCE) shared the general Greek abhorrence of the notion of infinity. Aristotle influenced subsequent thought for more than a millennium with his rejection of "actual" infinity (spatial, temporal, or numerical), which he distinguished from the "potential" infinity of being able to count without end. To avoid the use of actual infinity, Eudoxus of Cnidus (c. 400–350 BCE) and Archimedes (c. 285–212/211 BCE) developed a technique, later known as the method of exhaustion, whereby an area was calculated by halving the measuring unit at successive stages until the remaining area was below some fixed value (the remaining region having been "exhausted").

The issue of infinitely small numbers led to the discovery of calculus in the late 1600s by the English mathematician Isaac Newton and the German mathematician Gottfried Wilhelm Leibniz. Newton introduced his own theory of infinitely small numbers, or infinitesimals, to justify the calculation of derivatives, or slopes. In order to find the slope (that is, the change in y over the change in x) for a line touching a curve at a given point (x, y), he found it useful to look at the ratio between dy and dx, where dy is an infinitesimal change in y produced by moving an infinitesimal amount dx from x. Infinitesimals were heavily criticized, and much of the early history of analysis revolved around efforts to find an alternate, rigorous foundation for the subject. The use of infinitesimal numbers finally gained a firm footing with the development of nonstandard analysis by the German-born mathematician Abraham Robinson in the 1960s.

A more direct use of infinity in mathematics arises with efforts to compare the sizes of infinite sets, such as the set of points on a line (real numbers) or the set of counting numbers. Mathematicians are quickly struck by the fact that ordinary intuitions about numbers are

misleading when talk-
ing about infinite sizes.
Medieval thinkers were
aware of the paradoxical
fact that line segments of
varying lengths seemed to
have the same number of
points. For instance, draw
two concentric circles,
one twice the radius (and
thus twice the circumfer-

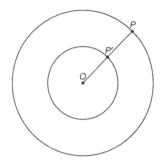

Concentric circles demonstrate that twice infinity is the same as infinity. Encyclopædia Britannica, Inc.

ence) of the other. Surprisingly, each point *P* on the outer
circle can be paired with a unique point *P'* on the inner circle by drawing a line from their common centre *O* to *P* and
labeling its intersection with the inner circle *P'*. Intuition
suggests that the outer circle should have twice as many
points as the inner circle, but in this case infinity seems to
be the same as twice infinity. In the early 1600s, the Italian
scientist Galileo Galilei addressed this and a similar non-
intuitive result now known as Galileo's paradox. Galileo
demonstrated that the set of counting numbers could be
put in a one-to-one correspondence with the apparently
much smaller set of their squares. He similarly showed
that the set of counting numbers and their doubles (i.e.,
the set of even numbers) could be paired up. Galileo concluded that "we cannot speak of infinite quantities as
being the one greater or less than or equal to another."
Such examples led the German mathematician Richard
Dedekind in 1872 to suggest a definition of an infinite set
as one that could be put in a one-to-one relationship with
some proper subset.

The confusion about infinite numbers was resolved
by the German mathematician Georg Cantor beginning
in 1873. First Cantor rigorously demonstrated that the
set of rational numbers (fractions) is the same size as the

counting numbers. Hence, they are called countable, or denumerable. Of course this came as no real shock, but later that same year Cantor proved the surprising result that not all infinities are equal. Using a so-called "diagonal argument," Cantor showed that the size of the counting numbers is strictly less than the size of the real numbers. This result is known as Cantor's theorem.

To compare sets, Cantor first distinguished between a specific set and the abstract notion of its size, or cardinality. Unlike a finite set, an infinite set can have the same cardinality as a proper subset of itself. Cantor used a diagonal argument to show that the cardinality of any set must be less than the cardinality of its power set—i.e., the set that contains all the given set's possible subsets. In general, a set with n elements has a power set with 2^n elements, and these two cardinalities are different even when n is infinite. Cantor called the sizes of his infinite sets "transfinite cardinals." His arguments showed that there are transfinite cardinals of endlessly many different sizes (such as the cardinals of the set of counting numbers and the set of real numbers).

The transfinite cardinals include aleph-null (the size of the set of whole numbers), aleph-one (the next larger infinity), and the continuum (the size of real numbers). These three numbers are also written as $\aleph_0$, $\aleph_1$, and c, respectively. By definition $\aleph_0$ is less than $\aleph_1$, and by Cantor's theorem $\aleph_1$ is less than or equal to c. Along with a principle known as the axiom of choice, the proof method of Cantor's theorem can be used to ensure an endless sequence of transfinite cardinals continuing past $\aleph_1$ to such numbers as $\aleph_2$ and $\aleph_{\aleph_0}$.

The continuum problem is the question of which of the alephs is equal to the continuum cardinality. Cantor conjectured that $c = \aleph_1$. This is known as Cantor's continuum hypothesis (CH). CH can also be thought of as stating that any set of points on the line either must be countable (of size less than or equal to $\aleph_o$) or must have a size as large as the entire space (be of size c).

In the early 1900s a thorough theory of infinite sets was developed. This theory is known as ZFC, which stands for Zermelo-Fraenkel set theory with the axiom of choice. CH is known to be undecidable on the basis of the axioms in ZFC. In 1940 the Austrian-born logician Kurt Gödel was able to show that ZFC cannot disprove CH, and in 1963 the American mathematician Paul Cohen showed that ZFC cannot prove CH. Set theorists continue to explore ways to extend the ZFC axioms in a reasonable way so as to resolve CH. Recent work suggests that CH may be false and that the true size of c may be the larger infinity $\aleph_2$.

INTEGRAL

An integral is either a numerical value equal to the area under the graph of a function for some interval (definite integral) or a new function the derivative of which is the original function (indefinite integral). These two meanings are related by the fact that a definite integral of any function that can be integrated can be found using the indefinite integral and a corollary to the fundamental theorem of calculus. The definite integral (also called Riemann integral) of a function $f(x)$ is denoted as

$$\int_a^b f(x)\, dx$$

and is equal to the area of the region bounded by the curve (if the function is positive between $x = a$ and $x = b$) $y = f(x)$, the x-axis, and the lines $x = a$ and $x = b$. An indefinite integral, sometimes called an antiderivative, of a function $f(x)$, denoted by

$$\int f(x)\,dx,$$

is a function the derivative of which is $f(x)$. Because the derivative of a constant is zero, the indefinite integral is not unique. The process of finding an indefinite integral is called integration.

INTEGRAL EQUATION

An equation in which the unknown function to be found lies within an integral sign is called an integral equation. An example of an integral equation is

$$f(x) = \int_{-\infty}^{\infty} \cos(xt)\, \varphi(t)\, dt,$$

in which $f(x)$ is known; if $f(x) = f(-x)$ for all x, one solution is

$$\varphi(x) = \frac{2}{\pi} \int_{0}^{\infty} \cos(ux) f(u)\, du.$$

INTEGRAL TRANSFORM

An integral transform is a mathematical operator that produces a new function $f(y)$ by integrating the product of an existing function $F(x)$ and a so-called kernel function $K(x, y)$ between suitable limits. The process, which is called transformation, is symbolized by the equation $f(y) = \int K(x,y)F(x)dx$. Several transforms are commonly named for the mathematicians who introduced them: in the Laplace transform, the kernel is e^{-xy} and the limits of integration are zero and plus infinity. In the Fourier transform, the kernel is $(2\pi)^{-1/2}e^{-ixy}$ and the limits are minus and plus infinity.

Integral transforms are valuable for the simplification that they bring about, most often in dealing with differential equations subject to particular boundary conditions. Proper choice of the class of transformation usually makes it possible to convert not only the derivatives in an intractable differential equation but also the boundary values into terms of an algebraic equation that can be easily solved. The solution obtained is, of course, the transform of the solution of the original differential equation, and it is necessary to invert this transform to complete the operation. For the common transformations, tables are available that list many functions and their transforms.

INTEGRAPH

The integraph is a mathematical instrument for plotting the integral of a graphically defined function. Two such instruments were invented independently about 1880 by the British physicist Sir Charles Vernon Boys and the Lithuanian mathematician Bruno Abdank Abakanowicz and were later modified and improved by others. The integraph draws the graph of the integral as the user traces the graph of the given function.

INTEGRATION

In mathematics, integration is the technique of finding a function $g(x)$ the derivative of which, $Dg(x)$, is equal to a given function $f(x)$. This is indicated by the integral sign "$\int$," as in $\int f(x)$, usually called the indefinite integral of the function. (The symbol dx is usually added, which merely identifies x as the variable.) The definite integral, written

$$\int_a^b f(x)\, dx$$

with a and b called the limits of integration, is equal to $g(b) - g(a)$, where $Dg(x) = f(x)$.

Some antiderivatives can be calculated by merely recalling which function has a given derivative, but the techniques of integration mostly involve classifying the functions according to which types of manipulations will change the function into a form the antiderivative of which can be more easily recognized. For example, if one is familiar with derivatives, the function $1/(x + 1)$ can be easily recognized as the derivative of $\log_e(x + 1)$. The antiderivative of $(x^2 + x + 1)/(x + 1)$ cannot be so easily recognized, but if written as $x(x + 1)/(x + 1) + 1/(x + 1) = x + 1/(x + 1)$, it then can be recognized as the derivative of $x^2/2 + \log_e(x + 1)$. One useful aid for integration is the theorem known as integration by parts. In symbols, the rule is $\int f Dg = fg - \int g Df$. That is, if a function is the product of two other functions, f and one that can be recognized as the derivative of some function g, then the original problem can be solved if one can integrate the product gDf. For example, if $f = x$, and $Dg = \cos x$, then $\int x \cdot \cos x = x \cdot \sin x - \int \sin x = x \cdot \sin x - \cos x + C$. Integrals are used to evaluate such quantities as area, volume, work, and, in general, any quantity that can be interpreted as the area under a curve.

INTEGRATOR

The integrator is an instrument for performing the mathematical operation of integration, important for the solution of differential and integral equations and the generation of many mathematical functions.

The earliest integrator was a mechanical instrument called the planimeter. A simple mechanical integrator of the disk-and-wheel variety has essential parts mounted on mutually perpendicular shafts, with a means of positioning the wheel in frictional contact with the disk, or turntable. In use, an angular displacement of the disk causes the wheel to turn correspondingly. The radius of the integrating wheel introduces a scale factor, and its positioning on the disk represents the integrand. Thus the rotations of the disk and the wheel are related through multiplicative factors and the number of turns made by the integrating wheel (for any number of turns of the disk) will be expressed as a definite integral of the function represented by the variable position of the wheel on the disk.

Electronic integrators or electrical integrating circuits have largely displaced mechanical integrators. For time-varying input, if the resistance R is very large compared with the capacitive reactance X_C of the capacitor C, the current will be almost in phase with the input voltage E_{IN}, but the output voltage E_{OUT} will lag the phase of the input voltage E_{IN} by almost $90°$. Thus the output voltage E_{OUT} is the time integral of the input voltage E_{IN}, as well as the product of the current and the capacitive reactance, X_C.

Viewed as analogues, many common devices can be considered as integrators—examples being the odometer and the watt-hour meter.

ISOPERIMETRIC PROBLEM

The determination of the shape of the closed plane curve having a given length and enclosing the maximum area is the isoperimetric problem. (In the absence of any restriction on shape, the curve is a circle.) The calculus of variations evolved from attempts to solve this problem and the brachistochrone ("least-time") problem.

In 1638 the Italian mathematician and astronomer Galileo Galilei first considered the brachistochrone problem, although his solution was flawed. With the discovery of calculus, a new approach to the solution became available, and the Swiss mathematician Johann Bernoulli issued a challenge in 1697 to mathematicians. Isoperimetrics was made the subject of an investigation in the 1690s by Johann and his older brother Jakob Bernoulli, who found and classified many curves having maximum or minimum properties. A major step in generalization was taken by the Swiss mathematician Leonhard Euler, who published the rule (1744) later known as Euler's differential equation, useful in the determination of a minimizing arc between two points on a curve having continuous second derivatives and second partial derivatives. His work was soon supplemented by that of the French mathematicians Joseph-Louis Lagrange and Adrien-Marie Legendre, among others.

Techniques of the calculus of variations are frequently applied in seeking a particular arc from some given class for which some parameter (length or other quantity dependent upon the entire arc) is minimal or maximal. Surfaces or functions of several variables may be involved. A problem in three-dimensional Euclidean space (that of finding a surface of minimal area having a given boundary) has received much attention and is called the Plateau problem. As a physical example, consider the shapes of soap bubbles and raindrops, which are determined by the surface tension and cohesive forces tending to maintain the fixed volume while decreasing the area to a minimum.

Other examples may be found in mechanics, electricity, relativity, and thermodynamics.

KERNEL

The kernel is a known function that appears in the integrand of an integral equation. Thus, in the equation

$$f(x) = g(x) + \int_a^b K(x,y)\, f(y)\, dy$$

both the kernel function, $K(x, y)$, and $g(x)$ are given, and $f(x)$ is the function sought. As an example, in Abel's equation for the curve followed by a particle moving in a vertical plane under the influence of gravity, which takes the form of the integral equation

$$f(x) = \int_0^x \frac{s(t)\,dt}{\sqrt{2g(x-t)}},$$

in which t is time, the kernel function is

$$\frac{1}{\sqrt{2g(x-t)}},$$

with g the acceleration of gravity. Other kernels in mathematics, such as the Dirichlet kernel and Fejér's kernel, are concerned with Fourier series.

LAGRANGIAN FUNCTION

The Lagrangian function (also called the Lagrangian) is a quantity that characterizes the state of a physical system. In mechanics, the Lagrangian function is just the kinetic energy (energy of motion) minus the potential energy (energy of position).

One may think of a physical system, changing as time goes on from one state or configuration to another, as progressing along a particular evolutionary path, and ask, from this point of view, why it selects that particular path out of all the paths imaginable. The answer is that the physical system sums the values of its Lagrangian function for all the points along each imaginable path and then selects that path with the smallest result. This answer suggests that the Lagrangian function measures something analogous to increments of distance, in which case one may say, in an abstract way, that physical systems always take the shortest paths.

In the special case of a ray of light, the path of system configurations is just the ordinary path of the light through space, and the Lagrangian function reduces simply to a measure of the passage of time. The particular curved path that a light ray takes through a refracting lens is therefore just the one that takes the least time.

The principle is, however, much more general than that, and it is a remarkable discovery that it seems to describe all phenomena equally well, including, for example, the travel of a rocket to the moon, and the likelihood that colliding subatomic particles will scatter each other in selected directions.

LAPLACE'S EQUATION

The second-order partial differential equation known as Laplace's equation is widely useful in physics because its solutions R (known as harmonic functions) occur in problems of electrical, magnetic, and gravitational potentials, of steady-state temperatures, and of hydrodynamics. The equation was discovered by the French mathematician and astronomer Pierre-Simon Laplace (1749–1827).

Laplace's equation states that the sum of the second-order partial derivatives of R, the unknown function, with respect to the Cartesian coordinates, equals zero:

$$\frac{\partial^2 R}{\partial x^2} + \frac{\partial^2 R}{\partial y^2} + \frac{\partial^2 R}{\partial z^2} = 0.$$

The sum on the left often is represented by the expression $\nabla^2 R$, in which the symbol ∇^2 is called the Laplacian, or the Laplace operator.

Many physical systems are more conveniently described by the use of spherical or cylindrical coordinate systems. Laplace's equation can be recast in these coordinates. For example, in cylindrical coordinates, Laplace's equation is

$$\nabla^2 R = \frac{\partial^2 R}{\partial r^2} + \frac{1}{r}\frac{\partial R}{\partial r} + \frac{1}{r^2}\frac{\partial^2 R}{\partial \theta^2} + \frac{\partial^2 R}{\partial z^2} = 0.$$

LAPLACE TRANSFORM

The Laplace transform is an integral transform invented by the French mathematician Pierre-Simon Laplace, and systematically developed by the British physicist Oliver Heaviside (1850–1925), to simplify the solution of many differential equations that describe physical processes. Today it is used most frequently by electrical engineers in the solution of various electronic circuit problems.

The Laplace transform $f(p)$, also denoted by $L\{F(t)\}$ or Lap $F(t)$, is defined by the integral

$$f(p) = \int_{0}^{\infty} e^{-pt} F(t)\,dt,$$

involving the exponential parameter p in the kernel $K = e^{-pt}$. The linear Laplace operator L thus transforms each function $F(t)$ of a certain set of functions into some function $f(p)$. The inverse transform $F(t)$ is written $L^{-1}\{f(p)\}$ or $Lap^{-1}f(p)$.

LEBESGUE INTEGRAL

The Lebesgue integral is a way of extending the concept of area inside a curve to include functions that do not have graphs that can be represented pictorially. The graph of a function is defined as the set of all pairs of x- and y-values of the function. A graph can be represented pictorially if the function is piecewise continuous, which means that the interval over which it is defined can be divided into subintervals on which the function has no sudden jumps. Because the Riemann integral is based on the Riemann sums, which involve subintervals, a function not definable in this way will not be Riemann integrable.

For example, the function that equals 1 when x is rational and equals 0 when x is irrational has no interval in which it does not jump back and forth. Consequently, the Riemann sum $f(c_1)\Delta x_1 + f(c_2)\Delta x_2 + \cdots + f(c_n)\Delta x_n$ has no limit but can have different values depending upon where the points c are chosen from the subintervals Δx.

Lebesgue sums are used to define the Lebesgue integral of a bounded function by partitioning the y-values instead of the x-values as is done with Riemann sums. Associated with the partition $\{y_i\}$ ($= y_0, y_1, y_2, ..., y_n$) are the sets E_i composed of all x-values for which the corresponding y-values of the function lie between the two successive y-values y_{i-1} and y_i. A number is associated with these sets E_i, written as $m(E_i)$ and called the measure of the set, which is simply its length when the set is composed of intervals. The following sums are then formed: $S = m(E_0)y_1 + m(E_1)y_2 + \cdots + m(E_{n-1})y_n$ and $s = m(E_0)y_0 + m(E_1)y_1 + \cdots + m(E_{n-1})y_{n-1}$.

As the subintervals in the y-partition approach o, these two sums approach a common value that is defined as the Lebesgue integral of the function.

The Lebesgue integral is the concept of the measure of the sets E_i in the cases in which these sets are not composed of intervals, as in the rational/irrational function above, which allows the Lebesgue integral to be more general than the Riemann integral.

LIMIT

The mathematical concept of the limit is based on the idea of closeness, used primarily to assign values to certain functions at points where no values are defined, in such a way as to be consistent with nearby values. For example, the function $(x^2 - 1)/(x - 1)$ is not defined when x is 1, because division by zero is not a valid mathematical operation. For any other value of x, the numerator can be factored and divided by the $(x - 1)$, giving $x + 1$. Thus, this quotient is equal to 2 for all values of x except 1, which has no value. However, 2 can be assigned to the function $(x^2 - 1)/(x - 1)$ not as its value when x equals 1 but as its limit when x approaches 1.

One way of defining the limit of a function $f(x)$ at a point x_o, written as

$$\lim_{x \to x_0} f(x),$$

is by the following: if there is a continuous (unbroken) function $g(x)$ such that $g(x) = f(x)$ in some interval around x_o, except possibly at x_o itself, then

$$\lim_{x \to x_0} f(x) = g(x_0).$$

The following more-basic definition of limit, independent of the concept of continuity, can also be given:

$$\lim_{x \to x_0} (x) = L$$

if, for any desired degree of closeness ε, one can find an interval around x_0 so that all values of $f(x)$ calculated here differ from L by an amount less than ε (i.e., if $|x - x_0| < \delta$, then $|f(x) - L| < \varepsilon$). This last definition can be used to determine whether or not a given number is in fact a limit. The calculation of limits, especially of quotients, usually involves manipulations of the function so that it can be written in a form in which the limit is more obvious, as in the above example of $(x^2 - 1)/(x - 1)$.

Limits are the method by which the derivative, or rate of change, of a function is calculated, and they are used throughout analysis as a way of making approximations into exact quantities, as when the area inside a curved region is defined to be the limit of approximations by rectangles.

LINE INTEGRAL

The line, or contour, integral is the integral of a function of several variables, defined on a line or curve C with respect to arc length s:

$$\int_C f(x, y)\, ds = \lim \sum_{i=1}^{n} f(x_i, y_i)\, \Delta_i s$$

as the maximum segment $\Delta_i s$ of C approaches 0. The line integrals

$$\int_C f(x, y)\, dx \text{ and } \int_C f(x, y)\, dy$$

are defined analogously. Line integrals are used extensively in the theory of functions of a complex variable.

MEAN-VALUE THEOREM

The mean-value theorem deals with a type of average useful for approximations and for establishing other theorems, such as the fundamental theorem of calculus.

The theorem states that the slope of a line connecting any two points on a "smooth" curve is the same as the slope of some line tangent to the curve at a point between the two points. In other words, at some point the slope of the curve must equal its average slope. In symbols, if the function $f(x)$ represents the curve, a and b the two endpoints, and c the point between, then $[f(b) - f(a)]/(b - a) = f'(c)$, in which $f'(c)$ represents the slope of the tangent line at c, as given by the derivative.

Although the mean-value theorem seemed obvious geometrically, proving the result without appeal to diagrams involved a deep examination of the properties of real numbers and continuous functions. Other mean-value theorems can be obtained from this basic one by letting $f(x)$ be some special function.

MEASURE

In mathematics, measure is a generalization of the concepts of length and area to arbitrary sets of points not composed of intervals or rectangles. Abstractly, a measure is any rule for associating with a set a number that retains the ordinary measurement properties of always being nonnegative and such that the sum of the parts equals the whole. More formally, the measure of the union of two nonoverlapping sets is equal to the sum of their individual measures. The measure of an elementary set composed of a finite number of nonoverlapping rectangles can be defined simply as the sum of their areas found in the usual manner. (And analogously, the measure of a finite union of nonoverlapping intervals is the sum of their lengths.)

For other sets, such as curved regions or vaporous regions with missing points, the concepts of outer and inner measure must first be defined. The outer measure of a set is the number that is the lower bound of the area of all elementary rectangular sets containing the given set, while the inner measure of a set is the upper bound of the areas of all such sets contained in the region. If the inner and outer measures of a set are equal, this number is called its Jordan measure, and the set is said to be Jordan measurable.

Unfortunately, many important sets are not Jordan measurable. For example, the set of rational numbers from zero to one does not have a Jordan measure because there does not exist a covering composed of a finite collection of intervals with a greatest lower bound (ever smaller intervals can always be chosen). It has a measure, however, that can be found in the following way: The rational numbers are countable (can be put in a one-to-one relationship with the counting numbers 1, 2, 3,...), and each successive number can be covered by intervals of length $1/8$, $1/16$, $1/32$,..., the total sum of which is $1/4$, calculated as the sum of the infinite geometric series. The rational numbers could also be covered by intervals of lengths $1/16$, $1/32$, $1/64$,..., the total sum of which is $1/8$. By starting with smaller and smaller intervals, the total length of intervals covering the rationals can be reduced to smaller and smaller values that approach the lower bound of zero, and so the outer measure is 0. The inner measure is always less than or equal to the outer measure, so it must also be 0. Therefore, although the set of rational numbers is infinite, their measure is 0. In contrast, the irrational numbers from zero to one have a measure equal to 1. Hence, the measure of the irrational numbers is equal to the measure of the real numbers. In other words, "almost all" real numbers are irrational numbers. The concept of measure based on countably infinite collections of rectangles is called Lebesgue measure.

MINIMUM

The minimum is the point at which the value of a function is less than or equal to the value at any nearby point (local minimum) or at any point (absolute minimum).

NEWTON AND INFINITE SERIES

Isaac Newton's calculus actually began in 1665 with his discovery of the general binomial series $(1 + x)^n = 1 + nx + \frac{n(n-1)}{2!} \cdot x^2 + \frac{n(n-1)(n-2)}{3!} \cdot x^3 + \cdots$ for arbitrary rational values of n. With this formula he was able to find infinite series for many algebraic functions (functions y of x that satisfy a polynomial equation $p(x, y) = 0$). For example, $(1 + x)^{-1} = 1 - x + x^2 - x^3 + x^4 - x^5 + \cdots$ and $\frac{1}{\sqrt{(1-x^2)}} = (1 + (-x^2))^{-1/2} = 1 + \frac{1}{2} \cdot x^2 + \frac{1 \cdot 3}{2 \cdot 4} \cdot x^4 + \frac{1 \cdot 3 \cdot 5}{2 \cdot 4 \cdot 6} \cdot x^6 + \cdots$.

In turn, this led Newton to infinite series for integrals of algebraic functions. For example, he obtained the logarithm by integrating the powers of x in the series for $(1 + x)^{-1}$ one by one, $\log (1 + x) = x - \frac{x^2}{2} + \frac{x^3}{3} - \frac{x^4}{4} + \frac{x^5}{5} - \frac{x^6}{6} + \cdots$, and the inverse sine series by integrating the series for $1/\sqrt{(1 - x^2)}$, $\sin^{-1}(x) = x + \frac{1}{2} \cdot \frac{x^3}{3} + \frac{1 \cdot 3}{2 \cdot 4} \cdot \frac{x^5}{5} + \frac{1 \cdot 3 \cdot 5}{2 \cdot 4 \cdot 6} \cdot \frac{x^7}{7} + \cdots$.

Finally, Newton crowned this virtuoso performance by calculating the inverse series for x as a series in powers of $y = \log (x)$ and $y = \sin^{-1} (x)$, respectively, finding the exponential series $x = 1 + \frac{y}{1!} + \frac{y^2}{2!} + \frac{y^3}{3!} + \frac{y^4}{4!} + \cdots$ and the sine series $x = y - \frac{y^3}{3!} + \frac{y^5}{5!} - \frac{y^7}{7!} + \cdots$.

Note that the only differentiation and integration Newton needed were for powers of x, and the real work involved algebraic calculation with infinite series. Indeed, Newton saw calculus as the algebraic analogue of arithmetic with infinite decimals, and he wrote in his *Tractatus de Methodis Serierum et Fluxionum* (1671; "Treatise on the Method of Series and Fluxions"):

> *I am amazed that it has occurred to no one (if you except N. Mercator and his quadrature of the hyperbola) to fit the doctrine recently established for decimal numbers to variables, especially since the way is then open to more striking consequences. For since this doctrine in species has the same relationship to Algebra that the doctrine of decimal numbers has to common Arithmetic, its operations of Addition, Subtraction, Multiplication, Division and Root extraction may be easily learnt from the latter's.*

For Newton, such computations were the epitome of calculus. They may be found in his *Tractatus* and the manuscript *De Analysi per Aequationes Numero Terminorum Infinitas* (1669; "On Analysis by Equations with an Infinite Number of Terms"), which he was stung into writing after his logarithmic series was rediscovered and published by Nicolaus Mercator. Newton offered the much more comprehensive *Tractatus* and *De Analysi* to Cambridge University Press and the Royal Society, but—amazing as it seems today—they were rejected. This experience left Newton reluctant to publish anything, which of course only hurt him in his priority dispute with Gottfried Wilhelm Leibniz.

ORDINARY DIFFERENTIAL EQUATION

An ordinary differential equation relates a function f of one variable to its derivatives. (The adjective *ordinary* here refers to those differential equations involving one variable, as distinguished from such equations involving several variables, called partial differential equations.)

The derivative, written f' or df/dx, of a function f expresses its rate of change at each point—that is, how fast the value of the function increases or decreases as the value of the variable increases or decreases. For the function $f = ax + b$ (representing a straight line), the rate of change is simply its slope, expressed as $f' = a$. For other functions, the rate of change varies along the curve of the function, and the precise way of defining and calculating it is the subject of differential calculus. In general, the derivative of a function is again a function, and therefore the derivative of the derivative can also be calculated, $(f')'$ or simply f'' or d^2f/dx^2, and is called the second-order derivative of the original function. Higher-order derivatives can be similarly defined.

The order of a differential equation is defined to be that of the highest order derivative it contains. The degree of a differential equation is defined as the power to which the highest order derivative is raised. The equation $(f''')^2 + (f'')^4 + f = x$ is an example of a second-degree, third-order differential equation. A first-degree equation is called linear if the function and all its derivatives occur to the first power and if the coefficient of each derivative in the equation involves only the independent variable x.

Some equations, such as $f' = x^2$, can be solved by merely recalling which function has a derivative that will satisfy the equation, but in most cases the solution is not obvious by inspection, and the subject of differential equations consists partly of classifying the numerous types of equations that can be solved by various techniques.

ORTHOGONAL TRAJECTORY

The family of curves that intersect another family of curves at right angles is called orthogonal trajectories.

Such families of mutually orthogonal curves occur in such branches of physics as electrostatics, in which the lines of force and the lines of constant potential are orthogonal. They also occur in hydrodynamics, in which the streamlines and the lines of constant velocity are orthogonal.

In two dimensions, a family of curves is given by the function $y = f(x, k)$, in which the value of k, called the parameter, determines the particular member of the family. Two lines are orthogonal, or perpendicular, if their slopes are negative reciprocals of each other. Curves are said to be perpendicular if their slopes at the point of intersection are perpendicular. Depending on context, the slope may also be called the tangent or the derivative, and it can be found using differential calculus. This derivative, written as y', will also be a function of x and k. Solving the original equation for k in terms of x and y and substituting this expression into the equation for y' will give y' in terms of x and y, as some function $y' = g(x, y)$.

A member of the family of orthogonal trajectories, y_1, must have a slope satisfying $y'_1 = -1/y' = -1/g(x, y)$, resulting in a differential equation that will have the orthogonal trajectory as its solution. To illustrate, if $y = kx^2$ represents a family of parabolas, then $y' = 2kx$, and, because $k = y/x^2$, a substitution of the latter in the former yields $y' = 2y/x$. Solving this for the orthogonal curve gives the solution $y^2 + (x^2/2) = k$, which represents a family of ellipses orthogonal to the family of parabolas.

PARABOLIC EQUATION

A parabolic equation is any of a class of partial differential equations arising in the mathematical analysis of diffusion phenomena, as in the heating of a slab. The simplest such equation in one dimension, $u_{xx} = u_t$, governs the temperature distribution at the various points along a thin rod from moment to moment. The solutions to even this simple problem are complicated, but they are constructed largely from a function called the fundamental solution of the equation, given by an exponential function, exp $[(-x^2/4t)/t^{1/2}]$. To determine the complete solution to this type of problem, the initial temperature distribution along the rod and the manner in which the temperature at the ends of the rod is changing must also be known. These additional conditions are called initial values and boundary values, respectively, and together are sometimes called auxiliary conditions.

In the analogous two- and three-dimensional problems, the initial temperature distribution throughout the region must be known, as well as the temperature distribution along the boundary from moment to moment. The differential equation in two dimensions is, in the simplest case, $u_{xx} + u_{yy} = u_t$, with an additional u_{zz} term added for the three-dimensional case. These equations are appropriate only if the medium is of uniform composition throughout, while, for problems of nonuniform composition or for some other diffusion-type problems, more complicated equations may arise. These equations are also called parabolic in the given region if they can be written in the simpler form described above by using a different coordinate system. An equation in one dimension the higher-order terms of which are $au_{xx} + bu_{xt} + cu_{tt}$ can be so transformed if $b^2 - 4ac = 0$. If the coefficients a, b, c depend on the values of x, the equation will be parabolic in a region if $b^2 - 4ac = 0$ at each point of the region.

PARTIAL DIFFERENTIAL EQUATION

A partial differential equation relates a function of several variables to its partial derivatives. A partial derivative of a function of several variables expresses how fast the function changes when one of its variables is changed, the others being held constant (*compare* ordinary differential equation). The partial derivative of a function is again a function, and, if $f(x, y)$ denotes the original function of the variables x and y, the partial derivative with respect to x—i.e., when only x is allowed to vary—is typically written as $f_x(x, y)$ or $\partial f/\partial x$. The operation of finding a partial derivative can be applied to a function that is itself a partial derivative of another function to get what is called a second-order partial derivative. For example, taking the partial derivative of $f_x(x, y)$ with respect to y produces a new function $f_{xy}(x, y)$, or $\partial^2 f/\partial y \partial x$. The order and degree of partial differential equations are defined the same as for ordinary differential equations.

In general, partial differential equations are difficult to solve, but techniques have been developed for simpler classes of equations called linear, and for classes known loosely as "almost" linear, in which all derivatives of an order higher than one occur to the first power and their coefficients involve only the independent variables.

Many physically important partial differential equations are second-order and linear. For example:

- $u_{xx} + u_{yy} = 0$ (two-dimensional Laplace equation)
- $u_{xx} = u_t$ (one-dimensional heat equation)
- $u_{xx} - u_{yy} = 0$ (one-dimensional wave equation)

The behaviour of such an equation depends heavily on the coefficients a, b, and c of $au_{xx} + bu_{xy} + cu_{yy}$. They are called elliptic, parabolic, or hyperbolic equations according as $b^2 - 4ac < 0$, $b^2 - 4ac = 0$, or $b^2 - 4ac > 0$, respectively. Thus, the Laplace equation is elliptic, the heat equation is parabolic, and the wave equation is hyperbolic.

PLANIMETER

The planimeter is a mathematical instrument for directly measuring the area bounded by an irregular curve, and hence the value of a definite integral.

The first such instrument, employing a disk-and-wheel principle to integrate, was invented in 1814 by J.H. Hermann, a Bavarian engineer. Improved mechanisms were invented by the British mathematical physicist James Clerk Maxwell (1855) and the Scottish engineer James Thomson (1876). So far as is known, Maxwell never actually built a working model of his invention, which he called a platometer, but Thomson's principle was not only applied in planimeters but adapted by his brother, the physicist William Thomson (later 1st Baron Kelvin), for a machine used in harmonic analysis of tides. A practical, inexpensive polar planimeter was invented by the Swiss mathematician Jacob Amsler about 1854. It consists of a pole arm, or bar, which has a weight at one end, and a tracer arm, the end of which has a point that the operator guides around the boundary of the area in question. Both arms rest in a carriage that moves as the tracer arm is moved. A vernier wheel within the carriage provides directly the area that is measured, calibration of vernier and area units being undertaken at the outset.

POWER SERIES

A power series is an infinite series that can be thought of as a polynomial with an infinite number of terms, such as $1 + x + x^2 + x^3 + \cdots$. Usually, a given power series will converge (that is, approach a finite sum) for all values of x within a certain interval around zero—in particular, whenever the absolute value of x is less than some positive number r, known as the radius of convergence. Outside of this interval the series diverges (is infinite), while the series may converge or diverge when $x = \pm r$. The radius of convergence can often be determined by a version of the ratio test for power series: given a general power series $a_0 + a_1x + a_2x^2 + \cdots$, in which the coefficients are known, the radius of convergence is equal to the limit of the ratio of successive coefficients. Symbolically, the series will converge for all values of x such that

$$|x| < \lim_{n \to \infty} |a_n / a_{n+1}| = r.$$

For instance, the infinite series $1 + x + x^2 + x^3 + \cdots$ has a radius of convergence of 1 (all the coefficients are 1)—that is, it converges for all $-1 < x < 1$—and within that interval the infinite series is equal to $1/(1 - x)$. Applying the ratio test to the series $1 + x/1! + x^2/2! + x^3/3! + \cdots$ (in which the factorial notation $n!$ means the product of the counting numbers from 1 to n) gives a radius of convergence of

$$\lim_{n \to \infty} |(1/n!)/(1/(n+1)!)| = \lim_{n \to \infty} |n + 1| = \infty,$$

so that the series converges for any value of x.

Most functions can be represented by a power series in some interval. Although a series may converge for all values of x, the convergence may be so slow for some values that using it to approximate a function will require calculating too many terms to make it useful. Instead of powers of x, sometimes a much faster convergence occurs for powers of $(x - c)$, where c is some value near the desired value of x. Power series have also been used for calculating constants such as π and the natural logarithm base e and for solving differential equations.

QUADRATURE

The process of determining the area of a plane geometric figure by dividing it into a collection of shapes of known area (usually rectangles) and then finding the limit (as the divisions become ever finer) of the sum of these areas is called quadrature. When this process is performed with solid figures to find volume, the process is called cubature. A similar process called rectification is used in determining the length of a curve. The curve is divided into a sequence of straight line segments of known length. Because the definite integral of a function determines the area under its curve, integration is still sometimes referred to as quadrature.

SEPARATION OF VARIABLES

One of the oldest and most widely used techniques for solving some types of partial differential equations is separation of variables. A partial differential equation is called linear if the unknown function and its derivatives have no exponent greater than one and there are no cross-terms—i.e., terms such as ff' or $f'f''$ in which the function or its derivatives appear more than once. An equation is called homogeneous if each term contains the function or one of its derivatives. For example, the equation $f' + f^2 = 0$ is homogeneous but not linear, $f' + x^2 = 0$ is linear but not homogeneous, and $f_{xx} + f_{yy} = 0$ is both homogeneous and linear.

   If a homogeneous linear equation in two variables has a solution $f(x, y)$ that consists of a product of factors $g(x)$ and $h(y)$, each involving only a single variable, the solution of the equation can sometimes be found by substituting the product of these unknown factors in place of the unknown composite function, obtaining in some cases an ordinary differential equation for each variable. For example, if $f(x, y)$ is to satisfy the equation $f_{xx} + f_{yy} = 0$, then by substituting $g(x)h(y)$ for $f(x, y)$ the equation becomes $g_{xx} h + g h_{yy} = 0$, or $-g_{xx}/g = h_{yy}/h$. Because the left side of the latter equation depends only on the variable x and the right side only on y, the two sides can be equal only if they are both constant. Therefore, $-g_{xx}/g = c$, or $g_{xx} + cg = 0$, which is an ordinary differential equation in one variable and which has the solutions $g = a \sin (xc^{1/2})$ and $g = a \cos (xc^{1/2})$. In a similar manner, $h_{yy}/h = c$, and $h = e^{\pm yc^{1/2}}$. Therefore, $f = gh = ae^{\pm yc^{1/2}} \sin (xc^{1/2})$ and $ae^{\pm yc^{1/2}} \sin (xc^{1/2})$ are solutions of the original equation $f_{xx} + f_{yy} = 0$. The constants a and c are arbitrary and will depend upon other auxiliary conditions (boundary and initial values) in the physical situation that the solution to the equation will have to satisfy. A sum of terms such as $ae^{\pm yc^{1/2}} \sin (xc^{1/2})$ with different constants a and c will also satisfy the given differential equation, and, if the sum of an infinite number of terms is taken (called a Fourier series), solutions can be found that will satisfy a wider variety of auxiliary conditions, giving rise to the subject known as Fourier analysis, or harmonic analysis. The method of separation of variables can also be applied to some equations with variable coefficients, such as $f_{xx} + x^2 f_y = 0$, and to higher-order equations and equations involving more variables.

SINGULAR SOLUTION

The singular solution of a differential equation cannot be obtained from the general solution gotten by the usual method of solving the differential equation. When a differential equation is solved, a general solution consisting of a family of curves is obtained. For example, $(y')^2 = 4y$ has the general solution $y = (x + c)^2$, which is a family of parabolas. The line $y = 0$ is also a solution of the differential equation, but it is not a member of the family constituting the general solution. The singular solution is related to the general solution by its being what is called the envelope of that family of curves representing the general solution. An envelope is defined as the curve that is tangent to a given family of curves. If the singular solution is an envelope, it can be found from the general solution by solving the maximum (or minimum) problem of finding the value of the parameter c for which y has a maximum (or minimum) value for a fixed x, and then substituting this value for c back into the general solution. In the example given, y has its minimum value for each x when $c = -x$, giving the singular solution as indicated.

SINGULARITY

In a function of the complex variable z, a point is called a singularity if the function is not analytic there (that is, the function cannot be expressed as an infinite series in powers of z) although, at points arbitrarily close to the singularity, the function may be analytic, in which case it is called an isolated singularity. In general, because a function behaves in an anomalous manner at singular points, singularities must be treated separately when analyzing the function, or mathematical model, in which they appear.

For example, the function $f(z) = e^z/z$ is analytic throughout the complex plane—for all values of z—except at the point $z = 0$, where the series expansion is not defined because it contains the term $1/z$. The series is $1/z + 1 + z/2 + z^2/6 + \cdots + z^n/(n+1)! + \cdots$ where the factorial symbol $(k!)$ indicates the product of the integers from k down to 1. When the function is bounded in a neighbourhood around a singularity, the function can be redefined at the point to remove it. Hence it is known as a removable singularity. In contrast, the above function tends to infinity as z approaches 0. Thus, it is not bounded and the singularity is not removable (in this case, it is known as a simple pole).

SPECIAL FUNCTION

A special function is any of a class of mathematical functions that arise in the solution of various classical problems of physics. These problems generally involve the flow of electromagnetic, acoustic, or thermal energy. Different scientists might not completely agree on which functions are to be included among the special functions, although there would certainly be very substantial overlap.

At first glance, the physical problems mentioned above seem to be very limited in scope. From a mathematical point of view, however, different representations have to be sought, depending on the configuration of the physical system for which these problems are to be solved. For example, in studying propagation of heat in a metallic bar, one could consider a bar with a rectangular cross section, a round cross section, an elliptical cross section, or even more-complicated cross sections. The bar might be straight or curved. Every one of these situations, while dealing with the same type of physical problem, leads to somewhat different mathematical equations.

The equations to be solved are partial differential equations. To apprehend how these equations come about, one can consider a straight rod along which there is a uniform flow of heat. Let $u(x, t)$ denote the temperature of the rod at time t and location x, and let $q(x, t)$ denote the rate of heat flow. The expression $\partial q/\partial x$ denotes the rate at which the rate of heat flow changes per unit length and therefore measures the rate at which heat is accumulating at a given point x at time t. If heat is accumulating, the temperature at that point is rising, and the rate is denoted by $\partial u/\partial t$. The principle of conservation of energy leads to $\partial q/\partial x = k(\partial u/\partial t)$, where k is the specific heat of the rod. This means that the rate at which heat is accumulating at a point is proportional to the rate at which the temperature is increasing. A second relationship between q and u is obtained from Newton's law of cooling, which states that $q = K(\partial u/\partial x)$. The latter is a mathematical way of asserting that the steeper the temperature gradient (the rate of change of temperature per unit length), the higher the rate of heat flow. Elimination of q between these equations leads to $\partial^2 u/\partial x^2 = (k/K)(\partial u/\partial t)$, the partial differential equation for one-dimensional heat flow.

The partial differential equation for heat flow in three dimensions takes the form $\partial^2 u/\partial x^2 + \partial^2 u/\partial y^2 + \partial^2 u/\partial z^2 = (k/K)(\partial u/\partial t)$. The latter equation is often written $\nabla^2 u = (k/K)(\partial u/\partial t)$, where the symbol ∇, called del or nabla, is known as the Laplace operator. ∇ also enters the partial differential equation dealing with wave-propagation problems, which has the form $\nabla^2 u = (1/c^2)(\partial^2 u/\partial t^2)$, where c is the speed at which the wave propagates.

Partial differential equations are harder to solve than ordinary differential equations, but the partial differential equations associated with wave propagation and heat flow can be reduced to a system of ordinary differential equations through a process known as separation of variables. These ordinary differential equations depend on the choice of coordinate system, which in turn is influenced by the physical configuration of the problem. The solutions of these ordinary differential equations form the majority of the special functions of mathematical physics.

For example, in solving the equations of heat flow or wave propagation in cylindrical coordinates, the method of separation of variables leads to Bessel's differential equation, a solution of which is the Bessel function, denoted by $J_n(x)$.

Among the many other special functions that satisfy second-order differential equations are the spherical harmonics (of which the Legendre polynomials are a special case), the Tchebychev polynomials, the Hermite polynomials, the Jacobi polynomials, the Laguerre polynomials, the Whittaker functions, and the parabolic cylinder functions. As with the Bessel functions, one can study their infinite series, recursion formulas, generating functions, asymptotic series, integral representations, and other properties. Attempts have been made to unify this rich topic, but not one has been completely successful. In spite of the many similarities among these functions, each has some unique properties that must be studied separately. But some relationships can be developed by introducing yet another special function, the hypergeometric function, which satisfies the differential equation $z(1 - z)d^2y/dx^2 + [c - (a + b + 1)z]\, dy/dx - aby = 0$. Some of the special functions can be expressed in terms of the hypergeometric function.

While it is true, both historically and practically, that the special functions and their applications arise primarily in mathematical physics, they do have many other uses in both pure and applied mathematics. Bessel functions are useful in solving certain types of random-walk problems. They also find application in the theory of numbers. The hypergeometric functions are useful in constructing so-called conformal mappings of polygonal regions whose sides are circular arcs.

SPIRAL

A spiral is a plane curve that, in general, winds around a point while moving ever farther from the point. Many kinds of spiral are known, the first dating from the days of ancient Greece. The curves are observed in nature, and human beings have used them in machines and in ornament, notably architectural—for example, the whorl in an Ionic capital. The two most famous spirals are described below.

Although Greek mathematician Archimedes did not discover the spiral that bears his name, he did employ it in his *On Spirals* (*c.* 225 BCE) to square the circle and trisect an angle. The equation of the spiral of Archimedes is $r = a\theta$, in which a is a constant, r is the length of the radius from the centre, or beginning, of the spiral, and θ is the angular position (amount of rotation) of the radius. Like the grooves in a phonograph record, the distance between successive turns of the spiral is a constant—$2\pi a$, if θ is measured in radians.

The equiangular, or logarithmic, spiral was discovered by the French scientist René Descartes in 1638. In 1692 the Swiss mathematician Jakob Bernoulli named it *spira mirabilis* ("miracle spiral") for its mathematical properties; it is carved on his tomb. The general equation of the logarithmic spiral is $r = ae^{\theta \cot b}$, in which r is the radius of each turn of the spiral, a and b are constants that depend on the particular spiral, θ is the angle of rotation as the curve spirals, and e is the base of the natural logarithm. Whereas successive turns of the spiral of Archimedes are equally spaced, the distance between successive turns of the logarithmic spiral increases in a geometric progression (such as 1, 2, 4, 8, ...). Among its other interesting properties, every ray from

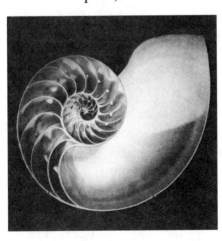

Section of pearly, or chambered, nautilus (Nautilus pomphius) with its naturally spiral-shaped shell. Courtesy of the American Museum of Natural History, New York

its centre intersects every turn of the spiral at a constant angle (equiangular), represented in the equation by b. Also, for $b = \pi/2$ the radius reduces to the constant a—in other words, to a circle of radius a. This approximate curve is observed in spider webs and, to a greater degree of accuracy, in the chambered nautilus, and in certain flowers.

STABILITY

The condition in which a slight disturbance in a system does not produce too disrupting an effect on that system is called stability. In terms of the solution of a differential equation, a function $f(x)$ is said to be stable if any other solution of the equation that starts out sufficiently close to it when $x = 0$ remains close to it for succeeding values of x. If the difference between the solutions approaches zero as x increases, the solution is called asymptotically stable. If a solution does not have either of these properties, it is called unstable.

For example, the solution $y = CE^{-x}$ of the equation $y' = -y$ is asymptotically stable, because the difference of any two solutions $c_1 e^{-x}$ and $c_2 e^{-x}$ is $(c_1 - c_2)e^{-x}$, which always approaches zero as x increases. The solution $y = ce^x$ of the equation $y' = y$, on the other hand, is unstable, because the difference of any two solutions is $(c_1 - c_2)e^x$, which increases without bound as x increases. A given equation can have both stable and unstable solutions. For example, the equation $y' = -y(1 - y)(2 - y)$ has the solutions $y = 1, y = 0$, $y = 2, y = 1 + (1 + c^2 e^{-2x})^{-1/2}$, and $y = 1 - (1 + c^2 e^{-2x})^{-1/2}$. All these solutions except $y = 1$ are stable because they all approach the lines $y = 0$ or $y = 2$ as x increases for any values of c that allow the solutions to start out close together. The solution $y = 1$ is unstable because the difference between this solution and other nearby ones is $(1 + c^2 e^{-2x})^{-1/2}$, which increases to

1 as x increases, no matter how close it is initially to the solution $y = 1$.

Stability of solutions is important in physical problems because if slight deviations from the mathematical model caused by unavoidable errors in measurement do not have a correspondingly slight effect on the solution, the mathematical equations describing the problem will not accurately predict the future outcome. Thus, one of the difficulties in predicting population growth is the fact that it is governed by the equation $y = ax^{ce}$, which is an unstable solution of the equation $y' = ay$. Relatively slight errors in the initial population count, c, or in the breeding rate, a, will cause quite large errors in prediction, even if no disturbing influences occur.

STURM-LIOUVILLE PROBLEM

The Sturm-Liouville problem, or eigenvalue problem, is a certain class of partial differential equations (PDEs) subject to extra constraints, known as boundary values, on the solutions. Such equations are common in both classical physics (e.g., thermal conduction) and quantum mechanics (e.g., Schrödinger equation) to describe processes where some external value (boundary value) is held constant while the system of interest transmits some form of energy.

In the mid-1830s the French mathematicians Charles-François Sturm and Joseph Liouville independently worked on the problem of heat conduction through a metal bar, in the process developing techniques for solving a large class of PDEs, the simplest of which take the form $[p(x)y']' + [q(x) - \lambda r(x)]y = 0$ where y is some physical quantity (or the quantum mechanical wave function) and λ is a parameter, or eigenvalue, that constrains the equation so that y satisfies the boundary values at the endpoints of the interval over which the variable x ranges. If the functions p, q, and r satisfy suitable conditions, the equation will have a family of solutions, called eigenfunctions, corresponding to the eigenvalue solutions.

For the more-complicated nonhomogeneous case in which the right side of the above equation is a function, $f(x)$, rather than zero, the eigenvalues of the corresponding homogeneous equation can be compared with the eigenvalues of the original equation. If these values are different, the problem will have a unique solution. On the other hand, if one of these eigenvalues matches, the problem will have either no solution or a whole family of solutions, depending on the properties of the function $f(x)$.

TAYLOR SERIES

The Taylor series is the expression of a function f— for which the derivatives of all orders exist—at a point a in the domain of f in the form of the power series $\sum_{n=0}^{\infty} f^{(n)}(a)(z-a)^n/n!$ in which Σ denotes the addition of each element in the series as n ranges from zero (0) to infinity (∞), $f^{(n)}$ denotes the nth derivative of f, and $n!$ is the standard factorial function. The series is named for the English mathematician Brook Taylor. If $a = 0$ the series is called a Maclaurin series, after the Scottish mathematician Colin Maclaurin.

VARIATION OF PARAMETERS

The variation of parameters is a general method for finding a particular solution of a differential equation by replacing the constants in the solution of a related (homogeneous) equation by functions and determining these functions so that the original differential equation will be satisfied.

To illustrate the method, suppose it is desired to find a particular solution of the equation $y'' + p(x)y' + q(x)y = g(x)$. To use this method, it is necessary first to know the general solution of the corresponding homogeneous equation— i.e., the related equation in which the right-hand side is zero. If $y_1(x)$ and $y_2(x)$ are two distinct solutions of the equation, then any combination $ay_1(x) + by_2(x)$ will also be a solution, called the general solution, for any constants a and b.

The variation of parameters consists of replacing the constants a and b by functions $u_1(x)$ and $u_2(x)$ and determining what these functions must be to satisfy the original nonhomogeneous equation. After some manipulations, it can be shown that if the functions $u_1(x)$ and $u_2(x)$ satisfy the equations $u'_1 y_1 + u'_2 y_2 = 0$ and $u_1' y_1' + u_2' y_2' = g$, then $u_1 y_1 + u_2 y_2$ will satisfy the original differential equation. These last two equations can be solved to give $u_1' = -y_2 g/(y_1 y_2' - y_1' y_2)$ and $u_2' = y_1 g/(y_1 y_2' - y_1' y_2)$. These last equations either will determine u_1 and u_2 or else will serve as a starting point for finding an approximate solution.

GLOSSARY

axiom A statement accepted as true as the basis for argument or inference; established rule or principle, or self-evident truth.

brachistochrone A cycloid, or the curve of fastest descent for a body moving from one point, and restricted to moving on the curve and assuming there is no gravity or other force acting on it, to a second point.

complex number Number made up of a real number and an imaginary one. It often takes the form of a+bi, where a and b are real numbers and i is imaginary (where i^2= -1).

conformal Having to do with a function that preserves angles, or leaves the size of the angle between corresponding curves unchanged.

derivative The limit of the ratio of the change in a function to the corresponding change in its independent variable as the latter change approaches zero.

dynamical systems theory This theory is part of applied mathematics and is used to describe the behaviour of complex dynamical systems, such as the flow of water in a pipe or the number of fish in a pond in a given season. It helps describe math rules where any object in a specific space is dependent on time.

factorial The product of all the positive integers from 1 to n, denoted by the symbol $n!$.

heuristic Involving or serving as an aid to learning, discovery, or problem-solving by experimental and especially trial-and-error methods.

hypergeometric series A probability function that gives the probability of obtaining exactly x elements of one kind and $n - x$ of another if n elements are chosen at random without replacement from a finite population containing N elements.

imaginary number A complex number, such as $2 + 3i$, in which the coefficient of the imaginary unit is not zero.

integral The area under the graph of a function over some defined interval or a new function of which the derivative is the original function.

irrational number A number` that can be expressed as an infinite decimal with no set of consecutive digits repeating itself indefinitely and that cannot be expressed as the quotient of two integers.

isocline Lines that indicate an equality of inclination or slope.

logarithm The exponent that indicates the power to which a number is raised to produce a given number.

manifold A topological space such that every point has a neighbourhood which is homeomorphic (or able to be mapped one-to-one between sets so both the function and its inverse are continuous) to the interior of a sphere in Euclidean space of the same number of dimensions.

monad An atom, or a unit.

natural number The number one or any number obtained by adding 1 to this number one or more times.

nutation Oscillatory motion of the axis of a rotating body, much like the wobble of a spinning top.

parabola A plane curve generated by a point so that its distance from a fixed point is equal to its distance from a fixed line.

power series An infinite series whose terms are successive integral powers of a variable multiplied by constants.

quotient The number resulting from the division of one number by another.

radian A unit of plane angular measurement that is equal to the angle at the centre of a circle subtended by an arc equal in length to the radius.

rational number An integer or the quotient of two integers.

real number One of the numbers that have no imaginary parts and are made up of the rational and irrational numbers.

secant In trigonometry, this is the function that for an acute angle is the ratio of the hypotenuse of a right triangle of which the angle is considered part and the leg adjacent to the triangle.

transcendental number Number that is not the root of any algebraic equation with rational coefficients.

BIBLIOGRAPHY

NONTECHNICAL WORKS

James R. Newman (ed.), *The World of Mathematics*, 4 vol. (1956, reprinted 1988), a gigantic and eclectic collection of writings about mathematics and mathematicians, contains many items related to analysis. Leo Zippin, *Uses of Infinity* (1962, reissued 2000), covers topics such as limits and sums of infinite series. Morris Kline, *Mathematical Thought from Ancient to Modern Times* (1972, reprinted in 3 vol., 1990), an enormous and comprehensive history of mathematics up to the early 20th century, contains a great deal of material on the development of analysis and the thinking behind it. Philip J. Davis and Reuben Hersh, *The Mathematical Experience* (1981, reprinted 1998), tells what mathematicians do and why. Ian Stewart, *From Here to Infinity* (1996), follows the historical development of many areas of mathematics, including several chapters on analysis, both standard and nonstandard, and his *Does God Play Dice?*, 2nd ed. (1997), explains the basic underlying ideas of chaos theory. John Stillwell, *Mathematics and Its History*, 2nd ed. (2002), emphasizes historical developments in order to unify and motivate mathematical theory at an undergraduate level. Frederick J. Almgren, Jr., and Jean E. Taylor, "The Geometry of Soap Films and Soap Bubbles," *Scientific American*, 235(1):82–93 (July 1976), is a highly illustrated introduction to the Plateau problem for the nonspecialist.

TECHNICAL WORKS

CALCULUS AND REAL ANALYSIS

E. Hairer and G. Wanner, *Analysis by Its History* (1996), a well-illustrated and readable account of the history of calculus from Descartes to the beginning of the 20th century, is particularly informative on the classical period of Newton, Leibniz, the Bernoullis, and Euler. Jerrold Marsden and Alan Weinstein, *Calculus*, 2nd ed., 3 vol. (1985, vol. 2 and 3 reprinted with corrections, 1996, 1991), a clear and well-organized calculus text, is typical of a vast literature but better than most. Tom M. Apostol, *Calculus*, 2nd. ed., 2 vol. (1967–69), is an introduction to rigorous analysis that is directed toward the topics usually featured in calculus courses. Walter Rudin, *Principles of Mathematical Analysis*, 3rd ed. (1976, reissued 1987), is a typical advanced undergraduate text on analysis. Bernard R. Gelbaum and John M.H. Olmsted, *Counterexamples in Analysis* (1964), contains a collection of problems that demonstrate just how counterintuitive rigorous analysis can be.

COMPLEX ANALYSIS

E.T. Whittaker and G.N. Watson, *A Course of Modern Analysis*, 4th ed. (1927, reprinted 1996), is a classic text on complex analysis that turns into a remarkably detailed survey of the most interesting special functions of mathematical physics. It is worth reading as a period piece alone, yet it is still relevant today. John B. Conway, *Functions of One Complex Variable*, 2nd ed. (1978, reprinted with corrections, 1995), is a beautifully organized introduction to the analysis of complex functions at an undergraduate level. Ian Stewart and David Tall, *Complex Analysis* (1983, reprinted with corrections, 1985), is an undergraduate textbook that includes historical material and an unusual amount of motivating discussion to bring out the geometric ideas behind the rigorous formalism. Lars V. Ahlfors, *Complex Analysis*, 3rd ed. (1979), is an advanced undergraduate text by one of the subject's leading authorities.

MEASURE THEORY

H.S. Bear, *A Primer of Lebesgue Integration*, 2nd ed. (2002), is an introduction to Henri Lebesgue's theory of measure and integration at an undergraduate level.

ORDINARY DIFFERENTIAL EQUATIONS AND DYNAMICAL SYSTEMS

Martin Braun, *Differential Equations and Their Applications*, 4th ed. (1993), is a typical undergraduate text on differential equations that is unusually clear and readable. Morris W. Hirsch and Stephen Smale, *Differential Equations, Dynamical Systems, and Linear Algebra* (1974), was the first textbook to bring the qualitative theory of differential equations into the modern era for classroom use. Martin Golubitsky and Michael Dellnitz, *Linear Algebra and Differential Equations Using MATLAB* (1999), includes computer software, MATLAB on a CD-ROM, for carrying out symbolic calculations to develop differential equations for beginning undergraduates. John H. Hubbard and Beverly H. West, *Differential Equations: A Dynamical Systems Approach*, 2 vol. (1991–95; vol. 1 reprinted with corrections, 1997), uses in vol. 1 the methods of the qualitative theory of differential equations to develop traditional and modern topics within the field and is computer-oriented and highly pictorial in its approach; vol. 2 presents the qualitative theory of differential equations when many variables are present. Robert L. Devaney, *An Introduction to Chaotic Dynamical Systems*, 2nd ed. (1989, reissued 1998), introduces rigorous mathematics of chaos theory in the setting of discrete-time dynamics in order to minimize technicalities.

PARTIAL DIFFERENTIAL EQUATIONS AND FOURIER ANALYSIS

Michael Renardy and Robert C. Rogers, *An Introduction to Partial Differential Equations* (1993, reprinted with corrections, 1996), on the theory and applications of partial differential equations, is a good starting point for serious mathematicians. T. W. Körner, *Fourier Analysis* (1988, reissued with corrections, 1989), is a clear and simple introduction to Fourier analysis, leading into more advanced topics.

OTHER AREAS OF ANALYSIS

John B. Conway, *A Course in Functional Analysis*, 2nd ed. (1990, reprinted with corrections, 1997), an excellent textbook; and Lawrence W. Baggett, *Functional Analysis: A Primer* (1992), a thorough introduction, are suitable for advanced undergraduates. Stefan Hildebrandt and Anthony Tromba, *The Parsimonious Universe: Shape and Form in the Natural World* (1996), is a popular account of the classical problems in the calculus of variations—the isoperimetric problem, shortest paths, brachistochrone, least action, and soap films—with magnificent illustrations. U. Brechtken-Manderscheid, *Introduction to the Calculus of Variations* (1991; originally published in German, 1983), is an undergraduate text on the calculus of variations and its uses in science. Frank Morgan, *Geometric Measure Theory: A Beginner's Guide*, 3rd ed. (2000), presents the Plateau problem from the modern geometric viewpoint, an excellent introduction to global analysis as applied to a classic variational problem. Errett Bishop and Douglas Bridges, *Constructive Analysis* (1985), offers a fairly accessible introduction to the ideas and methods of constructive analysis. Abraham Robinson, *Non-Standard Analysis*, rev. ed. (1974, reissued 1996), is a readable account by the mathematician who made the field of nonstandard analysis respectable.

INDEX

I

J

K

L